ENGLISH POTTERY AND PORCELAIN FIGURES

By G. Bernard Hughes:

ENGLISH DOMESTIC SILVER, 1500–1820
ENGLISH GLASS FOR THE COLLECTOR, 1660–1860
ENGLISH AND SCOTTISH EARTHENWARE, 1660–1860

By Therle Hughes:

OLD ENGLISH FURNITURE
SMALL DECORATIVE ANTIQUES
MORE SMALL DECORATIVE ANTIQUES
ENGLISH DOMESTIC NEEDLEWORK, 1560–1860

By Bernard and Therle Hughes:

ENGLISH PORCELAIN AND BONE CHINA, 1743–1850
SMALL ANTIQUE FURNITURE
COTTAGE ANTIQUES

Derby figure decorated with enamels and gilding by Stevenson and Hancock. Mark painted in purple enamel: crown over crossed swords and script D flanked by SH. Height 7 inches.

G. BERNARD HUGHES

ENGLISH POTTERY
AND PORCELAIN
FIGURES

LONDON
LUTTERWORTH PRESS

First published 1964
Second impression 1970
Copyright © 1964 G. Bernard Hughes

7188 0268 3

PRINTED IN GREAT BRITAIN PHOTOLITHO
BY EBENEZER BAYLIS AND SON, LTD.
THE TRINITY PRESS, WORCESTER, AND LONDON

*To Mary E. Ball
with appreciation*

CONTENTS

Introduction

LIST OF PLATES

Derby figure of a girl and dog decorated with enamels and
gilding (*in the collection of Mrs. B. E. James*)

Colour frontispiece

9

11

ENGLISH POTTERY AND PORCELAIN FIGURES

INTRODUCTION

WHEN Joseph Addison visited Miss Shepherd early in Queen Anne's reign he was invited into the library to wait. Here he was delighted to observe "inclosed in a kind of Square one of the prettiest grotesque works that I ever saw and made up of Scaramouches, Lions, Monkies, Mandarines, Trees, Shells and a thousand odd Figures in China ware". This was before Europe had begun to make porcelain: these figures must have been brought from China by the East India Company. Yet already collectors were discovering the charm of porcelain toys representing in miniature the bright world around them, idealised or caricatured to meet their moods and expressing above all the gay sophistication peculiar to figures created in ceramics.

Half a century later, however, when Benjamin Franklin fell a prey to the craze, he could marvel at the fine displays of English porcelain in the London shops. The result was a determination to take home to his wife in Philadelphia a unique collection of porcelain "from all the English china-makers who modelled figures", that is, from Chelsea, Bow, Derby and Longton Hall. A whim of mid-Georgian fashion prompted an intense interest in these porcelain figures. Dressing out the tables filled with sweetmeats and fruits for dessert was an accomplishment expected of the hostess or her professional confectioner, and delightful little idylls were composed with figures of dreamy gardeners, immaculate shepherds and shepherdesses, suave Turks, plump orientals, classical heroes, celebrity portraits, animals and birds.

Groups of figures specifically designed for the dessert table catalogued by Chelsea in 1756 included "a shepherd and flock of 2 ewes, 2 lambs, 2 goats, 2 dogs and a fox, for desart" and "four terms of the Seasons". Advertisements

15

also announced "beautiful Groups and large single Figures for wall Brackets", and engraving of the period show figures fashionably displayed on the mantel shelf.

Few collectors today can acquire figures in 18th-century porcelain, and the purpose of this book is to consider in detail the far wider range of figures prompted by such early successes and created through the 18th and 19th centuries in a wealth of different ceramics, different treatments, different styles. Even on the dessert table the vogue for figure ornament persisted far into the 19th century, and at the Great Exhibition, 1851, Henry Keogh of Grosvenor Square displayed "sets of dessert ornaments of eight pieces in white parian statuary enriched with gilding".

This book has been written for those with no specialist knowledge of ceramics, who want straightforward help with identification or a clearer understanding and fuller enjoyment of the splendid specimens displayed but all too seldom adequately explained in our museums. For outlines of the technical processes involved the reader may be referred to several chapters in a companion volume *English Porcelain and Bone China 1743–1850*, by Bernard and Therle Hughes (Lutterworth Press, 1955, 35s.). Such an outline is helpful for distinguishing fakes and reproductions from original work, and offers a glimpse of the materials that had to be selected and prepared, the techniques developed, the whole complexity of trial and error, high fortune and hovering bankruptcy that produced these delectable small ornaments with no purpose save diversion and delight.

Chapter One

CHELSEA

THE Chelsea Porcelain Manufactory was founded in the early 1740s by Thomas Briand. The year was probably 1742 for on February 11, 1743 Briand laid before the Royal Society some examples of soft-paste porcelain which he had made. The *Journal Book* of the Royal Society records: "Mr. Bryand, a Stranger, that was present, shew'd the Society several Specimens of a sort of fine Ware made here [in London] by himself from native materials of our own Country, which appear'd to be in all respects as good as any of the finest Porcelaine or China Ware: and he said that it was much preferable for its fineness to the ware of Dresden, and seem'd to answer the Character of the true Japan. For when broken, it appears like broken sugar, and not like Glass as the Dresden ware does: and that if it be heated red-hot, and immediately put into Cold water it will not fly or break. And that this ware, before it be glaz'd (a Specimen of which he shew'd) is firm enough to stand the heat of a Glass-house furnace." Briand had been introduced to the Royal Society by its secretary, Dr. Cromwell Mortimer of Chelsea. Despite this report, by the time commercial production began this had been evolved into a glassy milk-white porcelain.

Little is known regarding the early years of the Chelsea porcelain factory under Briand's control but much has been conjectured. From about 1747, however, the factory was directed by the Huguenot silversmith Nicholas Sprimont, who in 1742 had struck his mark at Goldsmiths' Hall as a plate worker. Sprimont was a man of flamboyant personality and Falstaffian proportions who drove through the streets of London in a gilded cabriolet and pair. The profits of Chelsea eventually made Sprimont a very rich man with a house in

Knightsbridge, another on the Terrace at Richmond, Surrey, and a country seat in Dorset.

Sprimont, it appears, was financed by Sir Edward Fawkener, secretary to the Duke of Cumberland, and upon Fawkener's death he became proprietor. Documents in the Royal Collection, however, suggest that the Duke of Cumberland himself may have held a financial interest in the Chelsea factory. Highly influential royal and court patronage enabled Sprimont to concentrate on costly ornamental ware. A document of about 1759, now in the British Museum, entitled "The case of the Undertaker of the Chelsea manufacture of Porcelain Ware", gives some details about Chelsea while complaining of cabinet ministers and others who abused their privilege concerning imported painted porcelain and earthenware which was liable to a duty of eightpence a pound. This document records that "the undertakers [of Chelsea] last winter sold to the value of more than £3,500, which is a great deal considering that the thing [porcelain strengthened with bone ash] is new . . . . the ground plot of his manufacture has gone on still increasing. He already employs at least one hundred hands, of which is a nursery of thirty lads, taken from the parishes and charity schools, and bred to designing and painting."

At this time Sprimont subleased from a Mr. Lagrave the land upon which "were erected several workshops and kilns for the manufacture of porcelain" at a yearly rental of £24. Miss Eliza Meteyard has recorded that the Chelsea manufactory was carried on in "an aggregation of old timber houses [workshops], added one to each other as the business has grown."

The factory premises were not extensive. William Bemrose in *Bow, Chelsea and Derby Porcelain,* 1898, quotes legal documents in his possession, dated 1769, which in their turn refer to agreements made in 1759. These show that the land occupied by Nicholas Sprimont measured about 90 feet north to south, 85 feet east to west, the eastern frontage facing Lawrence Street and the southern frontage bordering the Thames with a narrow wharf for unloading clay flints, wood billets and other materials. When the lease and premises were sold to James Cox on August 17, 1769 for £600 he acquired "all the Mills, Kilns, Bruisers, Moddells in Wax—in Lead— Presses, Moulds. All the manufactured and unmanufactured Porcelain, Workshop, Buildings and all the Materials and Utensils of what nature or kind so-ever and all the Chattles and Effects what so-ever of and belonging and now being in upon or about the Shops and Warehouses." All this is clear indication that production on a large scale was impossible. Cox resold to William Duesbury and John Heath of Derby February 9, 1770, for £801 10s.

Further deeds and a plan in the Bemrose collection show that by August 1779 certain alterations had been made under Duesbury, the land area being reduced by about a third to 112 feet by 50 feet. The lease, which expired early in 1784, required Duesbury to remove workshops, kilns and all other erections leaving the land clear for the lessor. In the sale of Chelsea buildings and fixtures in December 1783 the last lot included "a wood house and burning room", the latter containing plant for converting timber into the charcoal that fired the enamelling muffles.

Jewitt's collection of bills for 1770 included "100 Loads of Billet [short lengths of timber] at 7s. 9d. per Load, £38 15s." and "cord [wood] for the Kilns £1 17s. 4d.", the latter being used for starting the fires in the baking kilns. Fumes from the charcoal heating the muffles affected the surface appearance of the enamels, giving them a lustre not yet achieved by fakers.

A series of figures formerly believed to have been manufactured by Sprimont between 1747 and 1754 have now been shown to be the work of a second Chelsea factory operating for several years from 1749. This porcelain has been described comprehensively by Arthur Lane in *English Porcelain Figures of the 18th Century*. No more than about eighty examples have been recorded. An example in the British Museum, *Britannia Mourning for Frederick, Prince of Wales* (d. 1751) is in fine-grained porcelain coated with a thin, glassy glaze, easily distinguished from Sprimont's porcelain of the same period. The largest group so far known is *Hercules and Omphale*, measuring eight inches in height. This subject was also potted by Chelsea (see page 23).

Sprimont in 1750 advertised not only table-ware but "a great variety of Pieces for Ornament" and on December 4 the auctioneer Ford announced in *The General Advertiser* the sale of a "closet of fine old Japan china . . . and curious Dresden and Chelsea Figures". For Chelsea to be coupled with Dresden (Meissen) at this early date was honour indeed: modelling and decoration must have already reached a high standard, suggesting manufacture throughout the Sprimont period. The use of periodic auction sales to attract custom has confused some collectors who have assumed they concealed financial trouble. Thus in 1754 Sprimont announced that "having at very great Expense brought the Manufactory to that perfection, as to be allowed superior to any other attempts made in that way . . . will positively not open his Warehouses, nor exhibit any Article to Sale, after this, till next year." In fact, such "Sales to the Nobility and Gentry" proved so successful that they angered the "Gentlemen of the China Trade", that is, the china sellers, who later associated themselves as "Members of the China Society". Duesbury of Derby was the first of the porcelain potters to discontinue auction sales.

Like those of other porcelain potters, Sprimont's soft-paste displays progressive improvement. Collectors classify Chelsea porcelain into six groups in accordance with major changes made in the paste. To these groups the collector today must add the imitations and fakes.

Until 1747. Under Briand, Chelsea porcelain resembled opaque white glass, being creamy in appearance with a satiny texture marred by specks. It was probably derived from the formula used at St. Cloud in France where, it is conjectured, Briand had been employed. The 10 per cent of lead oxide in its composition suggests that flint-glass cullet was incorporated in the frit: hence its glassy nature. This caused distortion in the kiln and a high proportion of wasters. The glaze was applied thickly and age has invested it with a slightly yellowish tinge. It is soft and glassy with occasional bubbles and usually shows fine crazing.

1747–1750. Under Sprimont a porcelain was evolved from which glass was almost eliminated and a proportion of lime added. This paste was somewhat sandy and faintly greyish in tone. The percentage of wasters was appreciably decreased although its increased weight failed to prevent warping in the kiln, and firecracks are often noted. The glaze was creamy coloured and thick like candle grease, and inclined to choke the crevices in the modelling. It was applied in the form of powdered lead oxide which left a rim of exposed paste around the lower edge. The underside of the base was not glazed. Thomas Frye patented the glaze dipping process in 1749 (see page 35).

1750–1754. Chelsea porcelain was whitened during this period and its glaze resembled that of the previous period. Superficial blemishes and firecracks continued.

1754–1756. This porcelain was finer grained than formerly showing increased translucency in thin sections. Its fine quality enabled Sprimont to produce ceramic masterpieces which have seldom been equalled. The glaze was thinner than formerly and its cool white tone appears faintly blue against the white of the body. It is soft, seldom crazed, and the enamels sank into it with rich effect.

1758–1768. Reopening after a temporary closure, Sprimont incorporated bone ash with the frit as a strengthening ingredient. The resulting porcelain was denser of texture, harder, whiter, but tended to suffer from crackling, sometimes visible through the glaze. Warping was overcome. This suggests that Sprimont probably became a licensee of Thomas Frye, whose patent (page 33) gave him a monopoly in the use of bone ash for porcelain until the end of 1763. The glaze remained unchanged. It now became the standard practice to flatten the bases of figures by grinding, the paste thus exposed being greasily smooth ·to the touch. With minor variations this paste continued in use until the factory ceased production in 1768.

1770–1783. Porcelain made at Chelsea under the directorship of William Duesbury has a more waxy appearance than Sprimont's. The glaze was thinner than formerly and its surface smoothness almost equalled that of glass. Derby clay was now used at Chelsea. Work bills in the possession of Llewellyn Jewitt, dated 1770, specified that certain articles were "made with the Derby Clay". This suggests that clay mixtures were sent down from Derby to ensure secrecy of formulae.

Apart from variations in the paste, Chelsea porcelain may be classified in accordance with changes in the trade mark.

1. Under Briand until 1747 the mark was an incised—not impressed—triangle: the name Chelsea in script and the years were added on some early pieces.

2. Sprimont's first mark, 1747–1754, was the raised anchor, that is, a small anchor embossed in relief on an applied oval pad. Until 1752 the relief anchor was plain: afterwards it might be painted in red over the glaze. The anchor might appear on a circular pad with a raised edge.

3. From 1754 to 1756 a small plain bright red anchor was commonly painted on the glaze in various forms and sizes. Chelsea's red anchor must not be confused with those of Bow and Derby. It is also seen in brown and purple over-glaze, and in blue underglaze. An incised anchor with a cable, painted red, may be noted too, and also interlocked twin anchors, one inverted, painted in red.

4. 1758–1769. The factory was closed during 1757. When Sprimont re-opened in 1758 he changed the mark to a gold anchor which he continued with variations until the factory was sold in 1769. A pair of anchors in gold, one inverted but not interlocked, was an occasional mark during this period. Painted anchors were sometimes hidden in crevices and may be so insignificant as to be discovered only after careful search.

Figures decorated outside the factory did not bear the factory mark. But gold anchors were painted on some purely Derby soft-paste porcelain figures and on Chelsea reproductions in bone china made at Coalport in the mid-19th century. They are also found on modern figures made in Staffordshire, France and Germany.

5. During the Chelsea-Derby period, 1770 to 1783, a figure might be marked with a gold anchor traversing a cursive D. In 1773 appeared the crowned anchor, the anchor sometimes being replaced by a cursive D. An incised cursive N was occasionally used.

Perhaps the most familiar piece of Briand's glassy porcelain marked with the incised triangle is the pair of goats lying head to tail supporting a jug decorated with a bee. But collectors regard this piece with caution: many specimens noted bear little technical resemblance to the authenticated examples in the Victoria and Albert Museum. Some undoubtedly were made at Coalport; others are 20th century reproductions made by potters who have had no close contact with an original.

Very few figures may be attributed, either, to Sprimont's pre-1750 period. In the Schreiber Collection, Victoria and Albert Museum, is a figure group *Hercules and Omphale* in plain white porcelain, attributed in the catalogue to about 1750. This was adapted from an engraving by Laurent Cars after the picture painted in 1724 by François Lemoyne, now in the Louvre, Paris. Scantily clad Hercules is seated on a rock with Omphale, wearing a lion's skin, standing beside him, her right arm about his neck. This group obviously enjoyed long production for when the stock of Thomas Turner, china seller of Pall Mall, was sold by Christie in 1767 it included "a fine white Chelsea group of Hercules and Omphale which sold for a guinea".

Nurse with a Child of the same period continued as a best seller for several years, in the white and enamelled. This was adapted from one of the series of statuettes at Avon, near Fontainbleau, from a model attributed to Bertelemy de Blenod. The nurse, wearing Elizabethan costume, carries a child in swaddling clothes and is seated on a low nursing stool. Such stools were in common use until the mid-19th century: Queen Charlotte's, closely resembling the stool represented in this figure, is in the collection of H.M. the Queen. William Duesbury's account book records that in 1751 he decorated ten "Chellsea Nurs" figures.

Early Chelsea figure work is associated with porcelain left in the white but close inspection of a piece may disclose faint traces of paint and gilding. This suggests decoration with unfired or cold colours—that is, oil paints applied over the glaze to which no greater heat was applied for fixing than a few hours in a warm oven. These colours were used chiefly on soft-paste porcelains incapable of withstanding a second firing without developing flaws and cracks.

Chelsea overcame this defect during the early 1750s. An advertisement appearing in the *Public Advertiser* throughout April 1754 announced a sale of Chelsea porcelain "brought from the Manufactory there and the Warehouses in Pall-Mall" which included "beautiful Groups of Figures, &c. . . . *all warranted* TRUE ENAMEL".

Duesbury also recorded that he enamelled a pair of Chelsea "Mascorders" for two shillings. This was probably the model described in the sale catalogues of 1755 and 1756 as "the beautiful groupe of figures of a man and woman dancing". The *Masquerader* was adapted from a Meissen Kändler group modelled in 1740.

During this period figures began to be coloured with some attempt at realism in restrained tones such as warm opaque brown, translucent blue, a yellowish red and several tints of green. These were applied in flat washes leaving large areas of white glaze and touched with black. There was a characteristic method of tinting the cheeks bright red. The thin square plinths of early figures were superseded by simple mounds with sparsely applied flowers and foliage and a characteristic moss.

When figures of brilliantly coloured birds became dessert table favourites Duesbury's account book recorded that he enamelled many at the rate of two shillings a pair. His curiously spelled entries included "Flapwing Birds Chelsay; Boolfinchis Birds; Topnot Birds; Chelsay phesons; King Fishiars; Hostrigsis; peeping birds", as well as parrots and goldfinches. The Schreiber Collection also includes hen harrier, warbler, goose, ptarmigan, barn owl and scops owl, the last perched with a smaller bird grasped in its claws. Several of these birds were modelled from engravings in *The Natural History of Uncommon Birds* by George Edwards, 1743. Edwards observed soon after publication that "several of our manufacturers that imitate the China ware have filled the shops in London with images modelled after the figures in my *History of Birds*, most of which are sadly represented as to shape and colouring."

Animals for the dessert table were a less numerous group and included sheep lying on oval mounds with clover flowers and foliage, cows, goats, pug dogs and lions. The second day of the Chelsea sale of 1756 included the sale of "two ewes and 2 lambs of different sorts, 2 goats, a fox, and 2 dogs *for a desart*", and "a cow and 3 calves, one sucking, the other 2 lying down, *for a desart*".

24

Sets of monkeys were made at Chelsea, direct copies from Meissen figures modelled in about 1740 by J. J. Kändler, and declared without contemporaneous evidence to be caricatures of the Saxon Court Orchestra. The catalogue of 1756 contains several entries: "a set of five figures of *monkies in different attitudes* playing on Musick". Three figures from the Chelsea set are described in the *Catalogue of the Schreiber Collection*. "Two are dressed as men, and one as woman in costume of the period. Both the former are standing; one wearing a cocked hat, a yellow, short-sleeved tunic and purple breeches is playing a pipe and a side drum; the other, clothed in a green and purple cap, loose white shirt and purple breeches, carries two draped kettle-drums slung on his shoulders. The female wears a lace cap tied with ribbons and a flowered Watteau dress over a yellow bodice and skirt; she is seated on a folding chair, singing from a music book on her knee. These stand on gilt rococo-scrolled bases with applied flowers and foliage." This description is important as Derby made a monkey orchestra, "large Monkey musicals" selling at 7s. 6d. each figure, the small size at five shillings. They were made by Derby and Spode in bone china and in hard-paste porcelain by Meissen. They are still in production.

Figures of the red anchor period (1754 to 1756) are among the finest creations in European ceramics with the Meissen influence visible in modelling and painting. The colours blend with the glaze in a harmony more attractive than that of contemporaneous hard-paste glaze.

The most charming figures made during this period represented characters from the Italian Comedy adapted from the celebrated Meissen series modelled by Kändler. The serious air of the Doctor, the mirth of the Jester and the coyness of Columbine, the mischievous Harlequin, the grotesque Pantaloon and the intriguing servant Scaramouche, are finely portrayed in these little figures full of life and movement. The range of figures and groups was wide.

The 1,618 lots of Chelsea porcelain sold during the fifteen-day sale in 1756 included: "pair of figures in *Turkish dresses*, sitting with shells; a *fine group* of theatrical figures; Dutchman and his wife dancing; four beautiful *small cupids* for a dessert; six beautiful Cupids, *love in disguise* for a desart; a beautiful small group of a gardner and his wife with a basket of flowers; two large figures of Mercury and Diana [the moulds were used later by Derby and in bone china during the early-19th century]; an Indian prince and queen; two small Savoyard figures; a map seller and his box of toys; a cobler and his wife singing; two figures of pilgrims; a shepherd and shepherdess; a *groupe of figures*, representing Europe and Asia and another groupe Africa and America; two large figures of a gentleman and lady in riding breeches; group of a man and woman dancing; a most beautiful *groupe of figures* representing the 4 seasons; Perseus and Andromeda, finely group'd; *a beautiful figure of a woman holding a jar,* or perfume pot; a *beautiful* figure of a Bacchus with a vine leav'd hat as a perfume pot; five figures *representing the senses,* Seeing, Feeling, Smelling, Hearing, Tasting".

When Chelsea recommenced in 1758 following a temporary cessation of production, Sprimont was sole proprietor. Bone ash was now incorporated in the frit as a strengthening ingredient: this was obviously by arrangement with Thomas Frye of Bow whose patent gave him a monopoly in its use for porcelain until New Year's day 1764. Figures continued to be an important production at Chelsea and were marked with a gold anchor. An advertisement of April 12, 1759 announced "beautiful large Groups and single Figures for Brackets" and later "small Figures for deserts, large Figures for brackets and Groups of Figures". The wall brackets were elaborately carved and gilded to designs published by such mid-Georgian masters as Thomas Chippendale and Thomas Johnson.

Enamels in pastel shades were superseded by a blaze of gaudy colour lavishly enriched with thickly applied gilding. Previously gilding on Chelsea porcelain had been sparsely applied to figures and until 1755 the impermanent oil gilding method had been used. Chelsea then introduced the more permanent honey gilding. Gold leaf ground with honey and tempered with oil of lavender was applied with a pencil brush and fixed by low temperature firing. The presence of the honey destroyed the rich brilliance of the gold, resulting in a slightly dull appearance and burnishing failed to increase its lustre.

The catalogue of the Chelsea five-day sale April–May 1761 (illustrated page by page in *Apollo,* August 1940) listed nearly five hundred lots of which 134 were figures and groups, with three pairs of English and Prussian dwarfs. One "fine figure of an English dwarf" sold for 17*s.* 6*d.* The stock in trade of Thomas Turner, china seller, auctioned by Christie in 1767 included "Two Chelsea figures of the English and Prussian Dwarfs, enamelled", which sold for £2. Nightingale recorded the English dwarf as John Coan of Norfolk who died in 1764: "He is represented in the costume of a Yeoman of the Guard or Beefeater, and is shown to be a dwarf by the large dog at his side. The words 'John Coan, English Dwarf' are inscribed on a tablet at the base; near this, at the foot, are the letters C.O. in gold on two tablets. The mark is a gold anchor and the letters GR III are inscribed on the breast, also in gold."

The Prussian dwarf was the Callot dwarf, believed to have been modelled in about 1750, an adaptation from the engraving *Varie figure Gobbi* by Jacques Callot published in 1622. The Chelsea figure has a high conical hat with feathers on one side and a tunic with slashed sleeves and large buttons and wears a sword. The moulds for these figures continued in use at Derby in soft-paste porcelain and in bone china. These figures are entered in the Derby price list as "No 227 Pair of Grotesque Punches, height 7 inches, 18*s.*" The 5½ inch examples to be found are 20th century copies.

The priced catalogue of Turner's sale quoted by Nightingale includes several Chelsea figures: "four white groups of the 4 quarters of the world, £1; a large white figure of a Shepherd and 2 Shepherdesses, £1 18*s.*; a white figure of Cicero, 9*s.*; a white group of a Prussian Hussar, £1 7*s.*; two [white] figures of *Mrs. Clive,* in *the character of the* Fine Lady, and four Indian figures, 11*s.*; a beautiful enamelled figure of Apollo, on a pedestal, £2." Inclusion of the white glazed figures proves the sale of undecorated work throughout the Sprimont period.

27

The magnificent array of Chelsea gold anchor figures included the *Vauxhall Masqueraders*, differing entirely from the red anchor versions of the same subjects from the same moulds. Placed side by side with their Derby equivalents and modern reproductions they offer fascinating contrasts.

Shepherds and shepherdesses were highly fashionable, single and in pairs, standing beside flowering tree-stumps rising from rococo scrolled bases and measuring from six to fifteen inches in height. Both were radiantly dressed, the shepherd usually accompanied by one or two dogs, his companion by lambs. Shepherds and shepherdesses appear to belong mainly to the gold anchor period. Few are entered in the 1756 sale catalogue, but in 1761 several lots of three different types are recorded: "a singing shepherd and shepherdess; two figures of a piping shepherd and a shepherdess with a crown of flowers; a shepherd and shepherdess sitting, playing on different instruments."

Sportsman and Lady are frequent entries in sale catalogues. Those of the red anchor period are sparsely decorated and show a man and a woman, each with a gun and sitting on a mound. The sportswoman holds a shot bird aloft in her left hand and at her feet lie a dead rabbit and birds: at the feet of the man lie several dead partridge. The gold anchor version is entirely different showing more elaborate figures splendidly coloured and gilded, standing upon pierced rococo pedestals, the man only grasping a gun. At the 1771 sale these commanded prices ranging from 36*s.* to 48*s.* a pair.

Gold anchor figure groups include the important *Roman Charity* of which two examples were sold in the Chelsea sale of 1770. The catalogue description reads: "*one very large and curious group,* representing *Roman Charity,* upon a very magnificent blue and gold pedestal." This sold for £8 15*s.*: a second example on a pea-green and gold pedestal sold for £6 16*s.* 6*d.* This was modelled by Joseph Williams (originally Willems) after a painting by Rubens in the Rijks Museum, Amsterdam. This group represents the Roman legend of Cimon, sentenced to death by starvation and saved by his daughter Pera who fed him during daily visits to his cell. Williams's original models of *Roman Charity, Una and the Lion* and *Pieta* and *Flora* (after Sir Anthony Vandyck's

28

painting) were discovered in his studio after his death in 1766. It is believed that he modelled *Leda and the Swan*, adapted from the painting by François Boucher now in the National Museum, Stockholm. This figure was mentioned in the 1756 sale catalogue: an enamelled example in the Victoria and Albert Museum is marked with the red anchor. In 1760 Williams advertised in the *London Chronicle*: "JOSEPH WILLIAMS. Modeller. At the Brussels Coffee-house, Chelsea. This artist teaches drawing and Modelling: and has modelled for the Chelsea China Manufactory for many years." Other figures attributed to Williams by Major Tapp are *Ceres*, 1756; *Perseus and Andromeda, c.* 1755; *Apollo, c.* 1763; *Urania and Thalia*, 1763; and *Clio*, 1763.

Pairs of groups, two or more figures to each group, were richly gorgeous affairs. The pair emblematic of the *Four Seasons* were creations intended for Georgian collectors: the figures *Winter and Spring* standing before a holly bush consist of a skater and his companion carrying an apron full of flowers; *Summer and Autumn* are displayed against an apple tree, the woman with a sickle, the man carrying fruit in his apron. Single figures of the four seasons were also issued.

Leafy, heavily flowered bowers of hawthorn or apple surrounding figure groups were introduced in about 1760. Described by the Chelsea Porcelain Manufactory as "arbours" or "canopies curiously ornamented with flowers", they are known to collectors as *bocages*. One of the finest of these is known as the *Music Lesson* modelled from J. E. Nilson's engraving after François Boucher's painting *L'Agréable Leçon*. Several examples were entered in the 1770 catalogue as "a very large and curious group of a Shepherd teaching a Shepherdess to play on the Flute". These sold for eight guineas each. The example in the Schreiber collection is described in detail: "The figures are seated on a mound in front of a *bocage* consisting of a flowering hawthorn. The boy wears a wide blue hat with a spray of hawthorn in it, a richly patterned coat and breeches and red shoes: by his side is a dog. The shepherdess is dressed in a blue bodice, flowered skirt and petticoat, and green shoes; on her lap is a lamb. With her left hand she holds a ribbon attached to the

29

neck of one of two lambs which lie at her feet. The whole group is supported on a gilt rococo-scrolled base decorated with applied flowers and foliage. Height, 16 in.; width, 11 in. Mark an anchor in gold and R impressed."

Bocages in the form of "candlesticks, girandoles for two lights each, and branched lights" for toilet table use are named in catalogues. The *Aesop's Fables* series of *bocages* have loop handles behind for carrying and their three-footed rococo-scrolled bases are inscribed with their titles in gold.

Porcelain manufacture virtually ceased at Chelsea in the early months of 1768, although enamellers continued to be employed decorating the considerable stocks of unfinished porcelain. An editorial notice in the *Public Advertiser*, May 4, 1769, reported that "as the Chelsea Porcelain Manufactory is declined, and the Porcelain become scarce, Jones, on the Terras in St. James's Street, who was always the chief disposer of the same, is selling off his curious Collection, going into another Branch". The factory with its plant and stock in trade had already been offered for sale in January 1764, but another five years elapsed before Sprimont finally ceased manufacture. Josiah Wedgwood, who had established an enamelling department for his celebrated queen's ware in nearby Little Cheney Row, because of the available supply of experienced decorators, enclosed with a letter to his partner Bentley on April 14, 1769 a newspaper cutting announcing the imminent sale of the Chelsea factory.

A few days after its purchase by William Duesbury and John Heath in February 1770, James Christie held at his rooms a four-day sale of "Chelsea Porcelaine by Order of Mr. Nicholas Sprimont". A copy of the catalogue of 336 lots annotated with prices and reproduced by Nightingale included a few figures: "four Cupids on Pedestals, 16s. 6d.; Mower and haymaker, 17s.; four seasons, sitting, £1 5s.; two small Chinese figures, 4s. 6d.; two Masquerade figures, 10s. 6d.; large group of Seasons, £3 10s.; figure of a Cupid with a basket and a small piping shepherdess, 7s.; group of mercury and Nymph, £1 14s.; Mars, 10s.; two large figures of quarters of the world, £2 10s.; and a very large and magnificent group of figures, curiously ornamented with Jessamine flowers, £9 19s. 6d."

Duesbury operated the Chelsea factory in a small way for the number of employees was few. Typical is the weekly expense account for the period March 16–23, 1771, listing seven men, including Boreman, Jinks, Snowden and Wollams. There had been nine a year earlier. A single horse was sufficient for operating the machinery.

Honey in *Old English Porcelain*, 1948, states that Chelsea-Derby figures are as a rule enamelled in insipid, weak colours. "Amongst them unpleasant but distinctive pale 'watery' greens and pinks are noticeable, but a characteristic rich brown is an exception." As a rule, however, it is difficult to distinguish between the concurrent productions of Derby and those of Chelsea-Derby.

As many of the original Chelsea models and moulds had been sent to Derby by 1784 it is obvious that they were intended for use. Derby figures in soft-paste porcelain identical with Chelsea are known and many examples exist in 19th-century Derby bone china. An inventory of models and moulds in the possession of Duesbury in 1795 include: "Large Chelsea Seasons, 4 sizes; Standing Chelsea Seasons, 3 sizes; pair of old Chelsea basket figures, 2 sizes; four Chelsea boys; Pair grotesque boy and girl (Chelsea)."

Among the final requests for instructions sent to Duesbury at Derby in February 1784 was: "Will yow have the mold of the large figur of Brittannia sent to the warehous or broake?" Evidently it was sent to Derby for in the inventory of moulds taken in 1795 "Large Britannia" appears as No. 374: the figure itself is shown in the price list of 1830 (page 68), costing two guineas.

Chapter Two

BOW

THOMAS FRYE, well-known as a painter of miniature portraits and an engraver in mezzotint, displayed a profound interest in porcelain manufacture during the early 1740s. Long experimental work in association with Edward Heylyn, a London glass manufacturer, resulted in a porcelain formula being evolved containing bone ash as a new and important ingredient. The long-term economic value of this development to the English pottery industry cannot be over-estimated. The *Gentleman's Magazine*, 1762, named Frye as "the Inventor and first Manufacturer of Porcelain in England", a claim never disputed by the competing proprietors of Chelsea, Derby and Worcester.

Frye and Heylyn were first granted a patent in 1744 for manufacturing a porcelain described in the specification as "equal to, if not exceeding in goodness and beauty, China or Porcelain Ware imported from Abroad". Their experiments had been carried out at Edward Heylyn's glasshouse in Bow, well-known for its flint-glass from about 1730 and possessing the basic facilities essential for porcelain making; indeed the composition of their earliest porcelain was one-third glass.

The close association was long continued. On May 7, 1756, for instance, the Bow clerk John Bowcock enquired "whether any Windsor bricks were received at the glass house and charged to the porcelain works in error". Bowcock also recorded the despatch of many consignments of glass and china from Bow.

Edward Heylyn and Alderman George Arnold jointly bought land at Stratford le Bow, Middlesex, and this was probably the site of the Frye-Heylyn factory, for when

1. Chelsea porcelain figures marked with red anchor. (*Top*) In the centre is a Meissen figure of Shylock modelled by Kaendler and made in hard-paste porcelain. To the left is a lead master model taken by the Chelsea factory from such a figure. To the right is a figure of Shylock in Chelsea soft porcelain, taken from moulds from such a model. Note the shrinkage which took place in firing. (*Below*) "River God and Goddess", leaning on overturned urns from which water is pouring.

2. (*Top*) Pair of gold anchor Chelsea candelabra with figures of musicians seated in floral arbours, one playing a flute, the other a guitar. Height 13¼ inches. (*Left*) Hearing, a rare figure from the set of Senses by Chelsea. Mark: gold anchor. Height 15 inches. (*Right*) Chelsea chinoiserie group with perfume vase. Mark: red anchor at the back of the base.

Arnold died in 1751 it was disclosed in the newspapers that he was "one of the principal proprietors of the Porcelain Manufactory at Bow". Virtually nothing is known of this venture and productions remain unidentified: purported examples when analysed at the British Museum and the Victoria and Albert Museum have been found to contain phosphoric acid indicating the presence of bone ash, an ingredient called for by a further patent granted to Thomas Frye on November 11, 1749—not 1748 as stated by Jewitt and many other later authorities. The cost of a patent at that time was the equivalent of £300 today, proof that Frye's financiers were satisfied with the experimental productions.

Manufacture of porcelain to the new formula containing bone ash in the frit (see page 34) was sponsored by Weatherby and Crowther, but it is certain that Heylyn and Arnold were also partners. Thomas Frye was appointed works superintendent and doubtless received a royalty for the use of his patent. A new and larger factory was erected in Stratford Langthorne on the Essex side of the River Lea, opposite to Bow. The works were styled "New Canton" and the design of the façade was adapted from the celebrated porcelain warehouses at Canton in China.

Production cannot have begun earlier than 1750 and this is the date incised upon several figures. With years of practical experience behind him and a nucleus of trained workers, Frye could produce porcelain displaying a high standard of craftsmanship. Some early publicity was secured by the distribution of flat-topped, cylindrical inkpots $3\frac{1}{4}$–4 inches in diameter inscribed in red MADE AT NEW CANTON 1750. The pot was designed with a raised rim encircling the well and five holes for quill pens in the shoulder. Ornament on the sides was painted in the Japanese style with blue, green, yellow and red paints. Curiously, the bases of authenticated examples are unglazed (see page 35). Specimens may be seen in the British Museum and the Victoria and Albert Museum: 20th-century copies exist.

Under Frye's management the venture was a huge success. The first year's trading totalled £6,573 0s. 8d.: five years later this amount was almost trebled. A document in the British Museum written by a former employee, Thomas

Craft, records that in 1760 the Bow China Manufactory employed 300, including 90 decorators.

Close application to porcelain manufacture and years of experimental work undermined Frye's health, however, and in 1759 he was compelled to retire. Either silicosis or lead poisoning may have brought about his death in 1762.

The novelist Samuel Richardson, when editing Daniel Defoe's *Tour of Great Britain* during 1752, reported on the productions of New Canton "where a large Manufactory of Porcelain is carried on. They have already made large quantities of Tea-Cups, Saucers, Plates, Dishes, Tureens, and most other Sorts of useful Porcelain; which, though not so fine as some made at Chelsea, or as that brought from Dresden, is much stronger than either and therefore better for common use; and being much cheaper than any other China, there is a greater Demand for it. The Proprietors of this Manufactory have also procured some very good Artists in Painting, who are employed in painting some of their finest sort of Porcelain, which is so well performed as to equal Dresden in this Respect. If they can work this so as to undersell the foreign Porcelain, it may become a very profitable Business to the Undertakers and save great Sums to the Public, which are annually sent abroad for this Commodity."

Richardson made no reference to figures which must at that time have been a minor production. In November of the following year, however, *Aris's Birmingham Gazette* carried a small advertisement inserted by "The China-House, near Bow", which ended: "a Person is wanted who can model small Figures in Clay neatly".

Bow porcelain, although an artificial or frit porcelain, was heavy and strong. The frit was composed of two parts bone ash and one part crushed calcined flint. Water was worked into this to form a paste which was then shaped into balls. These were burned in a fierce fire and then ground to flour fineness. According to the patent this was mixed with one-third its weight in fireclay, but early in the 1750s this was replaced by some kind of china clay. Frye's porcelain is not to be confused with 19th-century bone china which was not a frit porcelain.

Frye's 1749 patent incorporated a method of glazing by dipping, the first recorded reference to liquid glaze in this country. As a patent was granted for the process it is obvious that Frye possessed a 14-year monopoly from November 1749, lapsing a year after his death in 1762, but it is probable that he licensed the glazing process to others. It will be noticed that Bow figures are glazed beneath the base in contradistinction to those of Derby where the base remained unglazed, probably because the old glazing was used. Frye's patent called for the biscuit porcelain to be "glazed with the following preparation: Take salt petre one part, red lead two parts, sand, flint or other white stones, three parts. To make a glass, melt it well and grind it, to every twenty pounds of which add six pounds of white lead, adding a small portion of smalt to clean the colour; mix it with water and glaze the ware, which is done by dipping it in a vessel of glaze and setting it on to dry, when it must be put in case [saggars] and burned with wood [charcoal] till the surface of the ware is clear and shining, and it is finished." This resulted in a thick creamy glaze.

Weatherby and Crowther embarked upon a venture of their own in 1753 by opening a wholesale and retail ware house at Cornhill, London. An advertisement published in the *Derby Mercury* of March 9, quoted by Jewitt, announced: "BOW CHINA WAREHOUSE was opened on *Wednesday*, the 7th of *February*, near the *Royal Exchange*, in *Cornhill, London*, with a Back Door facing the *Bank*, in *Threadneedle St.* for the convenience of all Customers, both in Town and Country; where it will continue to be sold in the same manner as formerly, at BOW, with Allowance made to Wholesale dealers."

The showrooms soon became one of London's fashionable china shops, so successful that in 1756 Weatherby and Crowther established a West End branch at St. James's Street Terrace, a favoured area for the trade. An announcement in the *Daily Advertiser* described the venture as "for the Convenience of the Nobility and Gentry, which is constantly supplied with every Thing new direct from the Factory, with the real Price marked on each Piece without Abatement". The show rooms did not prove profitable, however, and were closed in April 1758 when Lambe the auctioneer advertised that he was selling "the intire Stock of the Bow Warehouse, on the Terrass in St. James's Street, they having intirely quitted the same; consisting of fine Epergnes, Chandeliers, Branches decorated with Flowers and Figures, beautiful Groups and other figures of Birds, Beasts . . . beautifully painted by several of the finest Masters from Dresden."

Four years later the *London Chronicle*, October 14–16, 1762, announced that "Yesterday morning died, at his house on Tower-hill, Mr. Wetherby, one of the proprietors of the Bow-china-warehouse, Cornhill", and in November of the following year John Crowther filed his petition of bankruptcy. The stock was sold by auction, including "curious figures, girandoles, branches for chimney-pieces finely decorated with figures and flowers, dishes, compotiers, beautiful desserts of the fine old partridge and wheatsheaf patterns". Nevertheless, John Crowther continued the porcelain factory at Bow and established another china warehouse in St. Paul's Church Yard.

The celebrated sculptor John Bacon, R.A. (1740–99), may have modelled for Crowther. No direct evidence of this is known but the facts suggest some slight association between them. Bacon was apprenticed in 1754 to the Crispe brothers, jewellers and potters of Bow Church Yard, Cheapside, London. The Crispe family were recorded as potters in the reign of Charles II and are reputed to have made porcelain in the Lambeth-Vauxhall district. Bacon's obituary notice in the *Gentleman's Magazine*, 1799, states definitely that he worked in the Crispes' china factory where he modelled "Shepherds, Shepherdesses, and such like small ornamental pieces". Later, in 1831, Allan Cunningham in *Lives of the Most Eminent British Sculptors*, described the Crispes as "eminent makers of porcelain, who taught Bacon the art of modelling various groups of figures such as the *Deer and the Holly Tree,* the *Bird and the Bush,* the *Shepherd and Shepherdess* and birds of all shapes, beasts of every kind yet made for show or for use in our Manufactories".

A bankruptcy notice in the *London Chronicle*, November 22nd 1763, described the Crispe brothers as Thomas, Nicholas and Edward, Jewellers and Potters, who were to appear at Guildhall on January 3, 1764. An adjoining notice shows that on the same day "John Crowther, of Cornhill, Chinaman" appeared in bankruptcy. This coincidence certainly points to some business association between the two firms. Bacon is known to have modelled for Duesbury of Derby who in 1769 paid him £75 7s. 2d. for models.

Bow figures and groups modelled in the Meissen style acquired a high contemporaneous reputation. No examples earlier than 1750 have been authenticated. Early figures possessed none of the delicacy of Continental work, but were weighty, with a compact, vitreous, faintly greyish paste, and a glaze usually greyish-white. From 1754 the paste was softer and whiter than formerly but might be flawed with specks and firecracks. Great care was needed in firing to the biscuit state: new saggars were essential and only a single figure was contained in each for it was found that when two were fired together in a saggar, one was invariably a waster.

The glaze, containing lead oxide, might be either faintly blue or slightly greenish-yellow, cobalt being introduced to clear the colour. This is particularly noticeable where thick drops collected in crevices, often obliterating finer reliefs. Until 1760 glazé was applied lavishly.

Bow figures may be classified into five main groups according to their decoration: (1) white glazed from 1750; (2) first enamelled period, 1754 to 1758; (3) biscuit, from 1755; (4) second enamelled period, 1758 to 1765; (5) third enamelled period, from 1765.

Figures in white glazed porcelain made from 1750 usually stand on rectangular plinths and are characterised by vigorous though elementary modelling displaying technical imperfections. Supports are often crudely simple, sometimes no more than lumps of clay hand-modelled to resemble pillars or tree-stumps, and the plinths may be moulded to suggest rock-work with growing flowers in relief.

Well-known among this early work is the figure of *Kitty Clive* the celebrated actress in the character of the Fine Lady of Garrick's farce *Lethe*. This was modelled after the engraving by Charles Mosley published in 1750. The example in the Fitzwilliam Museum is incised "1750" beneath the glaze of the base and is unusual in that it is mounted on a square moulded plinth with a theatrical trophy on the front. This figure is also found on a thin, flat, square base, as in the British Museum example, and on a shaped base as in a Victoria and Albert Museum example. These are undated and measure 9¾ inches in height. Doubtless Kitty Clive was a popular Bow figure, long in production, for she gave her final performance in the part of the Fine Lady during 1769. This would account for the several versions differing in minor details and for variations in chemical composition as described in *The Catalogue of the Schreiber Collection*, Volume 1, Victoria and Albert Museum, 1928.

Kitty Clive's companion was *Henry Woodward* as the Fine Gentleman in *Lethe*, modelled from an engraving by James McArdell after James Hayman's painting. The actor stands with legs apart and hands thrust in pockets, upon a pedestal on a square base incised with lozenge diaper. These figures were sold in the white and decorated by independent enamellers: William Duesbury's account book for 1751 records that he charged three shilling each for "enamelling Mr Woodward and Kitty Clive". Another well-known actor represented in Bow porcelain was James Quin in the character of Falstaff, a part he played in 1746 to 1747. This was modelled from an engraving by James McArdell after a drawing prepared by Quin himself who is shown wearing a plumed hat, flourishing a sword in his right hand and carrying a circular shield on his left arm. A similar figure was made at Derby from about 1765.

The Bagpiper, wearing a wide-brimmed hat and loose cloak, was possibly adapted from an engraving by Daullé after J. Dumont le Rom, 1739, but more likely copied from the Meissen figure of the same subject modelled by J. J. Kändler in 1741. A pair of *sphinxes* represented couchant on scrolled pedestals with heads of the actress Peg Woffington were adapted from the painting by Arthur Pond, engraved in the late 1740s by James McArdell and now in the National Gallery. These sphinxes were made over a ten-year period, many of them enamelled and gilded by outside decorators.

Handsome figures of three of the nine Muses were made

during the period, names for identification incised in cursive characters on their columns: *Melpomene* (tragedy) wearing a crown, leaning against a column and holding a cup in her right hand, a dagger in her left; *Polyhymnia* (of the sublime hymn) seated on a rock with a trophy of arms; *Terpischore* (dance and song) in a dancing pose.

Fully authenticated white glazed Bow figures and groups exhibited at the British Museum in 1959 included the foregoing and a figure of a *Negress* with basket and cover inscribed 1750; *Fisher-girl and Gallant*; *Actor and Actress* in Turkish costume of which the catalogue notes "the female figure has a markedly creamy appearance, a plain square base, underside of which is glazed and has a caduceus mark under the glaze. The male figure is of greyish white appearance on a thicker square base than its companion: traces of unfired green and white paint remain."

Duesbury's account book for porcelain decorated from 1751 to 1753 contains entries recording the wide variety of figures made at Bow and sold in the white. These include: "2 large groups of Bow Birds, 4*s*.; 2 Pairs of Bogh sesons, 12*s*.; 1 large group of Bogh figars, 4*s*.; 6 Bow doggs, 6*s*.; 2 groups Bogh candlesticks, 3*s*. 6*d*.; 1 Pr. small figars Bow, 2*s*. 6*d*."

William Bemrose who illustrated eight holograph pages from Duesbury's account book also attributed to Bow the following figures decorated between 1751 and 1753: "Minerva of two sizes; Flora; imperial shepherd and shepherdess; the new shepherd and its companion; Cupid; gentleman and lady; boy and girl; fluter; fiddler; harlequin; Columbine and Period or clown; tamborine player; sportsman; cook; Dutch dancer; woman with chickens; Turk and companion; female figures; boars, squirrels; goat; buck and doe; swans; birds on pedestals." (A pheasant and crane are to be seen in the Schreiber Collection, Victoria and Albert Museum.)

Figures decorated with overglaze enamels within the factory date from late in 1753, their first period continuing until 1758. This early decoration is by no means comparable with contemporaneous Chelsea or Derby. The drapery is usually of solid colour, pale pink and yellow being common;

others are enriched with flowers and foliage, a costume with simple flower motifs in two of three colours being typical. Enamels and glaze were never applied so thickly as at Chelsea of the gold anchor period, but they are in marked contrast to the thinness of Derby work. Seen at their best, however, the Bow colours display remarkable beauty. In sunlight the colours sparkle with a radiance quite foreign to the many reproductions which abound, the effect being due to impurities in the metallic oxides. The diversity of tone in Bow enamels at this time resulted from haphazard preparation of the ingredients which had not yet been standardised.

The curious brownish-red enamel, known to some collectors as sealing wax red, is now lacking in gloss because of the poor quality of the iron oxide in its composition which has tended to powder away from the glaze. This dry red and yellowish-green were commonly used with the addition of puce in shades ranging from pink to crimson, a milky blue of lifeless opacity, yellow and slight gilding. The colours might be merged to produce marbling effects on the bases.

Copies and adaptations of Meissen figures were largely made, but until 1758 they usually stood upon flat, rectangular or shaped plinths entirely lacking in ornament or with scrollwork in low relief. The more elaborate and costly figures stood upon high rococo scroll bases which might be picked out with slight touches of colour, purple being a favourite. Heights of figures rarely exceeded ten inches.

Figures of this period in the British Museum include the group *Leopard and Naked Boy*. The boy is seated on the back of a reclining leopard and feeding it with grapes. His head is encircled with fruiting vines and he has drapery across his knees. The base is in rustic style, the underside only partly glazed. Colouring ranges through yellow, brown, green, blue and purple. In *Liberty and Matrimony* the man, Liberty, stands against a tree stump, holding a bird in his upraised hand while a dog jumps up on his left knee and a ram lies at his side. The woman, Matrimony, stands against a tree stump holding a bird cage in her right hand. These figures have rococo scroll bases. Other versions are known enamelled in the later style.

John Bowcock, formerly a purser in the Royal Navy, employed at "the Bow China Warehouse, Cornhill", from the time of its establishment in 1753, became accountant, sales representative and general clerk in the factory. His memoranda book for 1756, preserved in the British Museum with other relevant papers, recorded various figures then in production, sometimes with prices. Some extracts from this manuscript are: "January, Mr Fogg a china seller, 16 cooks, 2s. each; a swan; two harlequins, 7s. March, Mr Fahy, 9 gentlemen and ladies at 9s., £4 1s.; Mr White, 1 small fluter, white; 3 pairs boys and girls; 1 pair small fidler and companion; 1 pair tamberines; 1 cook. Mr Fogg, 6 swans; 6 white boars; 6 swans, wings open. Mr Williams, 1 pair sporters; 1 enamelled pero, 6s.; 1 shepherd imperial, 7s.; 1 pair of the new shepherd and companion; 1 pair Dutch dancers, 9s.; 1 gentleman and lady, 18s.; 1 cook, 7s.; 1 boy and girl, 12s.; 1 Paris Cries, 6s.; 1 woman with chicken, 7s.; a pair of birds on pedestals. June, a pair of Minervas of each size; a pair of coloured squirrels; set, harlequin, columbine and perio." Other figures noted were *Flora, Cupid, sportsman, Turk and companion, goat, buck and doe.*

The Bowcock papers include a drawing of the *Fluter and Companion*, 3s. and 4s. 6d. each. A pair of these in the British Museum is described in the catalogue: "a boy playing a flute, a girl playing the guitar; seated on flowering tree-stumps on rococo-scroll bases; enamelled and heavily gilt; two triangular holes at the back on either side of each for mounts, the metal remaining on one. The mark, on girl figure, an anchor and dagger in red, on back of tree stump. About 1770." Some interesting bills in the collection are from the independent enameller "Richard Dyer at Mr Bolton's, enameller, near the Church, Lambeth".

Bowcock's reference to 16 Cooks ordered by Fogg in January 1756 discredits the attribution made by several authorities. Existing examples of these figures are impressed B and this has prompted the assumption that they were modelled by John Bacon (1744 to 1790), afterwards R.A. Allan Cunningham has recorded that in 1754 Bacon was apprenticed to "one Crispe of Bow Churchyard an eminent maker of porcelain". Apart from Bacon's youthfulness at the time of Bowcock's records it is unlikely that the rule of anonymity laid down by master potters would have been relaxed for an apprentice.

Bow biscuit figures undoubtedly preceded those of Derby, but were not received with enthusiasm: in comparison they are crude and ill-proportioned. Biscuit figures of *Kitty Clive* and *Henry Woodward* are known, but are probably productions of the 1760s. John Bowcock, however, noted in his journal for May 1756: "Mrs Whitfield to have 1 pr white biscuit candlesticks."

The second enamel period extended from 1758 to about 1764 following an influx of Chelsea decorators and the retirement of Frye. A distinct improvement had been made in the glaze which became smooth and ivory-tinted, a rich ground for enamels and gilding. Figures now tended to become more colourful, two or three enamels being usual with the addition of slight gilding. This resulted in a great resemblance between Bow and Chelsea figures. Careful inspection of many enamelled Bow figures discloses slight flaws beneath the glaze in undecorated areas. This was caused by the assembler's use of a flat knife for sharpening the surface and a pointed tool for accentuating lines before firing. Colours are conspicuously brighter and more garish.

Modelling was carried out with greater delicacy than formerly. Plinths were elaborated with rococo scrollwork so designed that the four corners of the base became small supporting feet with a swag between the two front feet. Bow was the first English porcelain factory to make the footed pedestal a characteristic feature. This style of pedestal was progressively elaborated on the more handsome and costly figures and was enlivened with touches of colour, usually purple. Small figures generally stood, as formerly, upon circular flat-based plinths.

During this period Bow introduced and used exclusively a light blue, solidly opaque in appearance and described by some collectors as sealing wax blue. This enamel is seen on most Bow figures after 1760 and is easily distinguished from the blues of Chelsea and Derby. Additional colours in the enameller's palette were opaque purple, brick red and pale yellow, very sparingly applied. Hand-modelled conventional flowers, usually coloured in puce or crimson, might border feminine garments. Faces were but slightly tinted although the touch of colour on each cheek was more pronounced than formerly.

John Bowcock's papers include several bills for undecorated figures supplied to "Richard Dyer at Mr Bolton's, enameller, near the Church, Lambeth", between May 21 and August 2, 1760. These show factory prices to have been: "2 pair of Turks, @ 1s. 3d. each; 6 pair of Italian Comedy @ 3s. per pair; 2 sets of Small Seasons, no plinths @ 1s. each; 4 Dianas, 1s. 6d. each; 4 Grape-cutting Boys, 1s. each; 8 pipers and Companions, 1s. each; 2 Minervas @ 6s. each; 6 large Gardiners @ 1s. 6d. each; 1 pr of double birds @ 2s. each; 2 Boys on Lyon and Leopards @ 1s. each; 12 Nuns and Fryers @ 10d. each; 4 new Dancers with plinths @ 1s. 6d. each."

In some instances a Bow figure shows a triangular, circular or square hole cut into the clay before glazing and fitted with a brass socket. This was intended to the attachment of a leafy branch of ormolu or green-enamelled metal stalks surmounted by porcelain flowers or candle sockets. From about 1760 the factory sold figures complete with decorative branches.

Gradually, table chandeliers, candlesticks and branches "for Chimney Pieces and finely decorated with Flowers and Figures" advertised at this time, were modelled in numerous designs. A pair might have stems modelled as a splendidly enamelled shepherd and shepherdess, or a cherub might hold aloft a candlesocket or a branch for two, three or four candles. A group of birds masking a metal stem and candle socket delighted the wealthy, but few specimens survived. Candlesticks made to receive branches are recognised by their wide, heavy bases, designed to prevent overbalancing.

Renowned among Bow productions were little leafy bowers with figures of small cherubs against backgrounds of flowers and foliage. These *bocages* are smaller than those of Chelsea with twisted leaves and petals: in Chelsea *bocages* leaves are flatter and the outer petals of flowers are saucer-shaped. Pairs of standing figures as containers for comfits were made in several forms. These might carry baskets or shells in their arms or poised on their heads. Seated figures in Eastern costume offered scallop shell vessels: later seated figures held baskets on their knees or placed beside them.

A further influx of experienced potters and decorators from Chelsea in 1764 and 1765 made possible large-scale production of groups and figures displaying greater creative individuality: Continental work was seldom copied. The porcelain was of more workable texture, the glaze thinner and more harshly white.

Rich, deep, lustrous enamels gave these Bow figures a lavish appearance. Pedestals were designed with gracefully pierced scrollwork and enriched with crimson, yellow and pale blue enamel. Collectors revel in costumes with grounds of rich crimson underglaze blue, sealing wax red or turquoise surrounding white reserves in rococo outline, often gilded and patterned with delicate flowers in one or more colours. A blue or crimson dress might be patterned with yellow flowers and tiny gold leaves; waistcoat or breeches might display the handsome peacock's tail scale pattern.

During this period the Bow porcelain factory was operated by John Crowther, with showrooms and a warehouse in St. Paul's Church Yard. In 1776 he sold the entire concern to William Duesbury who removed plant, moulds, tools and stock to Derby.

The number of enamelled figures attributed to Bow of the 1750s is unreasonably large. The presence of a mark must not be accepted as proof without further and more important evidence of authenticity. Bow marks appear on modern copies, duly "antiqued", from Paris and elsewhere. Firecracks are no longer proof of Georgian manufacture as they can be produced artificially.

Bow figures were not invariably marked as so many were sold to the independent decorators. Marks might be incised or impressed in the paste, roughly painted in crimson, or inscribed in blue under the glaze. Among the marks used at Frye's New Canton until 1758 were dates incised into the base; several versions of upper case B incised, impressed or painted in crimson; three vertical lines crossed by three horizontal lines; pseudo-oriental marks in blue under the glaze; and the caduceus.

44

Marks used between 1758 and 1764 included a circle crossed by an arrow, sometimes modified to a C crossed by a stroke and occasionally resembling a crescent; crossed or single daggers in blue underglaze; the caduceus in blue underglaze or incised. From 1758 the well-established anchor and dagger in red was used and also the sword in blue; late in the period the anchor might have a cable. Daggers and anchors occur in several variations and the anchor is seen with and without ring and barbs.

The impressed marks T° and T have been noted on Bow figures and also on figures from Plymouth, Bristol and Worcester. This mark is found on Bow porcelain figures such as the *Marquess of Granby* and the *Bagpiper* in the British Museum, and *General Wolfe, Minerva* and other figures in the Victoria and Albert Museum. It has been conjectured to be the mark of an assembler—the contemporary term was repairer—named Tebo. He was probably one of the several jewellers who entered the new trade of porcelain making in England, such as Crispe of Bow, Sprimont of Chelsea, Planché of Derby. Mr. A. J. B. Kiddell discovered a news paragraph in *The Daily Advertiser*, November 13, 1747, in which the occupier of a tenement in Fetter Lane, London, was a jeweller named Teboe. This may have been the figure maker.

Marks of this kind are associated not with modellers but with repairers, the men who moulded and assembled the parts of a figure.

Severne Mackenna has suggested that Tebo probably modelled the *Three Muses* at Bow. These, however, were modelled before he joined the firm and in any case would seem to be beyond his capacity for Josiah Wedgwood, employing him nearly twenty years later at Etruria, held a very poor opinion of his work. On November 16, 1774, Wedgwood wrote to his partner Thomas Bentley: "Mr Tebo is modelling the two Lamps from St. Non—but goes on very slowly." On July 3, 1775 Wedgwood wrote scathingly of Tebo as a figure modeller: "I think we can manage to model them [some Greek and Roman profiles], & Mr Tebo has nothing else to do. *He is not equal to a Figure*, but I can make him bost out and others finish the heads." A

45

week later Wedgwood reported: "Mr Tebo has had a cast of a Hare's Head before him for some time, *but it is not a likeness*. The wet plaister in Casting presses down the hair upon the face, & makes it look like the head of a drown'd Puppy; & Mr Tebo cannot model anything like the face of a Hare." On October 28 Wedgwood wrote: "Mr Tebo leaves us on the 11th of this month and not before he has done us a very considerable mischief, for our Modelers do less by one half than they did before, charging double prices for their work, and when talk'd to about it have their reply ready that 'it is cheaper than Mr Tebo, and is finish'd which his work never is'."

Chapter Three

DERBY

WILLIAM DUESBURY, that most spectacular of Georgian potters, at the age of twenty-five was already established in London as an independent decorator of porcelain. He lived to become the proprietor of one of the most prosperous industrial concerns of his day, incorporating under his Derby trade mark the Chelsea and Bow porcelain factories. For more than ninety years the Derby Porcelain Manufactory made figures and groups, glazed and in the biscuit. More than a thousand original models were issued in addition to those made from moulds acquired from Chelsea and Bow and copied from Meissen.

The earliest reference to Derby porcelain is recorded in Duesbury's account book for 1751 where he carefully detailed the 382 articles he decorated in that year from "Darbishire", "Bogh", "Staffartshire" and elsewhere, including many "Darby Figars" of dancers and seasons. Notes regarding decoration are sometimes comprehensive, such as: "How to color the group, a gentleman Busing a Lady—gentlm a gold trim^d cote, a pink wastcot and trimmed with black Breeches and socs, the lade a flowrd sack with yellow robings, a black stomager, her hare black, his wig powdrd."

The entries distinguish between "painting" and "enamelling". Painting with unfired or cold pigments was common at that period and less costly as no greater heat was needed for fixing than a few hours in a warm oven. Such decoration was short-lived in wear as it adhered poorly to the smooth surface of the glaze and quickly flaked away. Both Chelsea and Worcester advertised their decorations were "*all warranted* True Enamel".

47

The first name so far associated with porcelain manufacture at Derby is that of André Planché whose brother Jacques had been employed in the porcelain factory at Meissen. Jacques was working in the Staffordshire Potteries during the late 1740s but so far as can be ascertained none of the master potters took advantage of the special skills he had acquired at Meissen. Several authorities perpetuate the impossible legend that in 1745 the seventeen-year-old André was in Derby making white-glazed figures and birds which he fired in a pipe-maker's oven. It has been established by Major William H. Tapp, however, that the youth was apprenticed to Edward Mountenay, a manufacturing jeweller of Foster's Lane, London, from July 3, 1740 until July 3, 1747. Major Tapp also discovered that Planché married Sarah Stone at St. Pancras Church on September 28, 1747.

It is probable that after his marriage he found work at Derby, then an important centre of the jewellery trade where Severne & Co. employed nearly one hundred men and women, and Simpson more than thirty. Whilst following his trade as a jeweller he would have been able to carry out research in porcelain manufacture with the aid of information supplied by his brother in the adjoining county of Staffordshire. No doubt these experimental pieces were fired in the kilns of Derby's long-established earthenware pottery known as the Cockpit Hill Pot Manufactory where they attracted the attention of its financier, John Heath, a local banker and one of the three partners in the firm which included Thomas Rivett, then Member of Parliament for Derby. By 1749 Planché was established at Cockpit Hill as the master potter in charge of a porcelain department operating under the name of the Derby Porcelain Manufactory. From here came the white glazed porcelain figures decorated by William Duesbury in his London studio. It seems that nothing more than a short range of figures and some hollow-ware was made. Authenticated specimens now appear as white, but some display slight traces of unfired oil paints.

The Planché-Heath venture operated successfully, if not profitably, until 1755. Meantime, Duesbury had joined

3. (*Top left*) Group usually regarded as Madonna and Child. The Madonna wears a yellow cloak and pale puce scarf: the Child, draped with a red cloth, stands on a globe entwined by a serpent. Height 18¼ inches. Chelsea, red anchor period. (*Top right*) This important figure, known as "Pomona, Goddess of Fruit", also represents Taste in the set of Senses. Chelsea, gold anchor period. (*Bottom*) Shepherd with dogs and shepherdess with sheep and lamb, against flowering bushes. Chelsea, gold anchor and impressed R.

4. (*Top*) A pair of figures coloured and gilt. Height 7¼ inches. Bow 1760–65. (*Lower left*) Chelsea-Derby figure of Summer; about 1770. (*Lower right*) Chelsea figure of a Reaper, emblematic of summer, on a scroll pedestal. At his feet among flowers and corn are a flail and a barrel-shaped flask. Height 12½ inches. About 1760. A similar figure in the British Museum is marked with a gold anchor.

William Littler of Longton Hall in 1754 as an enameller. Here, doubtless, he met Jacques Planché and an introduction was arranged with his brother André in Derby. The long term result of this meeting was that a deed of partnership was drawn up between Heath, Duesbury and Planché on January 1, 1756, Heath financing the venture to the extent of £1,000. They acquired property in Nottingham Road, Derby, and under Duesbury's forceful direction the existing seven tenements and a dwelling house were quickly converted into a porcelain factory. This traded as Duesbury & Heath but was advertised as the Derby Porcelain Company.

John Heath's Derby Porcelain Manufactory ceased manufacture but continued as wholesale merchants. On December 14, 1756 the *Public Advertiser* contained the following advertisement, which was several times repeated:

To be sold by Auction
By MR BELLAMY
By order of the Proprietor of the DERBY PORCELAIN Manufactory, at a commodious House in Prince's Street, Cavendish Square. This and the three following Days.
A curious Collection of fine *Figures, Jars, Sauceboats, Services for Deserts,* and great *Variety* of other useful and ornamental Porcelain, after the finest Dresden models, all exquisitely painted in Enamel, with Flowers, Insects, India Plants, &c. together with a Parcel of China Ware seized and condemn'd in his Majesty's Court of Exchequer; and a large Quantity of China lackquered Ware, Pictures and Curiosities of a Captain of an East Indiaman, consisting of a great Variety of useful and ornimental China, in Dishes and Plates, compleat Tea Equipages Jars, Beakers, and Variety of fine India Dressing Boxes, and several Curiosities.
This and the following Days will be sold some of the finest of the Derby Porcelain and foreign China.

Most writers, omitting the final sentence, have attributed the "curious collection" to Duesbury, an impossibility considering the few months that manufacture had been in progress.

At this time the choice of fashion was the porcelain produced by Meissen, near Dresden, Saxony, and now often called Dresden porcelain. This was characterised by anatomical accuracy, sharp modelling detail, thin glaze and unglazed undersurfaces. But a few months after the Derby Porcelain Co. started production the Continent became involved in the Seven Years War.

In September 1756 the Prussians overran the Dresden Porcelain Manufactory and rifled the warehouses after discovering that the plant had been destroyed and the potters had escaped to Frankfurt. Production virtually ceased until the close of the war in 1763. Duesbury saw this as a golden opportunity for seizing the Meissen figure trade and duplicated as closely as possible the hard porcelain figures that had been made there. Among the connoisseurs who lent him valuable Meissen originals were the Duke of Newcastle and the Countess Spencer.

Having set out to make himself a specialist in figures and groups, a year later he was well-known as the potter of "Second Dresden" figures. An editorial notice in the *Public Advertiser*, May 17, 1757, reported an auction sale of porcelain which included "the largest Variety of the Derby or Second Dresden", observing "the Numbers of Quality and Gentry who expressed satisfaction at the Great Perfection of the Derby Figures which many good judges could not distinguish from the Real Dresden". The London china dealers placed unexpectedly large orders and by the end of the year Duesbury had enlarged his factory and doubled the number of his employees. Prices were "much cheaper than any Thing of equal Quality made in England".

In 1770 William Duesbury acquired the goodwill, plant and stock-in-trade of the Chelsea porcelain factory which he kept in production until 1784 before transferring it to Derby on account of his own ill-health. Influenced by his Chelsea acquisition Duesbury in 1772 entered the profitable branch of figure-making in unglazed biscuit porcelain which remained in continual production until the factory closed. This is considered in detail in the next chapter.

Duesbury's son William joined him in partnership in 1786, but at this time their London manager, Joseph Lygo, reported to Derby that demand for their figures was declining. The firm then traded as William Duesbury & Son. When the elder Duesbury died a few months later his son became sole proprietor and controlled the factory until 1795 when failing health prompted him to seek a partner. He selected Michael Kean, a London miniature painter, and when he died in 1796, Kean was appointed director of the factory on behalf of Duesbury's widow and children. Shortly afterwards Kean married Mrs. Duesbury: the business then traded as Duesbury & Kean.

Wartime conditions in the 1790s drastically reduced the demand for porcelain, however, and exports became negligible. Conditions became even worse in the late 1790s, for the sale of table-ware was affected by Josiah Spode's introduction of whiter, stronger and less costly bone china. Facing competition from newcomers to the industry, such as John Rose of Coalport, John Davenport of Longport and Robert Chamberlain of Worcester, Kean converted production from soft-paste porcelain to the new non-frit bone china.

Kean proved himself a skilful designer of porcelain but seems to have had differences with the grown-up sons of Duesbury. He disposed of his share of the business in 1811 to William Sheffield, father-in-law of the third William Duesbury (see *Jewitt*, Vol. 2, page 86).

For four years Derby traded unsuccessfully as Duesbury & Sheffield. Then the business was sold to Robert Bloor who for many years had been commercial manager to the Duesburys. The price was £5,000 to be paid in instalments, plus various annuities to the Duesbury family. The lease of the premises to Bloor at £110 per annum is dated November 1815. Bloor revived the declining business and before the end of the decade Derby was operating once more on a successful financial basis. Following the lead of Josiah Spode he devoted his energies to marketing great quantities of bone china table-ware decorated with gay japan patterns and richly gilded.

The warehouses at Derby had accumulated several tons of badly flawed soft-paste porcelain, including many figures. Bloor ordered these stocks to be gaudily decorated in such a way that faults were concealed. The result is that collectors are sometimes faced with figures obviously potted during the 18th century but decorated in the florid style of the late-

Regency. This method of obtaining ready money at little cost was immediately profitable, but it introduced a lack of care into the Derby system which began an all-round deterioration of quality and precipitated the decline of Derby's high reputation. Despite this, Robert Bloor was appointed potter to George IV in 1820. But three years after Bloor's death in 1845 the factory was closed and demolished.

Plant and stock-in-trade, including models and moulds of Chelsea and Bow figures were bought by Samuel Boyle, Little Fenton, Staffordshire. Many moulds for useful wares were destroyed but the models and moulds for figures, groups and other ornamental wares, to the extent of twenty barge loads, were taken by water to Little Fenton where Boyle made figures in the styles of old Derby and Chelsea. When Boyle emigrated to Australia a few years later the models and moulds were sold to various other potters who also made figures.

As Derby figures were often in constant production, many of them for more than eighty-five years, it is essential that the collector should be able to distinguish between the pastes of the various periods.

Planché (*1749–55*). So little is known of his porcelain that identification so far has been little more than guesswork. It is generally accepted that it is of poor quality, the paste light in weight and the opaque glaze usually dirty white with a faintly yellowish tinge. Some figures are solid: in others there is a funnel-shaped hole cut in the centre of the base extending to the hollow body. In others again a small hole is pierced in the back to permit gases to escape during firing and thus avoid bursting. Some figures attributed to Planché display microscopic traces of unfired oil paints and may possibly have been decorated by William Duesbury.

Duesbury (*1756–70*). Derby paste of the first Duesbury period was composed of white-burning clays from Derbyshire and Dorset and a glassy frit. At first this was noticeably light in weight, chalky in appearance and sandy textured. Improvements during the early 1760s produced a porcelain of creamy translucency. These porcelains were coated with a glossy, colourless glaze which penetrated deeply. Glazing was carried out by sprinkling flour-fine lead oxide over

5. Figures and groups in Bow porcelain. (*Top left*) Shepherdess with flowers in her apron and a reclining lamb beside her. Enamelled and gilt, with hole at the back for mount. Height 10 inches. 1759–1776. (*Top right*) Girl with basket of fruit and flowers: in brilliantly coloured enamels, supported by the stump of a flowering tree, on a rococo scrolled base. 1755–1760. (*Lower left*) The Handel commemorative vase with three children representing Music, Drama and Dancing. The front panel of the vase displays an enamelled score of a "Minuet", a "Song" and other scores arranged in the form of a trophy, one of them headed TF. Many of Thomas Frye's engravings were signed in this way. Height 7 inches. 1959. (*Lower right*) "*The Fortune Teller*", inspired by a panel of Beauvais tapestry signed by Boucher, 1736. Decorated in enamel colours touched with gilt. About 1760.

6. Bow enamelled figures. (*Top left*) General John Manners, Marquess of Granby (1721–1770) in the uniform of Colonel of the Horse Guards, standing beside a tree stump on a rococo-scrolled base picked out in gold. Probably made to commemorate the Battle of Minden. Taken from a print by Richard Houston, after Sir Joshua Reynolds, published 1760. Mark, T impressed. (*Top right*) Cook, carrying two trussed birds on a dish, Mark, B impressed. 1756. (*Lower left*) Gardener, emblematic of Autumn, wearing a green-lined crimson coat, figured waistcoat, flowered breeches, and dark blue apron, with a black cocked hat in his left hand, and with his right holding up his apron laden with fruit. Height 14 inches. About 1770. (*Lower right*) General Wolfe, adapted from an engraving by Richard Houston. Impressed T°, the mark of Tebo. Height 13⅞ inches. About 1760.

the biscuit. When fired at a moderate temperature the lead oxide was converted into a thin film of glaze. This ended an appreciable distance above the lower edge of the base and the underside of the base remained unglazed. To collectors these are known as dry edge figures. It is probable that the lead oxide was of Derbyshire origin thus containing impurities responsible for the very faint tinge of greenish-blue often visible in the glaze. Its thinness accentuated sharp outlines in the modelling: folds of garments, for instance, were almost knife-edged. Duesbury laid down a rule that his modellers should rough out their figures in the nude and then drape them, thus achieving anatomical accuracy, a device continued throughout the 18th century in Derby work. Thus Duesbury achieved the Meissen characteristics of good anatomical modelling, clear, sharp outlines, thin glaze and unglazed undersurfaces.

Derby enamels, notably pale in hue, were applied over the glaze less thickly than those of Chelsea and Bow, thus appreciably reducing costs, an important consideration when enamels were expensive. To produce one ounce of enamel colour the final grinding alone occupied a boy eight working days, then totalling nearly a hundred hours. So thin might be the enamel that brushmarks were unable to float out. A characteristic feature of early Derby figures is the reddish-brown colour ringing a darker spot to represent the eye pupil: eyebrows and eyelashes were often in the same tint. Drapery might be decorated with flowers in natural colours on a yellow ground and lined with crushed straw-berry pink, a frequent Duesbury colour. Gilding was sparse and seldom decorated more than the edges of garments and buttons, with a few touches enriching the pedestal which was decorated with enamels rather than the more expensive hand-made flowers in the round used by other potters. In Derby *bocage* figures the fabric of petals and the light, grass green and bluish green leaves are appreciably thinner and sharper to the touch than are those of Chelsea and Bow. The tree stump may be pierced with a circular hole for the insertion of gilded brass candle branches.

The subjects of some early figures with their wholesale prices were extracted by Llewellyn Jewitt from lists describing the contents of forty-five cases of porcelain despatched from Derby to London during 1763. These were: "4 Large Britanias at 36*s*.; 6 Second-sized Huzzars at 12*s*.; 8 Large Quarters [of the globe] at 40*s*.; 6 Shakespeares at 42*s*.; 6 Miltons at 42*s*.; 2 Jupiters at 68*s*.; 5 Ledas at 36*s*.; 1 Europa at 30*s*.; 2 Bird-catchers at 10*s*. 6*d*.; 4 Large Pidgeons at 7*s*.; 12 small Rabbets at 2*s*.; 12 Chickens at 2*s*.; 24 Bucks on pedestals at 2*s*. 6*d*.; second-sized Boys at 1*s*. 6*d*." There were also sets of the *Elements, Mars, Minerva, Juno, Neptune, the Muses, Diana, Spaniards,* standing sheep, feeding sheep, cats, garlanded shepherds and Chelsea-pattern candlesticks. These all continued in production until the factory closed in 1848.

Duesbury I and II (1770–96). Immediately after his acquisition of the Chelsea factory in 1770 Duesbury introduced 40 per cent of bone ash into his frit formula. The improvement was obviously conspicuous for Josiah Wedgwood in a letter to his partner Thomas Bentley during April 1772 expressed concern at "the Glare of the Derby china shows" in London. Derby soft-paste porcelain was now close grained and of cream tinted translucency. The fired biscuit figures were dipped into liquid lead glaze, which covered the underside of the base. This glaze gave to the porcelain a thick, lustrous surface, soft and easily scratched. So deeply did enamels sink into it that decoration often suggests painting under glaze. The glazed underside of the pedestal usually displays three or four unglazed areas about half an inch in diameter, known to potters as stilt marks and to collectors as patches. These were caused by the stilts or pads of clay which supported the figures whilst in the glazing kiln. This porcelain, with minor variations, continued in production until the end of the century.

The modelling of glazed figures during this period was less sharply defined than formerly and often suggests provincial origin. They might be no more than slightly tinted with pale washes of colour, the greens and pinks being extremely uneven. Derby blue, however, was an exception. In 1771 it was advertised as "*Rich ultramarine* and *bleu celeste* which Mr. Duesbury has with great Labour and Expense brought to a State of Perfection equal to that of the

French". This blue, sometimes termed lapis lazuli, was a thickly applied, semi-matt overglaze enamel, dark in tint and of exceptional brilliance and not used elsewhere. This was prepared by John Smith, who had been one of Duesbury's first apprentices, and it was known to the Derby decorators as Smith's blue. It may be slightly raised above the glaze in contrast to other colours which sank into it. Not until about 1790 did Derby use the less costly underglaze cobalt blue. The presence of opaque chrome green on a figure indicates a date later than 1796: until then a translucent copper green was used.

New figure subjects during this period included gods and goddesses, muses and senses, arts and science, passions and virtues, grotesque and sentimental figures, birds and animals. Portrait figures of celebrities followed the style of contemporaneous sculpture. Few of these subjects display originality, most of them being modelled from engravings.

At the sale of Derby porcelain at Christie's on May 23, 1785, a pair of the well-known figures, *Harlequin and Columbine*, were sold. J. E. Nightingale comments on these figures: "Before 1800 Harlequin was dressed in a long loose jacket and in trousers, as seen in the 18th century statuettes. In this year, however, at Drury Lane in *Harlequin Amulet*, James Byrne introduced the tight-fitting spangled shape of the present [1881] British stage; the celebrated Grimaldi was Clown, and Miss Menage, Columbine in the pantomime."

Included in this sale were also "a group of 2 Bacchants dressing Pan with a garland of flowers, in biscuit", bought by Lady Duncomb for £2 4s. (the catalogue price of this 12½-inch group was three guineas); a large group of "3 graces distressing Cupid, in biscuit", sold to Lady Monson for £2 14s. was catalogued at £4 4s.; "a pair of groups representing Poetry and Music, in biscuit", bought by the Imperial Ambassador for £2 1s. were catalogued at £3 15s.; and "a group of 2 Virgins awakening Cupid, in biscuit, £1 11s. 6d." was catalogued at £3 3s. 6d. An inventory of models and moulds of figures and trinkets taken in 1795 lists about a thousand subjects valued at £2,181 3s.: the moulds of useful wares were valued at £137 10s. At this time about seventy people were employed.

Kean (*1795–1811*) and *Sheffield* (*1811–15*). When Michael Kean abandoned soft-paste porcelain within a few years of becoming director of the factory, he introduced a hard, white bone china displaying a greenish translucency when held against the light. The thin, hard glaze did not absorb the enamels so that they could be applied less thickly than formerly. James Haslem, a decorator at Derby in the early-19th century, has recorded the technical reasons for the change, as regards figures, and infers that this had taken place by 1805. Formerly figures and groups had been fired to the biscuit state in the same kiln as useful wares. "As they required less heat they were placed near the bottom and in the front of the oven where the temperature was lowest. This was ideal until the ordinary china body [bone china] was made harder and required greater heat. This was unsuitable for firing the soft-paste porcelain used for figures which frequently collapsed into shapeless lumps. Instead of constructing kilns specially for firing figures it was decided to discontinue making them in soft porcelain. Thus it was that figures and groups began to be made of the ordinary domestic china body."

Bloor (*1815–48*). The quality of figures made at Derby had already deteriorated before Bloor became proprietor and he made no effort to bring about an improvement. Their lifelessness is no doubt attributable to the heavy bone china of poor translucency. Even when Duesbury's moulds and those of Chelsea and Bow were brought into use the figures were inclined to be carelessly finished. The thin, hard glaze has often become badly crazed. It would take thinly applied enamels but after muffle stoves for enamelling had been abandoned in about 1820 in favour of a large enamelling kiln, the enamels tended to flake, leaving white spots.

Gilding dominated the Bloor period. Of the 129 men and women employed in 1832 (there were also nearly 50 boys on the pay roll) 41 men worked as gilders and 32 women as burnishers. Week after week Robert Bloor bought gold from Read & Lucas, Sheffield, whose records show that throughout the 1820s two months' interest was always added to the purchase price. In 1823 he bought 480 oz. of gold at 85*s*. an ounce, which was lower than the London price. It is probable that the gold was less than standard quality: hence its bronzy appearance today, a feature also of gilding by Rockingham whose gold was bought from the same source.

It has been stated that figures ceased to be made at Derby in 1830. Haslem records, however, that in 1832 six "Figure Makers called Ornamental Repairers" were employed there, John Whitaker being the overlooker of the department, his assistants, Robert Blore, James Goodsby, Thomas Hall, William Hopkinson and John Perkins. As John Whitaker is known to have been employed as overlooker at Derby until the factory's closure in 1848 it is evident that figure making continued to the end. Whitaker was responsible for the gracefully modelled *Peacock Among Flowers* in production from 1829 to 1847. James Haslem's researches into the Derby story appear to merit reproducing at some length. In *The Old Derby China Factory*, 1876, he reproduced a catalogue of figures issued by the Derby China Works and referred to in his text as "the old list". This appears to be a copy of a list first issued in the early 1790s, but with 19th-century additions by Haslem since it includes the Doctor Syntax figures. This price list is reproduced on pages 64–73. This gives the height of each figure and its price, enamelled, gilt and in biscuit.

A new firm in no way associated with the Duesbury-Bloor factory was established at Derby in 1876. *Cassells Magazine of Art* in the following year described the new pottery and noted: "The figures, too, are larger than those of the past and modelling more correct. While the quaint and grotesque patterns such as Dr. Syntax and the Mansion House Dwarfs have been revived, something more than mere duplication is aimed at. For instance, there is an original series of statuettes representing Tribulation, Supplication, Resignation with one or two spirited essays in the classic, and certain droll illustrations of Force and Persuasion, in which a monk and a mule are the leading characters."

For the most part Derby figures were not marked. Some of the Planché period, 1749 to 1755, have been recorded with the name *Derby* incised in script on the unglazed base, and a simple script D with the date 1750, also inscribed. "Second Dresden" ware until the late 1760s might be painted underneath with crossed swords in blue. But figures and groups of the Duesbury periods were rarely marked until 1775, the year in which William Duesbury was granted the appointment of Potter to His Majesty King George III. A figure might then be incised with a modelling tool (not impressed) with a jewelled crown above a script D. From 1782 this was amplified by the insertion of crossed batons with three dots on each side, between the jewelled crown and the script D. More frequently the model number was incised, such as N° 37 on *Jason and Medea*, or N° 217 for the group emblematic of *music*. This refers to the numbers in the Derby figure catalogue first issued in the 1790s (see pages 64–73). The numeral 1, 2 or 3 on a figure indicates merely the size—large, standard or small.

A jewelled crown with DERBY below in upper case letters, or *Bloor/Derby* in script painted in red or vermilion may identify a figure of the Bloor period.

Yet another occasional mark is a symbol used by an assembler or so-called repairer: these include the ★ used by Isaac Farnsworth. An incised triangle sometimes puzzles a collector. This was the symbol of the early ornamental repairer Joseph Hill but has been mistaken sometimes for the early Chelsea triangle. A similar triangle was used by one of Josiah Wedgwood's workmen (illustrated in *The Wedgwood Handbook* by Eliza Meteyard, 1875, page 49) and was also the Minton date symbol on bone china for 1843.

Modellers and ornamental repairers employed by William Duesbury in the factory at Derby or on a freelance basis were innumerable, but few names have been associated with their actual productions. In all, Derby issued more than a thousand different figures and groups and many of those entered in the price list were sold by the thousand. John Bacon, R.A., the celebrated sculptor, received many commissions: his account for 1769 amounted to £75 7s. 2d. The Derby price list records "Garrick as Richard II" in two sizes and "Four seasons, large" as by Bacon. Some of the more celebrated modellers who were also ornamental repairers are considered below.

Pierre Stephan modelled many intricate groups and lifelike statuettes for the Duesburys between 1770 and 1795. Llewellyn Jewitt's unrivalled collection of Derby manuscripts included articles of agreement dated September 17, 1770, "between Peter Stephane of Derby in the county of Derby Modeller and China or Porcelain Repairer of the one part and William Duesbury of the same place China or Porcelain Manufacturer of the other part" in which he bound himself for three years "to employ himself in the Art of Modelling and Repairing China or Porcelaine Ware" at 2½ guineas a week. In 1773 he joined Josiah Wedgwood at Etruria, but for a further twenty years he carried out modelling commissions for the Duesburys.

Three large figure groups adapted from stipple engravings by Bartolozzi after Angelica Kauffman, although actually modelled by Stephan, are often wrongly attributed to Spängler. Examples were sold during the Derby sales of 1778 and 1782, before Spängler's arrival in England. They are numbered 195, 196 and 235 in the factory price list where they are described as: "group of two Virgins awakening Cupid", 12½ inches, 2 guineas enamelled and gilt, 3 guineas biscuit; "group of two Bacchantes adorning Pan", 12½ inches, 2 guineas and 3 guineas; "group of Three Graces distressing Cupid", 14¾ inches, £3 13s. 6d. and £4 4s. Other figures ascribed to Stephan include "The Elements" in three sizes (No. 3); a set of "Four Antique Seasons", each in three sizes (No. 5); and "Elements in two groups" (No. 48). Stephan made several portrait statuettes of admirals and generals from contemporary prints, including Rodney, Howe, Hood, Conway and Drinkwater. In some examples Stephan's name is incised on the back of the plinth.

Jean Jacques Spängler, son of the director of the Zürich porcelain factory, was an erratic genius who proved himself the greatest of the Derby modellers. He was responsible for some of the most elaborate groups ever made in English porcelain, excelling in historical and classic themes. It is believed that he was introduced to William Duesbury II by the celebrated clockmaker Justin Vulliamy, also a Swiss. Since the early 1780s he had been mounting clock movements in biscuit figures designed and modelled to his commission in London, but made at Derby. In September 1790 Spängler signed an agreement to model for Duesbury for three years "and shall himself make an original in Porcelain from each of his Models". It was agreed that he should work in a room in Derby apart from the factory, paid for from his weekly wage of two guineas after the first month. He was required to work sixty hours to the six-day week in summer, forty-eight hours in winter. A witness to this document was Vulliamy's son Benjamin.

Spängler absconded from Derby in 1792 and was trying to reach the Continent via Ramsgate when arrested and imprisoned. Duesbury obtained his release, conditional upon his immediate return to Derby, but in November 1793, following the expiration of his agreement, he left Derby. Soon afterwards he was seen passing "through the town on tramp, dressed in the cast off clothes of a soldier, and he was in such low water that a little refreshment and money which his old colleague Isaac Farnsworth gave him was very acceptable". In February 1795 Spängler returned to Derby, working on a monthly basis, and modelled for another year.

Before signing the 1790 agreement Spängler modelled a figure of *Astronomy* for a fee of ten guineas: this was for Vulliamy. The models made during his first month at Derby were *Figure with a Vase* (*Morning*) and its companion *Figure with a Vase* (*Noon*) for each of which he was paid ten guineas, and *Three Graces* at six guineas. The price list names *Belisarius and his Daughter* (No. 370) as Spängler's work although available were only enamelled and gilt. *The Russian Shepherd*, a large group of four figures, *Paleman and Lavinia*, a small figure *Meditation* and "a pair of new lace figures" are attributed to Spängler. Twenty-five figures are listed as "Spängler's and Coffee's Figures and Groups" (Nos. 335 and 359).

William J. Coffee arrived at Derby from Coade's Lambeth Pottery in 1791 to work as a kilnman. Advantage was taken of his undoubted flair for modelling rustic and grotesque characters and animals, usually with a touch of the vulgar. In 1794 Duesbury's London agent complained: "I do not much admire Mr. Coffee's modelling from what I have seen. Figure 359 is one of the most stupid looking things I ever

7. Pairs of Bow porcelain figures. (*Top*) Pair of musicians, playing triangle and trumpet: each figure, dressed in brilliant colours, stands supported by the stump of a flowering tree, on a rococo-scrolled base. Marked anchor and dagger in red. About 1770. (*Bottom*) Harlequin and Columbine, adapted from the Dresden figures modelled in about 1740. The dress of Harlequin painted in triangular patches of crimson, blue and green, purple and yellow. Columbine has a flowered skirt and yellow bodice. About 1765.

8. Bow figures, undecorated, creamy-white, 1750–54. (*Top left*) Kitty Clive in the character of the "Fine Lady" in Garrick's farce *Lethe*: the actress stands with her head thrown back, a spaniel under her right arm, and a letter in her left hand. She is dressed in a wide lace cap, lace-trimmed bodice and a hooped skirt (*Delomosne & Son Ltd.*). (*Top right*) Lovers with a bird cage, seated group after Lancret. Height 7½ inches. (*Lower left*) James Quin, the actor, Falstaff: he wears a plumed hat and carries a basket-hilted sword in his right hand and a circu shield on his left arm. (*Lower right*) A charming composition belonging to the easily recogni class of early Bow figures.

saw, and the figure of *Apollo* in group No. 379 is very vulgar . . . although the design is pretty enough." In the Victoria and Albert Museum is a biscuit figure of Coffee's *Shepherd* modelled after the figure of Antinous. This is companion to Stephan's *Shepherdess* and is the more attractive of the two. Both are incised No. 396. Coffee also modelled a set of four *Elements* (No. 325); *Scotchman and Lass* (No. 378); and a number of excellent dogs including three pugs.

It is interesting to compare his rates of payment with those of Spängler. Jewitt quotes an agreement of 1794 entered into with William Duesbury II who had the option of paying Coffee 3*s*. 6*d*. for each working day of ten hours or "at the rate of 7*s*. for any single human figure 6 inches high, whether standing or in any other action, which if standing would be 6 inches high, and that all figures shall be in correct proportions before draped." Threepence for every half-inch of additional height was paid. A few months later Coffee left Derby to join Sir Nigel Gresley, Bart., at his Burton-on-Trent pottery, but returned later in the year.

Coffee again left the works in 1805 and with another modeller named William Duesbury established a pottery in Friar Gate, Derby. Here they made small and life-size portrait busts, rustic figures, and portrait statuettes of eccentric characters of the day. The venture proved unsuccessful and Duesbury returned to the Derby China Works. Coffee then ceased to make china, but made figures in terracotta. Later he removed to Oxford Market, London, where he made plaster figures and ornamental castings in terracotta.

Charles Holmes, referred to in Haslem's price list, modelled at Derby in the early 19th century. He worked mainly on domestic ware but was responsible for a series of sheep and lambs in many positions and other small animals, birds and a set of *Seasons*, unusual in that the figures were seated.

The brothers *Edward and Samuel Keys,* important modellers in the early Bloor period, were apprenticed as modellers and ornamental repairers and each in due time became over-looker of his department. Their father, Samuel Keys, was a gilder, an acknowledged master of gold arabesque work into which he introduced coloured scrolls, and also excelled in decorating figures in the Meissen style, some being marked with pseudo-Meissen crossed swords in blue.

Edward Keys modelled the series of fourteen Doctor Syntax figures after illustrations to *The Tour of Doctor Syntax* by William Coombe, 1815. It is interesting to compare the price of 12*s.* 6*d.* charged for the equestrian figure of Dr. Syntax with 5*s.* for *Dr. Syntax Scolding the Landlady.* The Syntax figures are listed on page 70: other subjects, which abound, have been made since the closure of Bloor's Derby. Edward Keys also modelled the grotesque monkey musicians, an idea adapted from Meissen, and a series of characters from illustrations in *Life in London, c.* 1815, by Pierce Egan. Portrait statuettes of celebrities included George IV, Nelson and Napoleon, each about a foot in height. Among his small animals were the now rare *Cats on Cushions* and *Cats with Prey.* Edward Keys left Derby in 1826 to model for Henry Daniel, Shelton, later moving to the Minton factory where his wages averaged 30*s.* a week.

Samuel Keys modelled many theatrical characters between 1820 and 1830. This proved a highly successful project, the figures selling at prices ranging from six to eight shillings. The series includes figures of *Madame Vestris* in *Buy a Broom*; *Miss Foote,* later Countess of Harrington, in *The Little Jockey*; *Liston* in the characters of Maw Worm and Domini Sampson, and of Paul Pry in the play of that name by John Poole, first produced in 1825. Haslem records that Liston himself was the first purchaser of a Paul Pry figure. On arrival of the box of figures at Bloor's Bond Street show rooms a copy was placed in the window and almost immediately attracted the attention of the comedian who at once bought it. In 1830 Samuel Keys modelled exceptionally tall figures of *Hebe* and *Innocence,* 28 inches high and lavishly decorated in enamels and gold by his father. A few months later he left Derby for Staffordshire where by the mid-1840s he was established at Stoke-on-Trent as a parian statuary potter in partnership with John Mountford.

Collectors of Derby figures must beware of early Victorian reproductions which are sometimes converted into fakes. Haslem, in 1876, was able to write: "Many of the old Derby figures have been reproduced, particularly a set of the *Four Seasons* and some have, at sales of old Derby china, realised considerable prices under the impression that they were 'old Derby'. Of late years attention has been specially directed to the making of a larger class of figures."

Haslem reported fakes in museums too, nearly a century ago. Recently I have noticed figures on exhibition in a museum that were marked with the crown, crossed batons, six dots and script D of Derby. When the pieces were held so that light struck at an angle, it was possible to distinguish clearly the mark of a modern factory imperfectly removed by fluoric acid. Haslem also reported in 1876 that several Staffordshire potters had been making figures from the original moulds acquired by Duesbury a century earlier from Chelsea and Bow.

PRICE LIST
OF
GROUPS AND SINGLE FIGURES
Enamelled and Gilt, and in Biscuit

No.	*Names of Figures and Groups*	*Size*	*Height, inches*	*Enamelled and gilt*	*Biscuit*
1	Group of the Virtues	1st	11½	£2 2 0	
	Ditto Ditto	2nd			
3	The Elements, Stephan	1st		3 3 0	£3 13 6
	Ditto	2nd		2 12 6	3 3 0
	Ditto	3rd	7⅛	1 16 0	2 2 0
4	Pastoral Group			2 12 6	3 3 0
5	Four Antique Seasons, in a set	1st	8	1 4 0	1 8 0
	Ditto Ditto	2nd	6½	– 16 –	
	Ditto Ditto	3rd	4⅛	– 12 –	
6	Four Seasons		4	– 10 6	
7	Gardening	1st	6¾	– 15 –	– 16 –
	Ditto	2nd	5	– 8 –	– 9 –
8	Fruit and Flowers		5⅜	– 10 6	– 12 –
9	Music	1st	6¼	– 14 –	– 16 –
	Ditto	2nd	6	– 10 6	– 12 –
	Ditto	3rd	4⅝	– 6 –	– 7 –
10	Flute and Cymbal	1st	6¼	– 14 –	– 16 –
	Ditto Ditto	2nd	5⅝	– 10 6	– 12 –
	Ditto Ditto	3rd	4¾	– 6 –	– 7 –
11	Flute and Guitar		6⅜	1 10 0	1 11 6
12	Pastoral Group		12¼	2 12 6	
13	Cupid and Bacchus riding		7	1 1 0	
14	Sacrifice Figures, pair			1 0 0	1 4 0
15	Small Prudence and Discretion, with urns		9¼	1 8 0	
16	Dancing Group		6⅝	– 16 –	
17	Ditto Ditto		6⅝	– 16 –	
18 & 19	Names of Figures not given				
20	Fruit and Flowers, Pair	1st	6¼	– 14 –	– 16 –
	Ditto Ditto	2nd	5¾	– 10 6	– 12 –
	Ditto Ditto	3rd		– 6 –	– 7 –
21	Garrick as Richard III, Bacon		9¾	1 5 0	1 5 0
22 & 23	Names not given				
25 to 34	Ten Figures of Apollo and Muses, 5 in. in height, 5*s.* 3*d.* each				
35	Four Seasons		6	1 1 0	1 4 0
36	Sitting Fruit		5	– 10 6	– 12 –
37	Jason and Medea	1st		3 3 0	3 13 6
	Ditto	2nd	12¾	2 2 0	3 3 0
	Ditto	3rd		1 11 6	2 12 6
38	Prudence and Discretion		5½	– 7 –	– 8 –

9. Derby figures. (*Top*) Justice wearing a flowered and gilt robe with a pink-lined greenish-blue cloak thrown over it. The pair of scales is missing. Height 10 inches. About 1765. Pair of statuettes known as the "Ranelagh figures". The young man holds a letter inscribed "Dominae Lucretiae". Height 11 inches. The lady wears a miniature of a gentleman suspended from her shoulder. Height 12 inches. About 1760. (*Bottom*) Pair, both offering and carrying flowers and with more enriching their supporting tree-stumps. The ground colour of the flowered skirt and breeches is yellow enamel. Height 8½ inches. About 1775.

10. Derby figures, enamelled. (*Top left*) John Wilkes standing beside a pedestal on which are scrolls inscribed "Magna Char^{TA}" and "Bill of Rights". Height 11¾ inches. About 1775. (*Centre*) James Quin in the character of Falstaff with plumed hat, pink coat, flowered doublet and green breeches. Height 13 inches. About 1765. Compare with Plate 8. (*Right*) Field-Marshal Conway in semi-military costume with baton in his right hand. Height 12 inches. About 1785. Compare with Plate 12. (*Bottom left*) Man with tambourine and pipes, mauve hat and shoes, pale yellow jacket and terracotta breeches. Height 9¾ inches. About 1760. (*Right*) Girl with flowers with green and terracotta bodice, pink hat and apron, pale yellow flowered skirt. Height 10 inches. About 1760.

PRICE LIST OF GROUPS AND SINGLE FIGURES

No.	*Names of Figures and Groups*	*Size*	*Height, inches*	*Enamelled and gilt*	*Biscuit*
39 to 45	Seven Groups of Art and Sciences, various at 16*s.* each, with Pedestals—14*s.* without				
46	Dancing Figures and Group		5½	– 9 –	
47	Grotesque Seasons		5¼	– 16 –	
48	Elements in two Groups		8¾	2 12 6	3 4 0
49	Cat and Dog Figures		5¾	– 13 –	
50	Sporting and Companion		5⅝	– 12 –	– 14 –
51	Cat and Dog Figures		5	– 10 6	– 14 –
52	Dragon Candlesticks				
53	Griffin Candlesticks				
54	Justice		9½	– 15 –	
55	Dresden Shepherd	1st	9¼	1 6 0	
	Ditto	2nd	8¾	1 2 0	
56	Garland Ditto	1st	9¾	1 6 0	
	Ditto Ditto	2nd	9	1 2 0	
	Ditto Ditto	3rd	7⅝	– 18 –	
	Ditto Ditto	4th	6¾	– 15 –	
57	French Shepherds, Pair	1st		1 8 0	
	Ditto Ditto	2nd		1 2 0	
	Ditto Ditto	3rd		– 18 –	
	Ditto Ditto	4th		– 14 –	
	Ditto Ditto	5th		– 10 6	– 12 –
	Ditto Ditto	6th		– 7 –	– 8 –
58	Piping Shepherd			– 15 –	
59	Set of Five Senses		7½	2 12 0	
60	Singers	1st		1 0 0	
	Ditto	2nd	7	– 16 –	
	Ditto	3rd	5⅜	– 9 –	
61	Four Sitting Seasons	1st		1 1 0	
62	Welch Taylor and Family, large size			2 12 6	
	Ditto Ditto small		5½	1 1 0	
63	Small Turks		3½	– 5 –	– 6 –
64	Four Standing Seasons		5½	– 18 –	
65	Diana	1st		1 1 0	1 4 0
	Ditto	2nd	8½	– 14 –	
66	Venus and Cupid		6½	– 10 6	– 12 –
67	Venus, Chelsea Model				
68	Group of Four Seasons		9¼	1 10 0	1 18 0
69	Sitting Flute Figures			– 6 –	
70	Figure of Christie		12⅛	1 5 0	
71	Pair Sitting Figures, with Cat and Dog		5½	– 16 –	1 5 0
72	Pastoral Group, with Goat		5⅜	– 12 –	
73	Ditto Ditto, with Dog		5⅜	– 12 –	
74	Dancing Group of two Figures		6½	– 12 –	
75	Group of Cephălus and Procris		8½	1 1 0	
76	Ditto of Renaldo and Armida		8½	1 1 0	
77	Stocking Mending			– 12 –	– 18 –
78	Shoemaker, Group of 2 Figures		5⅞	– 12 –	– 18 –
79	Complimenting Ditto		6¾	– 13 –	
80	Spinning Ditto			– 12 –	
81	Shoeblack Ditto			– 12 –	
82	Fury Group, Broken Fiddle				
83	Ditto, Broken Chair				
84	Ditto, Hairdresser, 2 figures			– 12 –	– 18 –
85	Macaroni			– 14 –	

No.	*Names of Figures and Groups*	*Size*	*Height, inches*	*Enamelled and gilt*	*Biscuit*
86	Set of Elements, in Groups of two Figures each			2 2 0	
87	Pair of Salutation Figures		4¾	– 7 –	
88	Mrs. Macaulay				
89	Fury Group, Family				
90	Cook and Companion				
91	Female Macaroni			– 14 –	
92	Three Figures learning Music				
93	Group of Three Figures playing at Hazard		6	1 1 0	
94	Group of Three Figures at a Raree Show		6	1 1 0	
95	Sphinx Candlestick				
96	Ditto of a Vase				
97	Griffin ditto				
98	Group of Prudence and Discretion		11½	2 2 0	
99	Pair of Figures, Æsculapius and Hygeia		7½	– 16 –	– 18 –
100	Andromache weeping over the ashes of Hector	1st		1 10 0	1 11 6
101	Pair, Grotesque Boy and Girl		4½	– 5 –	
102 to 113	Twelve Figures of Nuns and Monks				
114	Pair of Figures, Mars and Venus		6¼	– 16 –	– 18 –
115	Ditto Ditto			– 16 –	
116	Apollo		6¾	– 8 –	– 9 –
117 & 119	Pair of Figures, Jupiter and Juno		6½	– 16 –	– 18 –
118	Neptune		6¾	– 8 –	– 10 6
120	Diana		6½	– 9 –	– 10 6
121	Minerva		6½	– 8 –	– 9 –
122	Hercules		6¼	– 8 –	– 9 –
123	Set of Seasons, from French	1st		4 4 0	
	Ditto Ditto	2nd		3 13 6	4 4 0
	Ditto Ditto	3rd		3 3 0	3 13 6
	Ditto Ditto	4th	7½	1 16 0	2 2 0
124	Time and Cupid	1st		2 12 6	
	Ditto	2nd		1 11 6	
	Ditto	3rd	7¾	1 1 0	
125	Set of four Chelsea Standing Seasons	1st	6⅜	1 8 0	
	Ditto Ditto	2nd	6¼	1 4 0	
	Ditto Ditto	3rd	5⅛	– 14 –	– 16 –
126	Wilkes			1 5 0	
127	Small Figures				
128 to 136	Nine Figures, names not given				
137	Madonna, a Group		8¼	– 18 –	1 1 0
138	Prudent Mother, a Group		8¼	– 18 –	1 1 0
139	Music Group of two Figures		6½	– 12 –	
140	Ditto Ditto Ditto		6½	– 12 –	
141	Pair of Fighting Boys		3½	– 4 –	– 5 –
142 & 143	Pair of small Boys riding on a Dolphin and Swan	1st	5 to 5¼	– 12 –	
	Ditto Ditto	2nd		– 10 –	
	Ditto Ditto			– 7 6	

No.	Names of Figures and Groups	Size	Height, inches	Enamelled and gilt	Biscuit
144 to 158	Fifteen Figures, names not given				
159 & 160	Pair, Laughing and Crying Philosophers		5¾	– 10 6	
161	Antique Figure of Wisdom	1st	8½	– 12 –	– 18 –
	Ditto Ditto	2nd			
162	Ditto of Justice	1st	8½	– 12 –	– 18 –
	Ditto Ditto	2nd			
163	Antique Figure of Plenty	1st	8½	– 12 –	– 18 –
	Ditto Ditto	2nd			
164	Ditto of Peace	1st	8½		– 18 –
	Ditto Ditto	2nd			
165 to 174	Ten Figures, names not given				
175	Pair of Boy and Girl Figures		4	– 4 –	
176 to 178	Three Figures, names not given				
179	Music Group of four Figures		13¼	2 12 6	
180	Pairs of Boys, Autumn and Spring			– 3 –	
181	Name not given				
182	Pair of Cupids riding on Bucks			– 10 6	
183	Ditto Prudence and Discretion			– 4 –	
184	Ditto Boy and Girl Figures			– 4 –	– 5 –
185	Ditto Cupids riding on Swan and Dolphin			– 7 –	
186 to 188	Three Figures, names not given				
189	Boy riding on Sea-horse		4¼	– 4 6	
190	Triton		2¾	– 3 –	
191 & 192	Names not given				
193 & 194	Pair, large Bacchus and Ariadne	1st	9	1 8 0	1 11 6
	Ditto, Ditto Ditto	2nd	8¼	1 1 0	1 4 0
	Ditto, Ditto Ditto	3rd	7½	– 16 –	– 18 –
195	Group of two Virgins awaking Cupid		12½	2 2 0	3 3 6
196	Ditto of two Bacchantes adorning Pan		12½	2 2 0	3 3 0
197	Cupid riding on Sea-lion		2¾	– 4 –	
198	Pair of Haymakers		6½	– 15 –	– 16 –
199	Ditto Harlequin and Columbine		5½	– 10 6	– 12 –
200	Set of four Quarters of the Globe	1st	6	1 12 0	1 12 0
	Ditto Ditto Ditto	2nd	5¼	1 4 0	1 4 0
201 & 202	Pair of Cupids		4	– 5 –	– 7 –
203	Pair of Cupids, with Dog and Falcon			– 10 6	
204	Ditto of Gardeners		5	– 8 –	– 12 –
205 & 206	Pair of Cupids		4½	– 5 –	– 7 –
207	Sea Nymph riding on a Dolphin		4⅛	– 4 6	
208	Ditto playing the Tabor		3	– 2 6	
209	Syren with a Shell		2½	– 2 6	
210	Triton		3	– 2 6	

No.	Names of Figures and Groups	Size	Height, inches	Enamelled and gilt			Biscuit		
211 &									
212	Names not given								
213 &									
214	Pair of Cupids, with Dog and Falcon		4¾	–	10	–	–	10	6
215	Name not given								
216 &									
217	Pair, Groups, Music and Poetry	1st	9¾	3	3	0	3	15	0
	Ditto Ditto	2nd		2	16	0	3	3	0
	Ditto Ditto	3rd		2	10	0	2	16	0
218 &									
219	Names not given								
220	Pair Basket Figures	1st	6½	–	15	0			
221	Ditto Ditto	2nd	5¼	–	10	6			
222	Figure of Time		6½	–	9	–	–	10	6
223 to									
226	Four Figures, names not given								
227	Pair Grotesque Punches		7	–	18	–			
228 to									
230	Three Figures, names not given								
231	Large Falstaff								
232 &									
233	Names not given								
234	Group of four Cupids		10	1	1	0	1	11	6
235	Group of Three Graces distressing Cupid	1st	14¾	3	13	6	4	4	0
	Ditto Ditto Ditto	2nd		2	12	6	3	3	0
236 &									
237	Pair of Cupids		4	–	5	–	–	7	–
238	Name not given								
239	The Virgin Mary		10½	1	1	0			
240	Pastoral Group of two Figures		7¾	–	8	–			
241 &	Names not given								
243	Apollo		9½	1	1	0			
244	Plenty		9¾	1	4	0			
245	Peace		9¼	1	4	0	1	11	6
246	Name not given								
247	Pastoral Group of two Figures		12¼	2	5	0			
248	Group of four Seasons, Antique		11⅛	1	11	6	2	2	0
249 &									
250	Names not given								
251	Group of four Cupids		9	–	18	–	1	5	0
252	Ditto of three ditto			1	1	0	1	11	6
253	Pair of Cupids with Dog and Bird-cage		3¾	–	4	–	–	7	–
254	Pastoral Group of two Figures		13¼	2	10	0			
255	Ditto Ditto		12	2	–	–			
256	Ditto Ditto		12¼	2	–	–			
257	Group of four Cupids		9¾	1	1	0	1	11	6
258	Pair Sitting Boy Candlesticks		6½	–	16	–			
259	Britannia	1st		2	2	0			
	Ditto	2nd		1	11	6			
	Ditto	3rd		1	1	0			
260	Crying Boy and Laughing Girl	1st		–	14	–			
	Ditto Ditto	2nd	7⅝						
261	No name								

PRICE LIST OF GROUPS AND SINGLE FIGURES

No.	*Names of Figures and Groups*	*Size*	*Height, inches*	*Enamelled and gilt*	*Biscuit*
262 to 278	Seventeen Figures of Cupid in Disguise			– 2 6	
279	No name				
280	Pair Pipe and Guitar Candlesticks, with ornamental Branches		8½	1 10 0	
	Ditto, with Chandelier Branches		8½	1 16 0	
281	Pair Spring Candlesticks		6⅛	– 16 –	
282	Ditto, Small Fame and Mercury		8½	– 18 –	
283	Ditto, Gardener Candlesticks		6⅞	– 16 –	
284	Pair of Spring Candlesticks, Pipe and Guitar		9½	1 10 0	
285	Ditto Ditto Ditto		8	1 6 0	
286	No name				
287	Pair Garland Shepherd Candlesticks		9½	1 10 0	
288	Ditto Mars and Venus ditto		8	1 6 0	
289 & 290	Names not given				
291	Falstaff	1st		2 12 6	
	Ditto	2nd		1 11 6	
	Ditto	3rd		1 5 0	
	Ditto	4th		– 15 –	
	Ditto	5th		– 12 –	
292	Pair of Dessert Gardeners	1st		– 7 –	
	Ditto Ditto	2nd	4¾	– 6 –	
293	Tythe Pig Group, three Figures		7	– 15 –	
294	Group of the four Seasons, with an Obelisk		8	1 11 6	2 2 0
295	Ditto of the four Quarters of the Globe		10⅛	2 2 0	2 12 6
296	Pair of Haymakers		9¼	1 11 6	
297	Milton		10⅝	1 5 0	1 11 6
298	Minerva	1st		2 2 0	2 12 0
	Ditto	2nd		1 11 6	2 2 6
	Ditto	3rd		1 1 0	1 10 0
299	Neptune on Rock Pedestal	1st	9¼	1 1 0	1 4 0
	Ditto Ditto	2nd		– 16 –	– 18 –
300	Ditto without ditto			– 9 –	– 10 6
301	Pair, Sitting Pipe and Guitar	1st		1 – –	
	Ditto Ditto	2nd	6¼	– 16 –	
	Ditto Ditto	3rd	5⅜	– 12 –	– 18 –
302	Ditto of Fame and Mercury			1 1 0	1 11 6
303	Ditto of Pipe and Tabor	1st		– 17 –	
	Ditto Ditto	2nd	6⅛	– 14 –	
304	No name				
305	Shakespeare		10½	1 5 0	1 11 6
306	No name				
307	Set of four Seasons, sitting		4⅝	1 – –	
308	No name				
309	Music Group of four Figures, with an Obelisk		10	1 11 6	
310	No name				
311	Pair, Pipe and Tabor Figures		8¼	1 – –	
312	No name				
313	Pair of Sitting Figures		5¾	2 2 0	3 3 0
314	Ditto Ditto				
315	Set of four Seasons, sitting		7		

No.	Names of Figures and Groups	Size	Height, inches	Enamelled and gilt	Biscuit
316	Pair, Sailor and his Lass	1st		1 16 0	
	Ditto, Ditto	2nd			
	Ditto, Ditto	3rd			
317	Ditto, Dancing Figures			– 18 –	
318	Ditto, Ditto			– 14 –	
319 to					
321	Three Figures, names not given				
322	Pair, Hen and Chicken Candlesticks		6¼	1 1 0	
323	Ditto, Cupid and Flora ditto		8¼	2 2 0	
324	No name				
325	Set of four Elements		8¾	2 2 0	
326	Pair of Singers	1st			
	Ditto	2nd			
	Ditto	3rd			
	Ditto	4th	5¾		
327 to					
330.	Four Figures, names not given				
331	Pair of Candlesticks with Bird and Dog		11¼	3 3 0	
332	Set of the four Quarters of the Globe	1st			
	Ditto Ditto Ditto	2nd			
	Ditto Ditto Ditto	3rd		1 16 0	
333	Group of four Boys			1 11 6	2 2 0
	Ditto Ditto			1 11 6	2 2 0
335 to					
359	"Spängler's and Coffee's Figures and Groups"				
360	Johnny Wapstraw and Companion			1 16 0	
361	Pair, Gardener and ditto			1 16 0	2 2 0
362	Ditto, Sitting Cat and Dog, William and Mary			1 10 0	
363	Ditto, Figures, with dead Bird		8	1 5 0	
364	Group of Figures Waltzing		6½	1 1 0	
365	Pair of Dancing Figures			– 18 –	
366	Spanish Group			1 16 0	
367	No name				
368	Pair of Dancing Figures			– 18 0	1 1 0
369	Shepherd and Shepherdess			1 16 0	2 2 0
370	Belisarius and Daughter, Spängler			1 16 0	
371	No name				
372	Sailor and Lass		7¼	– 18 –	
373 to					
377	Five Figures, names not given				
378	Pair, Scotchman and Lass, Coffee			1 16 0	
379 to					
389	Eleven Figures, names not given. No. 384 is on a Statuette, probably of Lord Howe or Lord Hood, 12 inches in height; and 385 is on a Figure, probably of Hygeia, 10 ins.				
390	Group of Gaultherus and Griselda			1 11 6	

The following are also in the List but are not numbered.

Pointer and Setter, per pair, Coffee				– 7 –	
Large Pug Dogs, ditto ditto				– 4 –	
Less ditto ditto ditto				– 3 –	

PRICE LIST OF GROUPS AND SINGLE FIGURES

	Enamelled and gilt			Biscuit		
Small ditto ditto ditto	—	2	—			
Begging Pugs, ditto Chelsea	—	2	—			
Ditto French Dogs ditto ditto	—	2	—			
Large Sheep and Lambs, per pair, Holmes	—	7	—			
Sheep lying down ditto ditto	—	4	—			
Standing Sheep ditto ditto	—	4	—			
Ditto 2 smaller sizes ditto						
Lambs with Sprigs, per pair, Chelsea	—	2	—			
Ditto without each ditto	—	—	10			
Canary Birds, each , ditto	—	1	—			
Tomtit ditto ditto	—	1	—			
Linnet ditto ditto	—	1	—			
Birds on Branches, two sizes, ditto						

	Enamelled and gilt			Biscuit		
Large Stags, per pair	—	15	—			
Ditto, two smaller sizes						
Large Sitting Cat						
Cat lying down	—	—	6			
Ditto with gold collar	—	1	—			
Cow and Calf, per pair	—	6	6	—	9	—
Ditto, lying down						
Large Swan	—	1	3			
Two smaller sizes of same, 1s. and 10d. each						
Large Squirrel	—	1	3			
Two smaller sizes of same, 1s. and 10d. each						
Large Boy—Four other sizes of the same were made, prices respectively 1s. 9d., 1s. 6d., 1s. 3d., 1s. and 10d. each. This is a naked boy, standing with basket of flowers, usually white and gold.						
Satyrs Heads, each	—	7	—			
Small Neptune's Heads	—	6	—			
Large Duck Boats, gold dontil edges	—	3	—			
Small ditto ditto ditto	—	2	—			
Trouts' Heads, with mottoes—"Angler's Delight" &c.	—	6	—			
Ditto, two smaller sizes, 5s. and 3s. 6d. each						
Hares' Heads, each	—	7	—			
Foxes' ditto ditto	—	4	6			
Ditto, two other sizes 4s. and 3s. 6d.						
Mice, each	—	1	6	—	1	6
Poodle Dogs and Fleecy Sheep, each				—	5	—
Lowing Cow, each	—	5	—			
Sitting Foxes, per pair	—	7	—			
Pointers' Heads, each	—	7	—			
Tulip Egg Cups, each	—	4	—			
Inkstands, on Cats, &c., each	—	18	—			
Large Panthers						
Small ditto, per pair	—	3	—			
Large Duck Boats, and several smaller do.						
Pigeon Boats	—	12	—			
Set of five Senses	2	12	6			
Foxes, per pair	—	10	6			
Small Turks, each	—	2	6			
Basket Boys, enamelled and gilt, pair	—	5	—			
Set of Season Busts	—	14	—			

	Enamelled and gilt	Biscuit
Cupids grinding, from the Element group	- 5 3	
Dogs from the Dresden Shepherd, each	- 1 -	
London Pointer and Greyhound, each	- 1 6	
Season Vases, each		- 7 -
Vases, Common Festoons		- 12 -
Vases, Best Festoons		1 11 6
Fountain Vase, on Pedestal		5 5 0
Cupid Sleeping, on Pedestal, from Spängler's Group		- 10 6
THE FOLLOWING MODELLED BY EDWARD KEYS		
Paris Cries, Set of six figures	1 4 -	1 16 -
Archers, per pair	1 16 -	
Large Elephant, with Driver	- 10 6	
Ditto, with cloths, no Driver	- 9 -	
Peacock	- 2 -	- 3 6
Large Neptune		
Small Napoleon	- 3 -	
Lean Cows, per pair	- 3 6	
Small Elephant	- 1 6	
Key's Fancy Figures, per pair	- 9 -	
New Sitting Pugs, on Cushions	- 1 6	
Small Sitting Foxes	- 1 6	
Tragedy and Comedy	- 4 -	
Bust of Nelson	- 5 -	
Vicars, Curates and Wardens, each	- 6 -	
Large Monkey Musicians, each	- 7 6	
Small ditto ditto ditto	- 5 -	
Dusty Bob and African Sall, each	- 4 -	
Doctor Syntax Walking Height: 5 ins.	- 7 6	
Ditto in Green Room	- 7 6	
Ditto at York	- 7 6	
Ditto at Booksellers	- 7 6	
Ditto Drawing	- 5 -	
Ditto Going to Bed	- 5 -	
Ditto Tied to a Tree	- 5 -	
Ditto Scolding the Landlady	- 5 -	
Ditto Playing the Violin	- 4 -	
Ditto Attacked by a Bull	- 9 -	
Ditto Crossing the Lake	- 7 6	
Ditto Mounted on Horseback	- 12 6	
Ditto Landing at Calais	- 7 6	
Doctor Syntax's Landlady, No. 8	- 3 6	
Grimaldi as Clown, Thomas Griffin	- 7 6	
Liston as Paul Pry, S. Keys	- 8 -	
Ditto as Mawworm, S. Keys	- 7 -	
Vestris in Buy a Broom	- 6 -	
Bucks and Does	- 4 -	- 7 -
Small Standing Sheep		- 7 -
Rabbits on Plinths		
Ditto without Plinths	- 2 -	
Large Horses	- 1 6	
Pony	- 2 -	
Set of Tyrolese Minstrels, each	- 1 6	
Canton Girls	- 7 -	
Liston as Domine Sampson, S. Keys	- 7 6	
Industrious Boy and Girl ditto per pair	- 8 -	
Cats on Cushions, large ditto each	- 15 -	
Ditto ditto small ditto ditto	- 2 -	
	- 1 6	

PRICE LIST OF GROUPS AND SINGLE FIGURES

			Enamelled and gilt			Biscuit
Lion and Lioness	ditto	each	–	2	–	
Worcester Mice	ditto	ditto	–	2	–	
New Poodle Dogs	ditto	ditto	–	2	–	
New Cats with Prey	ditto	ditto	–	1	6	
Billy Waters, the Black Fiddler	ditto	ditto	–	4	–	
Small Fruit Basket	each		–	2	–	
Sheep in Fold	ditto		–	4	–	
Pair of Topers, Douglas Fox, each			–	5	–	

A number of other Figures were published which are not entered in this list, the keeping of the list probably having ceased at the time they were modelled. Thus Louis Bradley modelled two Dancing Figures, and John Whitaker, between 1830 and 1847, among others modelled the following:

An Eastern Lady	Boy with Greyhound
Guitar Player	Girl with Falcon
Child in Arm Chair	Bust of Queen Victoria
Virgin Mary	Ditto of Duke of Wellington
An Angel	Group of Stags
Boy and Dog	Ditto of Dogs
Girl and Dog	Leaping Stag
Sleeping Nymph	Peacock among Flowers
Mazeppa on Wild Horse	Parrot

Chapter Four

DERBY BISCUIT FIGURES

NO English potter created more exquisitely delicate figures and groups than those in unglazed biscuit porcelain made at Derby under the directorship of William Duesbury, father and son. Figure modelling in unglazed biscuit was evolved by Jean Jacques Bachelier, art director at Vincennes. Authorities differ regarding the year of its introduction, suggested dates ranging from 1749 to 1753. But in view of the obvious association between this work and that of Derby it is worth considering the venture in some detail.

Bachelier's underlying motive was to rival in soft-paste porcelain the white marble statuary then highly fashionable for interior decoration. The first groups made at Vincennes were hunting scenes modelled after Oudry by the sculptor Blondeau. Madame de Pompadour immediately showed her appreciation by ordering eight figures to be reproduced from a set she possessed in glazed porcelain, modelled by Blondeau after Boucher. It appears, however, that few biscuit figures were made until the factory removed to Sèvres in 1756. Exceptionally intricate figures and groups were then created, but their cost was so high that issues were small. Not for another decade were white biscuit figures made in numbers sufficient to be considered as serious competitors of glazed and enamelled figure work.

The superlative biscuit porcelain of Sèvres, white and flawless of surface, was prepared from Fontainebleau sand, long acknowledged by glass-makers as a source of silica with virtually no tinging impurities; sea-salt; nitre; soda; alum and crushed alabaster. Suitable proportions were mixed to a plastic paste with pure spring water and con-

74

verted into solid blocks of frit by firing for two days. These blocks were ground to flour fineness, sieved through lawn and mixed with marl from Argenteuil. This mixture was kneaded, with a trace of smalt, in a horse-operated pug-mill for weeks on end to ensure adequate intermingling. After drying in troughs it was crushed between heavy rollers and finely sifted. Spring water was added to make a paste of a texture suitable for modelling.

The biscuit figures of Sèvres obviously attracted the attention of the leading English potters. There is no evidence to prove that Duesbury was the first English potter to make biscuit porcelain: in fact Bow is known to have sold biscuit figures as early as 1756 (page 42). It is possible that Sprimont at Chelsea had carried out experimental work. William Duesbury made biscuit figures immediately after acquiring the Chelsea factory in 1770. The catalogue cover of the Chelsea-Derby sale of April 17, 1771, announced among other porcelain, "several Groups and single Figures, both in the Biscuit and Glaz'd, finely model'd and in the most pleasing attitudes, the Dresses and Embellishments resembling Lace of the finest Texture". Of the eighty-five lots sold on the first day twelve were pairs of biscuit figures, including four groups of "the Virtues, with a pyramid in the middle, Minerva crowning Constancy with laurel, and Hercules killing the Hydra, curiously finish'd in biscuit" sold at prices ranging from five to seven pounds each. A copy was also sold "richly enamel'd and highly finish'd in burnish'd gold" for six pounds. Two pairs of "Bacchus and Cupid, riding on a goat and panther, with oblong pedestals, emboss'd festoons, in biscuit" made three guineas. This is clear proof that Duesbury had mastered figure making in biscuit porcelain by 1770.

When Duesbury bought the Chelsea business he doubtless acquired Sprimont's book of experiments and formulas. Here he might have found a method of making soft-paste biscuit porcelain adapted from the Sèvres formula. It is more reasonable to assume, however, that he evolved his own paste for he was well acquainted with the vast deposits of alabaster in Derbyshire.

When James Christie held a sale of the last year's produce

75

of the Derby and Chelsea porcelain manufactories "at the Royal Academy, Pall Mall, in February 1773", he catalogued thirty-six figures and groups of which twenty-five were in biscuit, including "Apollo and the Four Muses" and "Lady playing on a Guitar, finish'd lace".

During the following June Duesbury opened new show rooms in London, advertising in *The London Chronicle* and elsewhere: "Duesbury & Co, Manufacturers of Derby and Chelsea Porcelain, most respectfully beg leave to inform the Nobility, Gentry and the Public in General that they have fitted up the large and elegant suit of Rooms at No 1, Bedford Street, Covent Garden, which are now opened with a great variety of capital as well as Useful and Ornamental Articles. A Fine Assortment of Biscuit Groups and single Figures; also a Collection of Derbyshire Fluors, Spars, Alabasters, Marbles, formed into Vases, Urns, Cup, Etc. N.B. The Rooms are well air'd." Duesbury was, then, in close contact with the quarry masters of Derbyshire who supplied him with alabaster.

In honour of the occasion Duesbury published a quarto catalogue of twenty pages containing two hundred entries of porcelain on sale. In the preamble he drew attention to "a great choice of Biscuit Groups and Figures in a grotesque style, elaborately finished even to the minutest imitation of lace." The first entry reads: "Their present majesties the King and Queen and Royal Family, in 3 grouped pieces of biscuit—the centre-piece represents the King in a Vandyke dress, on a blue and gold basement, supported by 4 lions, leaning on an altar richly ornamented, in blue and gold, with hanging trophies of the polite arts and sciences. The crown, orb and sceptre reposing on a cushion of crimson, embroidered, fringed and tasselled in gold. Height 14 inches." These groups were modelled from Zoffany's painting of the royal family, 1770: a large mezzotint was published later in the year by Earlom. Three sets are still in existence.

Derby biscuit figures may be grouped into three distinct types:

(*a*) to 1795, unglazed frit biscuit porcelain;
(*b*) 1795 to *c*. 1805, smear-glazed frit biscuit porcelain;

(c) 1805 to 1830s, non-frit, harder biscuit with a basis of bone china.

Duesbury's soft-paste biscuit never approached the whiteness of Sèvres, but resembled light ivory in colour, was of fine close texture, semi-translucent in thin places, with a flawless surface and was modelled with clean, distinct lines. The percentage of biscuit figures taken from the kiln in perfect condition was so small that costs of production exceeded those for ordinary porcelain by about a third (see factory selling prices, pages 64 to 73). Figures marred with firecracks and specks were glazed, enamelled and gilded, and included in the lower price range.

Smear-glazed biscuit, introduced by Michael Kean, is slightly velvety to the touch. The surface texture was produced, not by applying glaze directly to the figure, but by a vaporising process described on page 180.

James Haslem, writing in 1876 (the original manuscript, still in existence, is dated several years earlier) infers that manufacture of frit biscuit was abandoned in about 1805: "There was a large stock of prepared frit on hand. Kean had a quantity taken into Bridge Gate, a short distance from the factory, which street was being raised, and had it buried there. In 1851, during excavations by the Derby Water Works Company for the purpose of laying the pipes, this buried frit was brought to light."

The less costly and harder non-frit biscuit was obviously already in production. Haslem's reasons for the change-over were detailed in the previous chapter.

The bone china body was "slightly altered to take off the dry, somewhat harsh character which porcelain has before it is glazed. It lacked the ivory-like colour and semi-transparency of the true Derby biscuit and the figures were consequently whiter and more chalk-like in appearance."

Figures and groups tended to be modelled carelessly when original moulds from the 18th century were taken into use. Moulds specially made to meet the requirements of the new paste produced meticulous work following changing fashions in design.

George Cocker made large numbers of biscuit figures at

77

Derby between 1826 and 1840, closely resembling in quality the dry, chalky biscuit made by Bloor to whom he had been apprenticed. Llewellyn Jewitt states that in 1817 Cocker left the Derby China Works and "removed to Coalport where he is said to have been much employed in making raised flowers. He next, in connection with two partners, also workmen, commenced a small factory at Jackfield, which, however, closed in a few months. He was then employed at Worcester until 1821 when he returned to the Derby China Works." In 1825 in partnership with another employee, John Whitaker, he opened a china factory in Friar Gate, Derby, under the style of Cocker & Whitaker.

Here they produced a ceramic known as "pearl pottery". This was described in 1825 as "a superb kind of elegant and tasteful ornaments and is so much valued that the workmen are usually locked up and employed only on choice articles". The ingredients consisted of "blue clay; porcelain clay, Cornish stone, a little flint-glass cullet and red lead." The result was a dry body with a finely-textured unglazed surface and it was used only for figures and busts.

The following is the announcement of the opening of these works:

DERBY.—NEW CHINA WORKS, *for the Manufacture of Porcelain Figures, Ornaments, &c*—MESSRS COCKER & WHITAKER beg most respectfully to inform the nobility, gentry, and the public, that they have commenced the above business in Friar Gate, Derby, where manufacture has begun and have now ready for inspection, and sale, a numerous assortment of Goods in Biscuit and Enamel, such as they hope will be found of the kind at present produced in this kingdom.

N.B.—Ladies or Gentlemen may have Figures, Ornaments, &c., executed from models or drawings of their own.

Friar Gate, Derby, Feb. 28, 1826.

Cocker erected a kiln and provided other essential plant on land behind his home, with the retail establishment and office immediately opposite in Friar Gate. The partnership was a failure and ended in little more than a year. Cocker then continued on his own account assisted by his wife, two sons, three daughters and a nephew.

A wide variety of small figures and busts were potted

including ornamental figures of a rustic character, such as his *boys* series: boy with hurdy gurdy; boy with bird cage; boy with pitcher at a well, and so on. These are often attributed by collectors to Bloor's Derby. Portrait statuettes included Queen Victoria and Hannah More, but he was more prolific with small busts of celebrities such as Nelson, Wellington, Sir Robert Peel and Douglas Fox the advocate of teetotalism. He also potted small animals and birds, and small baskets filled with exquisitely modelled raised flowers. Some of his better work was incised COCKER and the biscuit figures have a cross incised beneath the plinth.

Cocker removed to London in 1840, operating a kiln at 8 Chenies Street, Tottenham Court Road, with a small retail shop in Regent's Quadrant. Competition from parian statuary during the late-1840s killed the fashionable trade in biscuit porcelain and by 1853 George Cocker had removed to Stoke-on-Trent where he continued as a manufacturer of biscuit figures until his death in 1868. London productions were sometimes signed by his nephew: D. COCKER.

Biscuit figures closely resembling those of Cocker were made by Robert Blore, an ornamental repairer who established a short-lived pottery at Bridge Gate, Derby, in the mid-1830s. On the rare occasions he marked a figure it was inscribed *Blore* in script.

Chapter Five

D R. JOHN WALL'S porcelain manufactory established at Worcester in 1751 was quickly celebrated for its carefully potted table-ware in a hard soapstone porcelain capable of withstanding the impact of boiling water. When Thomas Falconer visited the works in August 1766 he wrote to the Rev. C. Goodwyn-Chester that the "immense improvements made in the Worcester manufactory of China would have afforded you great pleasure. It is hardly surpassed by the Vincennes and much cheaper. They have not yet debased it by making vile attempts at human figures, but stick to the useful."

The firm, overburdened with fifteen partners, was at this time on the verge of a period of financial stress and was envious, no doubt, of Derby's prosperity in the figure-making branch of the trade. An endeavour was made, therefore, to widen its scope, very possibly influenced by the wandering and nebulous modeller and figure-maker known as Mr. Tebo whose employers included Bow, Worcester, Plymouth, Bristol and Wedgwood. The venture was unsuccessful, however, for no more than six models have been identified, all of them now rare and attributed to the years between 1769 and 1771.

If in fact Tebo was in charge of figure-making at Worcester that might account for the failure of the venture. He worked at Etruria for a year from October 1774 and time and again Josiah Wedgwood reported that he was a very poor figure modeller (see chapter 2). Tebo's mark T° is incised on a pair of Worcester Turks in the British Museum.

The earliest known reference to Worcester figures is in Christie's advertisement published by the *Public Advertiser*, December 1769:

11. (*Top left*) David Garrick as King Richard III modelled from an engraving by J. Dixon, published 1772 after the painting by Nathaniel Dance, exhibited at the Royal Academy 1771. This figure is No. 21 in the Derby price list, page 64. (*Top right*) Mrs. Cibber, the Georgian actress, in the character of Vivandière, carrying a basket of bottles. She wears a pink jacket over a red bodice, flowered skirt and pink shoes. Height 8⅝ inches. Derby about 1765. (*Lower left*) David Garrick in the character of Tancred, wearing a fur shako, green fur-lined dolman, purple tunic with gilt facings, flowered breeches and red boots. Height 8⅞ inches. Derby about 1765. (*Lower right*) Thames Waterman, an original model made at Bow in 1754, wearing Doggett's coat and badge. Height 7¾ inches.

12. Derby biscuit porcelain figures. (*Top left*) Admiral Lord Howe, probably modelled by Pierre Stephen. Mid-1790s. (*Top right*) Field-Marshal Conway in semi-military costume with a baton in his right hand and his left hand resting on a cannon. Height 12¾ inches. About 1775. (*Lower left*) Virgins distressing Cupid. Marked D235 and an incised triangle. About 1795. (*Lower right*) Shepherd, with the addition of clothing, modelled by William Coffee from a cast of an antique figure of Antinous in the collection of Joseph Wright of Derby. Marked crowned D and No. 396. Height 13¾ inches. About 1795.

To be Sold by Auction by Mr. Christie at his Great Room in Pall Mall, on Wednesday the 13th Instant and the five following Days.

A large and elegant Assortment of the WORCESTER PORCELAIN: consisting of a great Variety of Table, Desert, and Tea Services, rich sets of Jars and Beakers, Figures, Bowls, Basons and other Articles: a great Part of which are calculated to suit the Trade.

J. E. Nightingale, who possessed a copy of this catalogue, stated that the reference to figures in the sale was misleading, as no figures at all appear in the catalogue.

Two visitors to the factory during 1771 saw figures in production and recorded their impressions. Mrs. Philip Lybbe Powys in her *Diary* for August 1771 gave a long account of her visit to the Worcester China Manufactory, describing in detail the eleven departments which she passed through: ". . . In the seventh room they make the china ornamental figures: they are done in moulds, separate moulds for the limbs and stuck on with a kind of paste. . . ." Many years later Mrs. Powys noted the source of the silica used at Worcester. During a visit to Alum Bay in the Isle of Wight she referred to "the fine white sand, the vein of which runs entirely through the extremity of the point opposite Yarmouth to the Downs at Aston. It belongs to Mr. Urry of Yarmouth: the profit very great indeed. Vessels lie in Alum Bay to load with it, being the only sort in these kingdoms fit for making the white [flint] glass, and 'tis likewise used for the China manufacture at Worcester: nor will any other do for these uses."

The units from which they were built were made by pressing the paste into moulds as at Bow. Captain Joseph Roche, R.N., who visited the factory on October 21, 1771, noted this in the *Diary*: "They make very fine Figures of ornamental china, it being done so much better and also Cheaper at Derby: here they are obliged to mould it, but there it is cast, which is ten times as expedicious. The Derby compositions is, however, not so good for useful ware."

Artistically Worcester figures cannot be compared with those from Chelsea or Derby. The soapstone paste was difficult to manipulate to produce features and folds in

6

clothing, hence poses are stiff and the work appears unskilled. Soapstone, known also as talc and steatite, is a soft hydrated magnesium silicate not found in figures from other sources. The opinion is widely held that Worcester figures were not made from soapstone porcelain but analysis has proved otherwise. Herbert Eccles acquired a pair of gardener figures, one of which he gave to the Victoria and Albert Museum. Analysis showed them to contain 31½ per cent of soapstone. The precise analysis was recorded in *Analysed Specimens of English Porcelain* by Eccles and Rackham: "silica, 70.43; alumina, 4.82; lime, 4.64; magnesia 10.50; lead oxide 4.65." The colours used in the decoration, including bright turquoise blue and cobalt-blue enamels, as well as the gilding, are precisely those of marked Worcester porcelain of about 1770; the flowers on the base closely resemble in modelling those attached to the handles of Worcester fruit-baskets.

The Worcester figure subjects are: *Gardener and Companion; Sportsman and Companion; Turk and Companion;* an adaptation of Chelsea's *La Nourrice* after the model by Bertelemy de Blenod, Fontainebleau, the only known example being firecracked and highly glazed; and a kingfisher.

The gardener and his companion are known in glazed white and enamelled in various colours. He carries a pot containing a flowering plant in his right arm and a spade in his left hand, and his companion holds a basket of flowers and a posy. They measure about six inches in height. An example in the Worcester Works Museum, standing against a *bocage* background, supports a tulip-shaped candle-socket on a four-footed rococo base in the Bow manner. In the majority of Worcester figures, however, the base consists of a pad plinth decorated with applied leaves and flowers: this is closed and slightly concave beneath and perforated by a small hole. At a later period Derby made very similar gardeners but these were cast.

The long-necked sportsman holds a gun resting on the ground and his companion has a powder flask in one hand and a dead bird in the other. Each stands on a circular base with rococo and shell moulding supporting a low bank of blossom enamelled in colours. A pair were sold in the London sale rooms in 1949 for £1,800.

The Turk is a copy of a Meissen figure. He wears a long turquoise coat, ermine-lined, over a gilt-flowered red robe and has a white and red turban. His companion has a long ermine-lined pink coat over a pink and gilt flowered turquoise dress and red underskirt. One of a pair in the British Museum, attributed to 1770, is inscribed with Tebo's mark. Very similar figures were made seventy years later at Coalport but these were cast.

Some confusion has been caused by the attribution to Worcester of certain figures bearing the crescent mark in underglaze blue, sometimes in association with the red anchor and dagger mark of Bow. Analysis has proved the presence of bone ash in these figures, a substance not known to have been used at Worcester, but always present in Bow porcelain.

Chapter Six

LONGTON HALL, a Georgian Staffordshire country seat a few miles from Stoke-on-Trent, played a minor role in the history of English porcelain. In the parkland ran a stream capable of driving potter's crushing and mixing machines and here in 1749 William Jenkinson, a London speculator with mining interests, established a porcelain manufactory. Few facts have come to light regarding the first two years of its operation. Dr. Richard Pococke, later Bishop of Meath, made some interesting comments in a letter to his mother dated July 14, 1750. During a visit to a pottery near Newcastle-under-Lyme he had met a potter whom he had known at the porcelain factory that had operated for eighteen months at Dick's Shore, Limehouse. (The *Daily Advertiser* of January 1, 1747, had announced that "the new-invented blue and white Limehouse ware" was on sale.) Pococke wrote of ".... this man who seem'd to promise to make the best china-ware but disagreed with his employers. He has had a great quantity made of it here for the oven, but he cannot bake it with coal, which turns it yellow, wood being the fewel which is proper for it. I took a piece of what he had perfected here, but he makes what he calls japan'd ware, and of this he has made boxes for ladies' toilets and several other things: he also makes statues of elephants, lyons, birds, &c., in their natural colour, but they are of stone ware glaz'd."

Some authorities have wrongly interpreted this to mean that Doctor Pococke had observed porcelain figures. The doctor was capable of distinguishing between stoneware and porcelain for in the following November during a visit to the short-lived Bristol china factory he recorded the pro-

84

13. Biscuit statuette of Queen Victoria, 1837, made by Derby at the time of her accession in 1837.

14. Longton Hall porcelain figures. About 1775. (*Top*) Set of the Four Seasons, Spring, Summer, Autumn and Winter. The boys wear pink coats and green breeches; the girls wear pink dresses with white aprons and green and pink hats. Heights $4\frac{3}{4}$, $5\frac{1}{8}$, $4\frac{7}{8}$, $4\frac{7}{8}$ inches. (*Bottom*) Pair enamelled and gilt.

duction of "two sorts of ware, one called stone china which has a yellow cast both in the ware and the glazing. The other they call old china: this is whiter and made of calcined flint and the soapy rock of Lizard Point, which it is known they use." It is certain, then, that Pococke did not see porcelain in production at Longton Hall and that none was made until the end of 1750 or even later.

The potter responsible for this small venture appears to have been a man named Planché who had acquired his knowledge at Meissen, and moved to Staffordshire after the failure of the Limehouse factory. This "Limehouse potter" was the practical man, Jenkinson the financier. Planché's son André in the same year established a porcelain-making department at the Cockpit Hill Pottery, Derby, under the style of the Derby Porcelain Manufactory.

With this rather vague record must be associated the fact that William Littler, a successful manufacturer of white salt-glazed stoneware at Brownhills in partnership with Aaron Wedgwood, joined Jenkinson at Longton Hall in 1751. (See the partnership agreements 1751–57 in the Firmin collection, pages 52–64 *Longton Hall Porcelain*, Bernard Watney, 1957.)

The firm was then styled William Littler & Co., the earliest reference to this being in William Duesbury's London account book 1751–53, now in the British Museum. This shows that Duesbury, then an independent porcelain enameller, decorated "Staffordshire figars" for Littler & Co. in October 1751. Early in 1754 Duesbury moved to Longton Hall where he was employed as a full-time decorator. Deeds once in the possession of Llewellyn Jewitt and dated 1755 refer to him as "William Duesbury of Longton Hall" and as an "enameller". With his arrival Longton Hall decorations improved: enamels were brighter in colour and no longer flaked.

Longton Hall newspaper advertisements, ranging from 1752 to 1760 make no reference to figures until June 20, 1757 when "William Littler, at Longton Hall, near New-castle, Staffordshire" offered among other items "a Variety of curious and useful Ornaments for Deserts with Figures and Flowers of all Sorts, made exactly to Nature". A year

85

later he advertised "Images" adding that "The LONGTON Porcelain is vastly improv'd, and is now allow'd by all Judges, to be the best made in England".

Within two years, however, the costly venture was discontinued, the final record being an advertisement in the *Salisbury Journal*, September 8, 1760, announcing the sale of "the genuine large and valuable stock of the Longton Porcelaine China Factory, which, as the partnership is dissolved will be sold without Reserve or the least Addition; containing upwards of ninety thousand Pieces".

The figures made at Longton Hall during its twelve years of production may be grouped into three classes: (1) those made before the arrival of Duesbury early in 1754; (2) the period showing Duesbury's influence, 1754–57; the third and finest period, 1757 until production ceased in 1760. The majority were unskilfully potted and virtually all show technical faults, including firecracks.

Longton Hall used two types of soft porcelain in figure work, quality variations occurring in each. Early figures were in a soft creamy-white, glassy porcelain, highly translucent in thickly potted sections. It rather resembles contemporaneous Chelsea but is coarser of texture with inferior plastic properties, resulting in poorly defined detail. The majority were made by the slip casting technique introduced by Ralph Daniel in the mid-1740s and used first in connection with Staffordshire white salt-glazed stoneware.

The glaze, containing tin oxide to produce white opacity, is faintly tinged with green and contains a mass of minute air bubbles. It was thickly and unevenly applied and fired to a surface not unlike that of paraffin wax. The glaze ended a fraction of an inch above the base and is known to collectors as the dry edge. The exposed biscuit has absorbed two centuries of dust and now appears as a dark line encircling the edge of the base.

The thick white glaze so obscured modelling details that collectors have named the early series of figures as the "snowman family". Excavations on the Longton Hall site revealed examples of the snowman type of figure. About forty models have been collated including Chinese deities, birds such as pheasants and herons, reclining horses, sheep

86

and cows. Most of them are hollow such as the Meissen pug dog sitting on a plinth of rococo scrolls scratching his ear with a hind paw. A few of these dogs display a little under-glaze manganese decoration and sometimes show traces of gilding on collars and plinths. A few have been noted marked with the Longton Hall crossed Ls in underglaze blue—the only marked figures so far known. Plinths might be circular pads, or flat squares or oblongs. It became customary to apply flowers in the round to the bases, usually in a characteristic shape described by W. B. Honey as "markedly double, unlike the large flat flowers on early Derby figures, or the smaller ones on Chelsea bases".

Additional to the crude one-piece snowmen were figures and groups similarly glazed, but modelled instead of cast. These include variations of *Cupid at Vulcan's Forge* in which a small boy is seated on a mound beside a forge in the form of a scrolled pedestal with flames issuing from the top: a shovel and tongs lean against one side. The oblong base is studded with blossoms. A turkey cock tobacco taper-stick in the Fitzwilliam Museum depicts the bird with its left leg raised on a base studded with large blossoms. A wreath thrown over the turkey's back forms the taper socket.

By about 1754 Longton Hall paste had been much im-proved and was less difficult to work. It displayed a faintly greyish hue and is noticeably heavier in weight than formerly owing to the incorporation of lead oxide, the result of using flint-glass cullet as an ingredient. This porcelain has a greenish-cream translucency in thin sections which also display irregularly shaped moons when held against the light. Black specks and a sanded appearance are common defects: chips and cracks show the specks to penetrate throughout the porcelain.

Enamel decorations were used throughout the period although an advertisement shows that Longton Hall por-celain was still sold in the white. Early pigments were poorly prepared and muffle firing inefficient with the result that enamel tended to flake with the passing of years, a fact which probably accounts for some now white figures also found in well developed colours, such as the statuette of

David Garrick. Characteristic colours were a harsh crimson, a poor but strong red, uneven yellow and a dry yellowish-green.

After Duesbury's appointment as head decorator enamelling vastly improved. Colours now included a bright purplish pink, orange red, opaque blue, greens in several tints and a reddish brown used by no other porcelain decorator. Heads and costumes were more capably modelled. Faces were distinguished by the use of a characteristic red to mark the features. Eyes copied the Meissen technique with a black pupil in the centre of a red iris and two lines above each eye for lashes and eyebrows in black. Dresses were typically decorated with star or diaper patterns: rarely were flower patterns used.

Gilding was introduced to enamelled work in about 1755 and was sparsely used. Thick gold leaf was attached with impermanent size and unskilfully fired, resulting in a dull granular surface that could not be burnished. The majority of this gilding has thus worn away.

There is little indication of modelling development in Longton Hall figures between the crude snowmen and the vigorously shaped figures of the late 1750s although many new models were designed. These competently enamelled figures have flattish faces as in the set of *Four Seasons* in the Fitzwilliam Museum. They are supported on heavily potted scrollwork bases and are characteristically enlivened with a few lines of red enamel on the edges of the scrolls with a few applied flowers in the round. The undersides are lumpy and firecracks common.

One modeller at this period appears to have been responsible for several pairs of seated figures turned and leaning slightly towards each other such as the pair of *Cooks, Boys with a Barrel* and *Boys with Grapes*. The *Market-Woman Selling Butter* is from the same hand. The Victoria and Albert Museum example is described in the Schreiber Catalogue as "seated with legs crossed on a rock with rococo scrollwork and applied flowers on the front and wears a yellow hood, a pink cape over a red bodice, and a white skirt with a pattern of stars. A basket containing pats of butter is suspended from the rock, whilst the woman holds a small dish of butter in her right hand; on her cap are flowers. Slight gilding. Height 5⅞ in."

The same modeller was fond of depicting grapes in his groups such as *Cupids Feeding a Goat* with one boy carrying a basket of grapes under his right arm and a goat standing nearby with its mouth full of grapes: his companion reclines beside him. Others in the grape series include *Fruit Seller, Infant Bacchus* and *Boy with a Basket of Grapes*.

An experienced modeller of outstanding skill appears to have arrived at Longton Hall during 1757, probably a former employee of Chelsea which had temporarily ceased production from 1756 to 1758. Littler had introduced this modeller into his workshops in response to the fashionable demand through the London china sellers for fine figure groups. There was a considerable shortage of such figures following the temporary closure of Chelsea and of Meissen which had ceased production after being overrun by the Prussians early in the Seven Years War (1756–63). Some Longton Hall figures and groups during its final period are counted among the finest to have been made in English soft-paste porcelain.

Longton Hall paste continued harsh of texture with technical problems unsolved that made it difficult to obtain clear-cut, detailed modelling. Distortions in the kiln were too numerous for the venture into handsome figure work to be profitable. Thin sections held against the light now displayed an opalescent green tint and surface flaws were less conspicuous than formerly.

Several outstanding equestrian figures were made. The British Museum and the Victoria and Albert Museum possess examples of a naked boy seated on a galloping horse with a baying hound running alongside. This Longton Hall group was adapted from a bronze made by Francesci Fanelli more than a century earlier. The oblong porcelain plinths with rounded ends are encrusted with flowers and foliage in the round. The equestrian groups include a pair of rearing horses, one led by a Turk, the other by a Blackamoor, after Meissen models originated by Kändler.

Longton Hall's masterpiece was an equestrian figure of Ferdinand, Duke of Brunswick, seated on a charger trampling upon military trophies captured from the French. The duke wears the ribbon and Order of the Garter: he was created a Knight of the Garter on August 16, 1759 for his services at the battle of Minden. These figures, enamelled and in the white, were made between that date and early in 1760.

To this period belongs the figure of Britannia with a loose three-cornered pedestal. Britannia supports an oval medallion displaying a relief bust of George II. The example in the Schreiber collection is catalogued as "with pedestal with designs printed in black and painted over in colours, amongst which is a trophy with a shield bearing the arms of Prussia. . . . Britannia sits on a mound, wearing a loose robe painted with bouquets of flowers: she holds the medallion with her left hand and with her right supports a shield behind which a lion is crouching. Beside the mound are a globe, weapons and a standard. The pedestal is elaborately moulded with rococo scrollwork, leaving three spaces in which are printed designs: these include a camp scene and a landscape with equestrian figures. Slight gilding. Height, including pedestal, 16⅛ inches." The presence of victory wreaths in one of the transfer-printed scenes shows the figure to have been made in 1759 to commemorate a series of victories by the combined British-Prussian forces. Another example is in the British Museum. Transfer-prints have been noted on Longton Hall porcelain signed "John Sadler Liverpool". Two-colour and three-colour transfer-prints had not yet been invented. Longton Hall is known to have made stands for a few other figures such as *Hercules Wrestling with the Nemean Lion,* but rarely have they remained intact.

The late period was also responsible for *The Dancers,* probably the most competently modelled of the Longton Hall figures. Measuring nearly eleven inches in height, it was probably the first attempt at large-size figure-making. This group is found in the white and lightly coloured in purples, yellows, greens and opaque reddish-brown and gold.

The handsome *Four Continents,* colourfully enamelled and measuring more than a foot in height, were probably Littler's swansong. These stand on high pedestals lavishly gilded by an improved method. These figures, with slight adaptations, were later reproduced at Plymouth in hard-paste porcelain. Dr. Bernard Watney points out that the Longton Hall set are flat beneath the base: the Plymouth versions are hollow. Other Longton Hall figures reproduced by William Cookworthy at Plymouth after 1768 were *Putti Feeding a Goat,* a set of boys as *Seasons* and various seated figures.

Twentieth-century reproductions of Longton Hall figures have been made, but none display the original potting techniques. The enamels, too, contain purer metallic oxides than were available in the 18th century and have been fired in more efficient muffle kilns. Chrome green has been noted, a metallic oxide not used in enamels until the 1790s.

Chapter Seven

ENGLISH potters from the days of Henry VIII had dreamed of making a hard translucent porcelain equal to that imported from China. As early as 1712 they were aware that Cornwall possessed large deposits of clays resembling those used by the Chinese for their fine porcelains. Hamilton, discussing the porcelain clays of China in 1727, commented: "We have the same sort of Clay in Great Britain, that porcelain is made of, but we want the warm sun to prepare it."

Working on such theories, William Cookworthy (1705–1780), a Quaker chemist of Plymouth, set out to match the oriental kaolin and petuntze with clays from Cornwall and evolve a process to remove impurities. Eventually he did find a suitable china clay, which is usually regarded as kaolin although differing in many respects. Also, near at hand, he found china stone, the fluxing element known to the Chinese as petuntze and essential to the manufacture of hard porcelain.

Cookworthy's interest in porcelain manufacture had been aroused while he was studying in London to become a druggist. Here he became absorbed in Baron Réamur's scientific treatise which described experiments carried out with a consignment of Chinese kaolin and petuntze sent to him in Paris by Père d'Entrecolles, a Jesuit missionary at Ching-tê-Chên, one of China's most important porcelain centres. The Jesuit's report on Chinese methods of manufacturing porcelain was included as an appendix to Réamur's book. Eventually more accurate and more detailed information was published in Du Halde's *History of China*, 1738. After reading this Cookworthy was determined to devote his energies to the manufacture of porcelain in England.

15. Longton Hall porcelain figures, about 1755. (*Top left*) Statuette of Britannia on a loose pedestal and holding a relief medallion of George II. She is seated on a mound with a globe, weapons and a standard behind. The pedestal is decorated with three printed designs including a camp scene and a landscape with equestrian figures. Height, including pedestal, 6¼ inches. (*Top right*) Group of a gallant and lady in fancy dress: behind is a tree stump with a flowering stem applied. High rococo-scrolled base with four feet. Height 10½ inches. (*Bottom*) Figures of an actor, believed to be David Garrick, with a cloak thrown over his left shoulder and his right hand resting on an open book; on the left in white porcelain, height 8¼ inches; on the right painted in enamel colours, height 7¾ inches.

16. (*Top*) Bristol porcelain figures, 1772 or later. Autumn wears a pink-lined mantle over a loose robe and a belt decorated with the signs of Libra, Scorpio and Sagittarius. Height 10 inches. Summer wears a yellow-lined flowered classical robe secured by a band passing over his shoulder, bearing the signs Cancer, Leo and Virgo. Height 9¾ inches. (*Lower left*) Bow shepherdess, closely adapted from a Meissen original, the rococo moulding on the base is outlined in purplish black. Height 10⅜ inches. 1755–6. (*Lower right*) Group in Plymouth hard porcelain with wreaths of applied flowers painted in colours. About 1770.

One contributory factor to his success—its importance difficult now to assess—was the pioneer work of Andrew Duché who in 1744 brought to London samples of Virginian "china earth", known to the American Indians as Unaker. Duché had recognised this as the kaolin mentioned in d'Entrecolles' reports. He had also discovered deposits of petuntze in Virginia and for more than two years had been producing hard porcelain in America. Samples examined by Cookworthy were pronounced by him to be "equal to the Asiatic".

William Cookworthy numbered many celebrities among his friends: Captain Cook, Sir Joseph Banks and Dr. Solander dined with him on the day before starting their voyage round the world. Another friend was John Nancarrow, superintendent of the tin mines at St. Austell and an engineer renowned for his improvements to steam engines. Under his guidance Cookworthy was introduced to large deposits of a clay used locally for repairing fireplaces and engine furnaces. This was known locally as moor stone and was capable of withstanding intense heat without disintegrating. When this clay was freed from mica and other impurities Cookworthy found it better than the American unaker. But more than twenty years of costly experiment were required before he evolved a satisfactory method of removing the impurities on a commercial scale.

In about 1757 he recognised in the growan stone of Cornwall a mineral resembling the Chinese petuntze used as a fluxing agent by the porcelain potters. Known to present-day potters as china stone, this is a partially felspathic granite.

With china clay and china stone at his disposal Cookworthy considered himself all set for pioneering the manufacture of true porcelain in England. In 1761 he established at Bristol a small pottery kiln capable of raising a temperature 200–300 degrees F. higher than was necessary for the soft-paste porcelains of Chelsea and elsewhere. Early in 1764 he formed a company in which he held three of the fourteen shares: one share was held by his brother and one by Richard Champion (1743–1791).

Champion's important and ill-fated venture into the manufacture of hard-paste porcelain is considered later in this chapter. Here it is enough to note in passing that he, too, belonged to a Quaker family. Inheriting a modest fortune when he came of age, he launched into business as a general merchant trading with America and had every prospect of becoming one of the most influential men of his day.

Cookworthy has recorded that his pioneer hard-paste consisted of "about equal parts of washed moor stone and growan stone obtained from Tregonnis Hill in Cornwall". This pioneer porcelain was of poor quality, the collapses and distortions too numerous for the venture to prove profitable: reluctantly he abandoned work early in 1766. That the factory actually operated is proved by a letter written by Richard Champion to Lord Hyndford later in the same year: "I therefore had it tried out at a manufactory set up here some time ago on the principle of the Chinese Porcelain, but not being successful is given up. . . . The Proprietors of the work in Bristol imagined that they had discovered in Cornwall all the materials similar to the Chinese: but though they burnt the body part tolerably well, yet there were impurities in the Glaze or Stone which were insurmountable. The body is perfectly white within but not without which is always smoky."

Cookworthy, undaunted, thereupon established a pottery at Plymouth, choosing a waterside site at Coxside. The British Museum possesses a mug in hard porcelain, flawed with many black specks and decorated under the glaze with the arms of Plymouth in a pale, blackish blue and inscribed "Plymouth Manufactory March 14 1768 CF". Three days later Cookworthy enrolled at the Patent Office in London a specification for a fourteen-year patent to give him the sole rights "to Make and Vend a Kind of Porcellain newly Invented by Me". The patent, No. 898, was granted on the following July 14 and Cookworthy traded as The Plymouth New Invented Porcelain Company. He was financed by Thomas Pitt, later created Lord Camelford, whose land had been found to contain a large deposit of moor stone and growan stone already mixed by nature.

Cookworthy has recorded that this "burned to a degree of transparence without the addition of petuntze, making a body much whiter than the Asiatic, and, I think, full as white as the ancient China ware or that of Dresden". Again, however, wastage through distortion in the kiln and fire-cracks proved costly. The formula was changed to a mixture of china clay and china stone from separate deposits. Soon the factory was employing between fifty and sixty workers, but lack of expert knowledge and experienced workmen from other pottery centres inevitably resulted in financial failure.

The white paste of Plymouth porcelain made under the patent verges slightly towards grey and translucency varies from a faintly yellowish green to a grey compared by William Turner to sodden snow. It breaks with a granular fracture. Firecracks, warping, pinholes and specks are common. Minute bubbles visible on the surface, known as pigskin pitting, were caused by imperfect wedging—that is, slapping the pieces of clay together to remove all the air. Cookworthy's potters failed to carry out this work skilfully and in the kiln the air bubbles expanded and disfigured the surface.

Although wood charcoal fuel was used the smoky appearance caused by "those tinging vapours" so characteristic of Cookworthy's porcelain, seems never to have been overcome. The result was a faintly brownish hue on the surface of the biscuit. Few figures are without this defect.

Glazing, too, brought problems. On early Plymouth figures the glaze was thickly applied and imperfect fusion caused uneven patches. Where the glaze has collected in crevices it displays a tint varying from pale greenish yellow to faint cobalt blue.

At first the Chinese method of glazing was used: the dried, unbaked "green" ware was covered with glaze. This had the advantage of needing only a single firing, but technical difficulties could not be overcome. At Plymouth, and later at Bristol, Cookworthy used standard glaze of the frit variety composed almost entirely of china stone: one part quick lime and two parts of fern ashes were fritted and one part of the frit added to fifteen of powdered china stone. This glaze, brilliant and thin, incorporated with the body to make the porcelain appear dense and semi-opaque, but

95

possessed the peculiar smoothness of surface found on true oriental porcelain.

Early Cookworthy figures might be of plain white glazed porcelain such as the goat in the British Museum, cleverly modelled but much disfigured by smoke. The majority, however, were clumsily decorated with enamels, judicious colour placement tending to disguise flaws. Small motifs widely spaced were characteristic. Cookworthy figures for the most part are open-based, their rococo scroll plinths touched with red or brownish crimson. Many display Staffordshire influence and a few have Longton Hall counterparts. It has been suggested that Cookworthy may have acquired moulds from an auction sale of some 90,000 pieces of Longton Hall porcelain advertised in the *Salisbury Chronicle* on September 8, 1760, six months or so before he established his Bristol factory in 1761. The advertisement, however, makes no reference to the sale of plant and tools.

Cookworthy's enamelled and gilded version of *The Four Continents* from Longton Hall achieved a considerable circulation. *Two Boys Feeding a Goat* is an attractive group: skilfully modelled *bocages* and birds such as pheasants and finches may be noted among other Longton Hall models, and such animals as cows, sheep, goats, lions and hares.

In the Schreiber collection at the Victoria and Albert Museum are several figures that were formerly in the possession of Cookworthy's relatives. These include male and female musicians, each seated between the branches of a flowering tree on a high pedestal—the man playing a flute, the woman a mandoline.

Another pair of six-inch figures in the Schreiber collection are known as *The Topers*. The youth sits astride a cask and holds up a tankard: he wears blue jacket, red breeches and black hat and shoes. His companion is a young woman reclining on a tree trunk and raising a wine-glass to her lips: her dress consists of purple bodice, flowered skirt and red shoes matching a plume in her hair. Here again each figure is placed between branches bearing applied flowers and leaves and their high pedestal bases are ornamented with leafy scroll work in relief.

In the September of 1770 William Cookworthy decided to

17. (*Top*) Longton Hall. On the left, a man reclining on a rococo-scrolled base with applied flowers. Attired in a pink coat over a white waistcoat with a pattern of stars, red breeches and black shoes. Height 6¼ inches. About 1755. On the right, two boys feeding a goat with grapes. The flesh is tinted a reddish pink. Height 5⅛ inches. About 1755. (*Bottom*) Plymouth. Pair of candlesticks with figures of a gardener with fruit and a woman with flowers, emblematic of Autumn and Spring. The trunks of trees form supports for candle sockets. Height 10⅝ inches and 9⅝ inches. About 1770.

18. Bristol hard-paste porcelain, about 1775. (*Top*) Summer and Autumn, two of a set of four children emblematic of the Seasons. The boy wears gold-flowered white knee-breeches, his green-lined purple coat is thrown over the beehive. The girl wears a gold-flowered dress with pink lining, a blue belt, gold and white petticoat. Impressed T°. Height 10½ inches. (*Bottom*) Shepherd and shepherdess, on square bases painted with leafy scrolls in dull crimson. The shepherd, holding out a brightly coloured bird, wears a yellow-lined pink coat and knee-breeches decorated with sprays of flowers in colour. The shepherdess wears a blue and red hat, a white bodice, gold-laced in front, and a white petticoat with a pattern of gold flowers.

transfer plant and material from his unprofitable Plymouth factory to 15 Castle Green, Bristol, where ample experienced labour was available. An advertisement published in *Berrows Worcester Journal*, February 22, 1770, shows that the move was already contemplated: "China Ware Painters wanted for the Plymouth New Invented Porcelain Manufactory. A number of sober, ingenious artists capable of painting in enamel or blue, may hear of constant employment by sending their proposals to Thomas Frank, Castle Street, Bristol."

The move was made with the knowledge that Richard Champion would join the firm, which would continue trading as the Plymouth New Invented Porcelain Company under the proprietorship of William Cookworthy and Company. Early in 1773, however, the aging Cookworthy conveyed his interest in the porcelain company to Richard Champion who thereupon became sole proprietor and styled the firm Champion & Company although the legal transfer was delayed until May 6, 1774 when Cookworthy's patent was assigned to him. Manufacturing hazards were slowly mastered and at the date of the transfer it was recorded that Bristol porcelain had not become "a marketable commodity so as to furnish an order until the last Six Months, but that sometimes they succeeded and at other times not; but that now they can execute any order". This shows that from the date of taking out the patent the advance to technical competence had taken six years.

The improved quality of Bristol porcelain was announced in an advertisement published in *Felix Farley's Journal*, January 1773, which stated that "The True Porcelain . . . is now brought to Great Perfection, Its texture not to be distinguished from East India China." It was also reported that "The Enamell of the Bristol China is as hard as the Dresden and harder than the Chinese" and "they can render this China in most Articles as cheap as the Asiatic and much Cheaper than the Dresden." Yet the extended patent granted to Champion contained a clause placing a tariff of 150 per cent on imported hard-paste porcelain, thus emphasising Champion's monopoly.

There is little doubt that Champion played an important part in the direction of the company before it came under

7
97

his entire control. The hard paste, now suggestive of Dresden, contained substantially the same ingredients that had been used at Plymouth. It was now milky white in colour with a surface suggesting the faintly greyish tint of newly cut ivory and showing scarcely any discolourations apart from occasional dark brown spots with black centres caused by particles of iron. Surface appearance throughout figures is fairly constant, however. Grit is often to be noted on the underside of the base. Sir Arthur Church in his monograph *English Porcelain*, 1885, described fractures in Bristol porcelain as "sub-conchoidal, slightly flaky, and the lustre of a fractured surface something between greasy and vitreous: apparently compact and homogeneous". This agrees with a statement made in 1774 by John Britain, Champion's factory manager. Translucency varies with the quality of the paste, the result of variations in the quality of the raw materials and changes in blending. This porcelain is very durable: several figures passed undamaged through the fierce fire at Alexandra Palace which reduced all examples of English soft-paste porcelain into shapeless masses.

Bristol glaze is thin, brilliant, with a non-undulating surface and in colour is almost identical with the paste. Champion appears to have overcome difficulties met with by Cookworthy in "dipping raw". This glaze has withstood the wear and surface stains of two centuries. It does not appear as a separate layer on the body, but appears to have amalgamated with it. Enamels have not sunk into this glaze as into those of Chelsea, Bow and elsewhere, but rise slightly above the level of the glazed surface, being in danger of peeling off with the passage of years.

Gilding is always handsome and has proved permanent. The parts to be gilded were first painted with unfired glaze tinged with thick vermilion. This made the gilded patterns stand out in slight relief after firing. The red tinge enriched the colour of the gold, always thickly applied.

A glimpse into Champion's careful managerial methods is disclosed in a letter illustrated in Champion's own handwriting in *Two Centuries of Ceramic Art in Bristol*, by Hugh Owen, 1873, sent by him to the modeller of the set of figures emblematic of the *Four Elements*: *Earth, Air, Fire and Water*,

98

the most distinguished figures made at Bristol. "I have seen", wrote Champion, "the four Elements which are made at Derby, they are very Beautifull, the dress easy, the forms fine, two in particular Air and Water are Charming figures. I apprehend that you made ye models & therefore hope from your Execution the following fancies will not look amiss." Champion then described at length and in minute detail how he wished the models to appear.

The Elements

Fire. A Vulcan forging a Thunderbolt in the attitude of striking with his anvil and Hammer, some pieces of Iron or Coals or anything peculiar to a Blacksmith's Shop to be scatter'd about.

Neither Champion nor his modeller could have been familiar with the blacksmith's craft. Vulcan is presented, not as the blacksmith but as the smith's striker, with arms raised to swing a sledge hammer, forging a thunderbolt on an anvil; at his feet lies a breast-plate with a lion's head shoulder-piece. He is placed incorrectly, standing end on to the anvil, facing one side with the pointed end or bick to his right. Lacking the blacksmith himself to steady the red-hot thunderbolt in his tongs, Vulcan would displace it from the face of the anvil with every blow.

Water. A Naiad crown'd with rushes, leaning with her arm on an urn from which gushes out Water. In the other hand she holds a fishing Net with Fishes enclos'd in it, the ground ornamented with rushes, shells, Fish or the Fancies peculiar to Water.

Earth. An husbandman digging with a spade, a Baskett fill'd with Implements of Husbandry on ye Ground. Ye ground ornamented with corns, acorns or fruits.

Air. A winged Zyphyr crown'd with Flowr's treding on clouds, which rise naturally about him, his robes flowing & flying behind him. He holds in one Hand a Branch of a Tree, if any ornaments behind are wanting, some Cherabim's heads blowing would not be amiss.

After describing *The Seasons* in similar detail, Champion continued: "All these figures to be about 10 inches high. After having seen the Derby Figures, I did not recommend Ease and Elegance in the shape and dress, but the latter I shall just mention as the antique Robes, are very easy and have a Propriety which is not to be met with in foreign Dresses, and as these figures are of a serious Cast I think such dresses will carry with them a greater Elegance. I shall be oblig'd to you to carry the designs into execution as soon as possible." This is proof enough that neither the *Elements* nor the *Seasons* may be attributed to a period earlier than mid-1772.

Despite technical shortcomings Bristol figures of the 1770s, usually modelled in pairs or sets of four, are among the most skilfully potted in England during the 18th century, carefully modelled and coloured with restraint. Some were inspired by Dresden, a few being exact copies, but about three-quarters of the size of originals. Plymouth and early Bristol figures have scrolled bases, but Champion quickly abandoned these in favour of the less elaborate rectangular or circular rock work style then fashionable in France. These may be decorated in high relief with ferns and leaves or motifs associated with the figures they bear. Their sides may be streaked pale yellow and brown with dull turquoise on top. Others are marbled. Bases may be hollow and covered with a thin sheet of porcelain pierced with a vent hole.

Characteristic decoration includes a tendency to ornament dresses with widely spaced flower sprays and arrangements of spots in a manner reminiscent of some Dresden shepherdesses. Unlike other makers of porcelain figures Champion, with Quaker restraint, refused to permit them to be dressed in gaudy splendour. Ground colours on clothing usually include vermilion, bluish green, pale yellow and pink. Champion's figures are decorated according to their station in life: rustics are differentiated from the well-to-do by striped clothing and conventional flowers. Competing potters usually gave all their figures handsomely painted attire. The flesh is usually very slightly tinted, with hair, eyes and lips touched in colour.

Figure groups were rarely made at Bristol. In the Victoria and Albert Museum, however, is a three-figure group *Venus and Adonis with Cupid* on a rectangular base decorated in front with symmetrical gilt scrollwork. This is obviously a mantel or side-table ornament. Typically, the flesh is very slightly tinted and the hair of Venus and Cupid is reddish-brown with that of Adonis greyish-brown. Venus is partly draped in yellow-lined bluish-green patterned with flower sprig medallions encircled by wreaths in gold. Adonis has drapery over his knees in dull crimson patterned with gilt sprays and lined in bluish-green.

Among other Bristol figures searched for by collectors are: *Shepherd and Milkman*; *Love Subdued by Time*; *Goatherd holding a Kid*; *Shepherd Bagpiper and Shepherdess*; *Boy and Girl Musicians* playing hurdy-gurdy and triangle; *Shepherd and Shepherdess* in several models; *Shepherd and Gardener*; set of four children emblematic of the *Seasons*; *Boy and Girl with Dogs*. Busts were made also and include *Shakespeare* and *Milton*.

Cookworthy's figures were rarely marked, but at Plymouth he used the alchemist's sign for tin, resembling a combination of the numerals 2 and 4. This appears in underglaze and in blue, red or reddish-brown enamel, and on fine pieces in gold. This mark was no doubt selected because of the association of the Cornish tin mines with the minerals used for his porcelain. An early Bristol mark is an X in blue under the glaze or incised.

At Bristol from 1770 the two marks were amalgamated, the cross placed below the symbol for tin. When the crossed swords of Meissen are included in a mark they indicate the source of the original model.

Reproductions of Champion's Bristol figures in hard-paste porcelain were imported from Kloster Veilsdorf, Thuringia, Germany, in the years immediately following 1874. So closely do these resemble the originals that experts are still deceived although they are marked with a cross containing S in its lower angle. More recently reproductions of Plymouth and Bristol figures have been made in England and imported from France.

Chapter Eight

SOONER or later most of the ceramics worked by potters of useful wares have been applied to figure making. The result is a range of ornament unparalleled among the media of other artist-craftsmen and unique, surely, in the pleasure it has afforded in palace and villa and cottage. For almost three centuries materials have reflected the potter's long advance in substance and technique while subject matter, design and execution have ranged from superb to trivial and absurd and who can say which have proved most endearing. But their story has an unusual beginning. Pre-requisite for any figure work beyond primitive "toys" was a clay body that could emerge from the kiln hard and white and delicately detailed. In England the man who first achieved this triumph also acquired the services of at least one notably skilful modeller so that the craft was stimulated by a brief spell of magnificence quite out of keeping with the general story of a slow-growing native craft. The fine clay body required for delicacy of modelling was white stoneware, and manufacture in England dates back no earlier than 1671 and was the pioneer work of John Dwight (1640–1703), now counted as one of the great potters of Europe. Dwight's Fulham Pottery issued vast quantities of domestic articles in brown salt-glazed stoneware. These were made by a patented process different from the centuries-old methods used in Germany, but were wholly commercial productions. Dwight is remembered today not for these but for a range of stoneware figures, masterpieces of the potter's art, now ranking as the finest works of their kind.

Stoneware is an almost vitrified pottery, halfway between hard porcelain and earthenware, and composed of plastic clay and silica. Firing at a high temperature causes partial vitrification, resulting in a close texture that makes it hard as stone. It will emit a ringing sound when struck and displays a near-glassy texture when fractured. The shaped clay was glazed at a single firing, the finished surface until 1847 acquiring an attractive granular texture suggesting orange skin (see page 108). The hard transparent glaze was produced by introducing into the kiln common rock salt which vaporised and settled in minute drops, forming a film on the surface (see page 108).

John Dwight was educated for the church at Christ Church College, Oxford, leaving in 1661 with the degree of B.C.L. to become "registrar and scribe" to Brian Walton, appointed Bishop of Chester after the Restoration. He continued under successive bishops, finally as secretary to Bishop Hall, who in those days of plurality of livings was also rector of Wigan where he resided. Dwight remained at Wigan during 1669 and 1670 and only then, at the age of thirty, turned his energies towards becoming a master potter.

In April 1671 Dwight, described as gentleman, was granted a patent (No. 164) in which the specification stated that he had discovered "the Mistery of Transparent Earthenware, commonly Known by the Names of Porcelaine or China, and Persian Ware, as alsoe the misterie of the Stone Ware vulgarly called Cologne Ware; and that he designed to introduce a Manufacture of the said Wares into our Kingdome of England where they have not hitherto been wrought or made."

A patent is a legal document which at that time cost £300, equivalent to more than £4,000 in present-day currency. It would have been impossible for a patent to have passed the scrutiny of the Lord Chief Justice had any of these ceramics formerly been potted successfully in England.

Dr. Robert Plot, the first keeper of the Ashmolean Museum, wrote in his *Natural History of Oxfordshire*, 1677, that "the ingenious John Dwight hath discovered the mystery of the stone of Cologne wares heretofore made only in Germany . . . and hath set up a manufacture of the same, which (by methods and contrivances of his own altogether unlike those used by the Germans) in three of four years he hath brought to greater perfection than it has attained where it has been used for ages." Dr. Plot also recorded that Dwight "hath caused to be modelled statues or figures (a thing not done elsewhere for China afford us only imperfect mouldings) which he diversified with great variety of colours, making them the colour of iron, copper, bronze and party colour'd as some Achat [agate] stones."

Here then is contemporaneous evidence that Dwight made notable stoneware figures more than eight years before applying for a further patent, No. 234, which was granted in June 1684, thus continuing the monopoly until 1698. In the specification "statues and figures" of stoneware are listed among his productions.

Surviving examples of Dwight's stoneware figures display high technical skill. They obviously followed the sculptor's technique of direct carving on stone. Unlike those of later porcelain, stoneware and earthenware potters they were not cast, pressed nor built from numerous units, but were hand modelled individually and without duplication. Most of them reveal the use of modelling tools.

Three types of stoneware have been noted in Dwight's existing figures:

1. A white body, translucent in the thinnest parts such as sharp folds of drapery. Such figures appear to be glazed by the vaporising process known as smear-glazing. *Flora* and *The Sportsman,* both in the British Museum, are of this quality.
2. A similar white body covered with fairly thick salt glaze, such as *Prince Rupert* and *Mrs. Pepys,* also in the British Museum.
3. A body covered with a thin wash of ferruginous clay, producing the effect of fine bronze, such as the mythological series of *Jupiter, Saturn, Mars* and *Meleager.*

The modelling of Dwight's spectacular life-size bust of Prince Rupert and other portrait busts has been attributed to Grinling Gibbons (1648–1721), but this is very improbable. The style and carving reflect the hand of John

Bushnell (1619–1682) whose terracotta bust of Charles II is in the Fitzwilliam Museum, Cambridge. It is known that in 1675 Bushnell carved the statue of Lord Mordant (d. 1675) at Fulham Parish Church, close to Dwight's pottery. Bushnell also carved the bust of Mrs. Pepys in St. Olave's Church, London and Dwight's stoneware model of Mrs. Pepys bears a close resemblance to this.

Dwight's stoneware figures were not commercially profitable. Tradition has it that eventually he buried all the equipment associated with this enterprise. This conformed with his character for the existing note books in Dwight's handwriting record that he was his own banker, concealing large quantities of gold coin about his home and pottery.

There is more than a passing interest in the thirteen note book entries he made in November 1693 which include the following: "In ye garret in a hole vnder ye fireplace 240 G [guineas] in a wooden box; in ye old Laboratory at the old house, in two holes vnder the fireplace on both sides ye ffurnace in 2 half pint Gor: Covered [pitcher] 460 Gui; in severall holes of ye ffurnace in ye middle of the kitchen opening at ye top where the sands lyes in a purse of 100 Gui: & severall Cans of Gs cover'd; at ye further End of the bottome hole of my furnace in the little parlour a box of 200 G; in two holes of that great furnace running in almost to the Oven, 2 boxes full of mill'd money. May be drawn out wth a long crooked Iron standing behind ye kitchen door." Milled guineas, specified in four of the hoards, were first minted in 1663 and preferred to the earlier hammered gold coinage which was notoriously light in weight.

Several entries regarding these hoards of guineas show that Dwight carried out experimental work in the privacy of his own home, thus confounding the suggestion made by some authorities that he merely financed skilled German potters of stoneware. He twice refers to his laboratory and also to furnaces in the garret, in the little parlour and in the kitchen which contained a "little ffurnace", a "great ffurnace in ye middle" and an oven.

About thirty beautifully modelled statuettes and busts

were preserved in the Dwight family as heirlooms until 1862, when they were sold and eventually acquired by C. W. Reynolds who lent them to the South Kensington Museum, now the Victoria and Albert Museum. After his death in 1871 twenty-seven lots were sold at Christie's including: "A life-size bust of James II since re-named Prince Rupert with the gold collar of the Order of the Garter and its pendent George, £39 18s.; Flora, £14 0s.; bust of Charles II in large wig and lace necktie, £27; bust of Lydia Dwight John Dwight's infant daughter lying on a couch, her head resting on a pillow, a broad lace over her forehead, in her hands a bouquet of flowers, with an inscription 'Lydia Dwight, dyd March 3, 1673', £158."

The Fulham Pottery continued under the control of Dwight's descendants until 1861 and is still in production. Figures, however, were not made until the late-1860s when a few outstanding examples were potted in terracotta under the direction of C. J. C. Bailey. The Fulham terracotta is richly red and light pink and a combination of the two displays a really attractive effect. As had been the case during John Dwight's regime, each figure was hand-carved individually and no identical copies made by industrial methods. The name R. W. Martin fecit appears on the bases of a few figures made in 1872 when Wallace Martin, one of the four celebrated brothers who later worked the Southall Pottery, was engaged as a modeller and designer.

Figures in white salt-glazed stoneware were in production by 1873 under the direction of E. Bennet, a well-known sculptor of the period. In 1877 Llewellyn Jewitt placed on record regarding Fulham figures that "the body, it may be well to note, is made from Dwight's original recipe—the very body from which the first figures were produced in England. Therefore the Fulham china of today has an intense historical interest."

It was not until the 18th century that salt-glazed white stoneware was developed on a commercial scale: this was in Staffordshire and it was never made so successfully elsewhere.

This development is associated, somewhat vaguely, with

Astbury of Shelton (1688–1743, his first name possibly Robert or John), father of Thomas Astbury (b. 1719), who is thought to have established himself as a master potter between 1715 and 1718. The long-familiar brown "drain pipe" stoneware had already evolved into a grey or drab-coloured stoneware. This was known to the potters of Staffordshire as crouch ware. Several unconvincing reasons for this name have been offered, but the fact has been overlooked that at Kreussen, in the Cologne district of Germany, tall jugs in grey salt-glazed stoneware with applied relief decorations were known as *crüches* and imported into England under this name. When similar jugs were made in Staffordshire the dialect modified the word to crouch and soon other articles of the same material became known under the generic term of crouch ware.

Astbury or others achieved progressive improvements in the grey crouch ware until the resultant white salt-glazed stoneware was strong and fine-grained for figure making. In an endeavour to whiten the ware the potter first covered its surface with a carefully lawned engobe or dip of fine white pipe clay from Bideford in Devonshire. Then, in the early 1720s, he hardened and whitened the body itself throughout its texture by incorporating pulverised calcined flints which greatly reduced warping hazards in the kiln. This stoneware, while still of a dull tint known to collectors as "drab", was nevertheless so translucent, when thin, that it was sold expensively by many dealers as porcelain.

Astbury's final improvement was made in the early 1730s, produced stoneware with a whiter body: this discovery gave half a century of high prosperity to about eighty Staffordshire master potters. While retaining a proportion of calcined flint, he discarded local marl in favour of the Devonshire pipe clay, thus obtaining increased plasticity and improved vitreous properties, particularly when it was weathered for a few months before use. This clay was eventually transported to the Potteries in the form of balls— hence the familiar term ball clay. It was in this white salt-glazed stoneware that Staffordshire potters made many of their most delightful figures or image toys.

The hard, translucent non-porous salt-glaze was imposed by the action of rock salt upon the red-hot surface of the clay. This glaze formed better and more thickly upon a body rich in silica—hence the improved glazing that followed the introduction of calcined flints to the clay, resulting in a highly vitreous ware. The figures were enclosed in fireclay saggars perforated with large holes and piled one upon the other in a specially designed kiln.

When the figures were red hot the draught was reduced and rock salt vaporised by throwing it into the fires. This reacted with the body in the presence of steam to form a thin coating of sodium alumino silicate. The salt was thrown when trials removed from the kiln showed that the ware was not quite vitreous. This was important: had the ware been too porous the salt vapour would have penetrated the body and the glaze would have been dull. Three saltings were required, an average charge being about 15 lb. of rock salt to one ton of stoneware. When cold this vapour glaze appeared as a thin, intensely hard film of soda glass, about 0.1. mm. thick and fused to the stoneware.

Brilliant when new and of long durability, early salt-glaze was characterised by its "orange skin" or "egg-shell" surface, caused by minute pinholes or pores left in the glazed surface. Wide variations of "grain" are found, even on different parts of a single piece. From about 1750 it was possible, at some extra cost, to avoid this effect by smearing the ware with red lead before placing it in the kiln. This glaze was softer but thicker and smoother than ordinary salt-glaze and often fails to be recognised.

At first, salt-glazed stoneware figures were modelled by hand with a few simple tools. The various anatomical sections were formed by rolling, cutting and pinching the clay. For instance, a woman from the waist up was based on a solid core, almost a plain cylinder, shaped by rolling clay between the palms of the hands. The upper end was thinned into a neck and a ball of clay rolled and modelled into a head, topped by a pleated cap. Arms of rolled clay were attached, their flattened ends tooled to represent hands and fingers. The figure was then dressed, garments being cut from clay rolled into flat sheets which were eventually fired to about $\frac{1}{16}$-inch thick. Dark ruffs might be wrapped around forearms and wrists to give the illusion of sleeves. No legs were hidden beneath the billowing skirt, which might be composed of alternating strips of dark and light clay, the surfaces of the white stripes often ornamented with milled lines. Over this elaborate skirt there might be a long white apron, then high fashion wear. Eyes, necklace and other trimmings were dots of black or dark brown slip.

Men were more completely modelled than women since their dress less thoroughly enveloped the figure, but clothing was fitted over a skeleton core in the same way. Narrow strips of clay shaped into heavy ringlets were attached to the head often under a tricorn hat. Clay stained a dark tint was used for the hat, neck ribbons, cuffs and shoes, set off by touches of white such as the edges of the hat brim and buckles on the shoes. The man might hold a musical instrument such as a violin or bagpipes. This method of modelling precluded exact duplication in the mass-production manner, each unit of the figure being individually created so that the potter had full scope to vary the standard model from which he worked. Such figures fashioned singly are usually attributed to the 1730s but technical details suggest many to have been made in the 1740s and later.

Salt-glazed figures of this type include horsemen, musicians, bell-shaped women and so-called pew groups. The pew group served the same purpose as the porcelain maker's *bocage*. Two or three figures were united into a substantial and comparatively strong entity with a minimum of vulnerable projections by being mounted on a background, in this case a high-backed settle. This, combined with the vivid dark and light tones of their material, ensured maximum display value in the smoky half-light of the mantel shelf in a small early-Georgian house. The settle formed a convenient background since seated figures could suggest many familiar, homely activities. One or two men and a woman compose the most usual groups: three-figure groups are rare. The settles might sometimes slightly resemble church pews but no religious significance should be inferred from the name given to them by collectors. Themes vary, love and music being the most common.

Pew groups may be considered in three classes: those of salt-glazed stoneware, those of lead-glazed earthenware, and the most numerous reproductions. Salt-glazed pew groups appear to be the productions of a single pottery, not more than half-a-dozen modellers being concerned. The figures, with minor variations, wear similar clothing. The rigidly posed women wear ruffed caps, tight bodices and wide skirts, partly hidden beneath long aprons. The men wear skirted coats over frogged and buttoned waistcoats, their heads bewigged with tightly twisted roll curls.

These fashions considered alone might place pew groups early in the reign of George II (1727–60). But the use of the white body containing calcined flint indicates a date no earlier than its introduction during the early 1730s. And technical details fix the date more precisely to the years preceding the introduction and gradual widespread acceptance of casting from plaster of paris moulds in the mid-1740s by Ralph Daniel of Cobridge (see page 112). Incised or scratched decoration is found on some examples. In these a pattern, incised with a sharp tool on the back of the settle before firing, is emphasised by a filling of powdered cobalt blue.

Some authorities suggest that Aaron Wood was responsible for the salt-glazed pew groups. Wood, formerly an apprentice with Dr. Thomas Wedgwood, was reputed to be the most skilful block cutter for moulds of his day. It is difficult to correlate the meticulously fine craftsmanship this would imply with the naïve designs of existing pew groups.

Astbury appears a more possible choice if a potter must be named for these anonymous groups. Astbury is associated with the improvement in the stoneware that rendered it suitable for figure modelling and a series of figures representing musicians playing their instruments, generally credited to him, bear resemblances to certain figures contained in musical pew groups.

Clays of two contrasting colours were skilfully used for these salt-glazed stoneware figures—white and a brownish-black. The black areas were produced, not by painting, or glazing, but by superimposing dark clay on the white body. The settle was the first unit to be prepared. This was constructed from five sections—base, back, sides and seat—cut as though it were pastry from a sheet of white clay $\frac{1}{4}$-inch thick: this reduced to $\frac{3}{16}$-inch or less during firing. Moulding applied around the top and sides of the settle-back increased its strength and prevented warping in the kiln. Decorative arm rests were added, often made by twisting together rolled lengths of black and white clay. Into the back of the settle below the seat two or more irregular arches were cut.

The back of the seat might be decorated with grotesque masks or modelled in relief or show simple cut-out designs composed of spades, circles and hearts. Solon in his *Art of the English Potter* suggests that these cut-out motifs imitated a German style of decoration in brown salt-glazed stoneware popular in England during the second quarter of the 18th century. In some instances flower and foliage ornament was incised and the hollows picked out in more fluid clay known as slip that would bake to a rich brown. There is no record of any salt-glazed white stoneware pew groups painted with enamels.

Cream-coloured earthenware figures will be considered in a later chapter but here it may be mentioned that the pew groups in this material consisted of a later series of crudely formed two-figure models with rounded seats. They were made by—or more probably for—Josiah Wedgwood and have his name impressed on the base. This places them between 1759 when he started in business on his own account and the beginning of his partnership with Thomas Bentley in 1769 when the mark became "Wedgwood & Bentley". These were lead-glazed and touched with manganese purple and brown. One Wedgwood group shows two youths on the settle, one reading a book, the other holding a scroll in his left hand and a glass of ale in his right.

The number of salt-glazed pew groups that have come to light during the past thirty years has reached significant proportions. It is therefore essential for the collector to be familiar with the constructional technique used by the pew group potter of George II's reign. Reproduction salt-glazed pew groups appear to have been copied from photographs of genuine examples. Modelling is laboured, lacking the apparent easy carelessness of originals, and white clay only is used. Decoration is in black slip, as a superficial wash, brush-applied, instead of being built into the piece. The potting technique displays other discrepancies when compared with that of Georgian pew groups.

Other figures in salt-glazed stoneware are of great interest to collectors. These include mounted soldiers shaped by hand and placed upon rectangular press-moulded plinths. The Marianne Wood collection of Staffordshire figures in the Hanley Museum contains two mounted hussars, one in white salt-glazed stoneware, the other in earthenware. These are so nearly alike that they suggest production by the same potter. Further evidence of this practice was discovered when wasters of both types were found among the the excavated potsherds from the site of Thomas Whieldon's pottery two centuries after its establishment in 1740.

The success of the porcelain figures from Meissen and later made at Chelsea, Derby and elsewhere soon prompted the Staffordshire potters to copy them as closely as possible in salt-glazed white stoneware. This entailed changing from the hand-modelling technique to shaping by means of moulds and decorating with enamels. Early moulds were elaborate. A model of the figure was made in wax and from this a block-cutter carved a master mould in a block of alabaster, a soft type of gypsum plentiful in Derbyshire. This was cut into separate units, each forming an individual mould. From these were made working moulds of clay, which when dried and fired were known as pitchers. Worn pitchers could be replaced from the original alabaster blocks as required. The most highly skilled block cutters were the brothers Ralph and Aaron Wood of Burslem, whose work was in continuous demand by all the leading potters of salt-glazed stoneware.

Figures could be shaped by casting from these "pitcher" moulds as required. The final step in casting dates from the mid-1740s: Ralph Daniel of Cobridge, who had been working in France, introduced plaster of paris moulds. Eventually

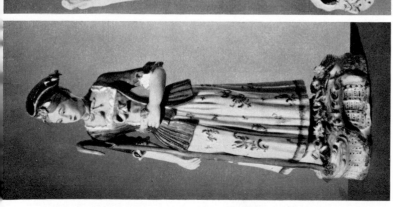

19. (*Left to right*) Bristol figure of a shepherdess wearing a blue hat with flowers below the brim and a green bodice with blue insertion at the front. The flesh has been left white. Height 12⅞ inches. Early 1770s. Plymouth figure of a negress holding a spear, emblematic of Africa. A lion and a crocodile are on her left. Height 12 inches. About 1770. Plymouth figure emblematic of Asia, enamelled in colours and gilt. A camel crouches at her side. Height 12½ inches. About 1770. Plymouth figure of an Indian huntress, emblematic of America. The miniature animal at her feet is a prairie dog. Height 12½ inches. About 1770.

20. Worcester figures of gardener and companion. Here they are standing on circular pad bases with applied flowers and foliage: an example is known with a bocage setting and a four-footed scroll pedestal. The gardener wears a mauve three-cornered hat, puce coat, white shirt, blue apron, mauve shoes with yellow bows, his left hand holding a spade. Height 7 inches. 1769–71.

plaster was used for the master moulds, shaped directly from models in oily clay, as well as for the working moulds, although results were less sharply cut as in continuous use the soft plaster of paris became blunted on corners and edges. The process of casting consisted of pouring the clay mixture in a liquid state into the mould, allowing an even layer to cover all sides. The absorbent plaster quickly drew out the moisture so that the clay formed into a shell of the required model and surplus could be poured away. Shrinkage of the clay while drying facilitated removal from the mould.

Among salt-glazed stoneware figures, collectors may find small specimens such as would have cost no more than a penny or twopence each at fairs. These were shaped in simple two-piece moulds: some were given additional ornament with hand tools. They included animals such as horses, dogs, cats, cows, sheep, rabbits and monkeys, and birds such as peacocks, hawks, cocks, hens and other natives. Eyes and other details were accentuated in brown or blue. Figures of the Chinese Shou Lao and the dog of Foo were produced in several sizes, being copies of Chinese originals. Busts of royalty were made such as those of the Empress Maria Theresa and her Consort, dating later than 1745.

An interesting series of small figures was moulded from salt-glazed stoneware variegated throughout its texture by markings superficially resembling the striations of marble or agate. This was known as agate ware and similar effects were achieved with lead-glazed earthenware. Bats of white clay were "wedged" with clays stained brown, green and blue, thus producing attractive veinings throughout the body.

Salt-glazed stoneware figures from 1750 to the 1780s might be decorated with an opaque glaze of brilliant blue of royal or lapis lazuli tint. This glaze is thought to have been discovered in the late 1740s by William Littler and his brother-in-law Aaron Wedgwood who were originally salt-glaze potters at Brownhills. It was secured by dipping the unfired stoneware into a carefully lawned mixture of flint and clay exactly similar to that used for the body but stained with zaffre or cobalt oxide and sometimes also with a little manganese. This produced a bright royal blue and when fired with salt-glaze acquired a glossy sheen of great brilliance free from the usual pittings of salt-glaze.

William Pitt in his *History of Staffordshire*, 1817, claimed that "this glaze possessed all the beauty of the finest lapis lazuli: others from the admixture of a small proportion of manganese have the appearance of the finest oriental lapis lazuli." This was used by Littler, first on his white stoneware and then on his Longton Hall porcelain. Sometimes the blue remained undecorated: in other examples it was ornamented with enamels or gilded. This blue glaze, known to collectors as Littler's blue, was not a Longton Hall monopoly, however. This is shown by two entries in *Bailey's Western Directory*, 1784: "Bourne & Malkin, Burslem, Manufacturers of China glazed blue, and cream-coloured ware"; and "Thomas & Benjamin Godwin, Cobridge. Manufacturers of Queen's ware and China glazed blue."

The glaze has been reproduced, but the original attractive tints have eluded the copyists. Zaffre in the 18th century contained such impurities as traces of copper, lead, iron and bismuth. These were removed from early in the 19th century and the zaffre gave a less attractive tint.

Salt-glazed stoneware figures in imitation of hard-paste porcelain of Meissen and China were probably Littler's work. Figures assembled from several units, shaped in separate moulds as in porcelain, date from the early 1750s and may be enamelled in brilliant green, blue, crimson and yellow. Figures adapted from Meissen originals included birds, dancers, Italian Comedy actors and such figures as a Turk and companion modelled in 1745 by J. J. Kändler from an engraving by M. de Ferriol, Paris, 1714. Figure makers became more ambitious as the century progressed. In the mid-1780s appeared the 18½-inch figure of Shakespeare after the statue carved by Peter Scheermaker for Westminster Abbey. An earthenware figure from the same model but painted in enamels is attributed to Enoch Wood who started his pottery in 1783.

Nottingham was long associated with less ambitious

stoneware, washed with a brown-burning clay slip. Specimens in the Fitzwilliam Museum include animals dating to the late 18th century despite the fact that by then stoneware figures were losing their popularity to more delicate English porcelains and cheaper lead-glazed earthenwares.

In the third quarter of the 19th century there was a revival of ornamental salt-glazed stoneware for display cabinets. These figures were sold under the name of "Elizabethan ware" and were not intended to deceive, but their impressed marks have since been removed and prices enhanced.

With the development of inexpensive moulded image toys in earthenware (Chapter 10) the demand for salt-glazed white stoneware figures virtually ceased. Early in the 19th century, however, the potters of salt-glazed brown stoneware, known as "brown stone potters", in Lambeth and Derbyshire began to compete with yet cheaper image toys sold at fairs and elsewhere at a few pence each. This durable, inexpensive "drainpipe" stoneware is wholly opaque, intensely hard and virtually non-porous. Fractures display a glassy texture. It was generally made from a plastic clay of local origin with the addition of felspar and quartz in the form of sand or powdered calcined flint. When fired at a high temperature the mixture became highly vitrified, ensuring a close, hard texture. The colours to which clays of suitable quality usually burned ranged from yellowish buff to dark brown—somewhat mottled until 1830—and the salt-glaze gave the surface an attractive sheen.

Image toys and portrait busts were made until the mid-19th century when larger and more colourful Staffordshire chimney ornaments in white earthenware were preferred. Early examples were crudely finished although considerable skill went into their manufacture.

A 6-inch figure of George IV wearing his crown, and probably a coronation souvenir, has been noted marked *Amatt* in script beneath the plinth. This was probably the work of Antony Amatt of Bristol, described in his bill heading of 1813 as "Iron Stoneware Manufacturer, Crew's Hole, Bristol". But most of the early figures were made by Doulton & Watts, established at Vauxhall Walk, Lambeth, in 1815. An old account book of 1818 in the possession of Doulton & Co. Ltd records that the kiln man was paid 18s. for burning the kiln, plus sixpence for beer and one penny for candles. Their first issue was the popular figure of Queen Caroline, consort of George IV. She is seen standing on a deep oval plinth, wearing her crown, although she was never crowned, her husband excluding her from the coronation. She holds a scroll with the familiar declaration "My Hope is in the People"—who were nine-tenths in her favour. Doulton & Watts followed this with portraits of the Duke of York, commander-in-chief of the army (d. 1827), and his successor in this office, the Duke of Cumberland, later king of Hanover.

Portrait figures issued from the early 1830s were in a finer clay, better modelled and more clear-cut, due to progressive technical improvements in kiln construction. The first improvement was the invention by William Bourne of Belper in 1823 of a stoneware kiln known as the Chesterfield brown ware kiln. This doubled the capacity of former salt-glazed stoneware kilns and also used less fuel, drastically reducing cost. The resulting ware was harder, more compact, with a more durable glaze. It was not in general use, however, until the 1830s. Figures showing such improvement included William IV and his consort Queen Adelaide, Sir Walter Scott, Sir Robert Peel, Lord Nelson and Napoleon. Queen Victoria's marriage to Prince Albert in 1840 prompted the issue of portrait figures in matching pairs of two sizes, nine inches and six inches tall, Prince Albert wearing the star and ribbon of the Garter. The oval plinths display their names in relief. A special range of portrait figures was introduced at this period but is more usefully considered as a separate group at the end of this chapter: this consists of flasks for spirits shaped as well-known figures, frequently with a political significance.

Yet another change in kiln design was introduced in 1847, entirely altering salt-glaze kiln technique. As a result figures were more meticulously finished in a harder brown stoneware more smoothly glazed. Three qualities of brown stoneware could be fired in these kilns and it is possible for collectors to distinguish these from earlier stonewares, both

21. Parian statuary. (*Top left*) Parian figure supporting coral branches covered in mother-of-pearl glaze. Belleek. Height 18 inches. About 1880. (*Top right*) *The Prisoner of Love* by Belleek. Height 25¼ inches. Impressed BELLEEK CO. FERMANAGH and transfer-printed with the wolf-hound and harp trade mark. (*Lower left*) *The Greek Slave* after the life-size marble by Hiram Powers. Impressed COPELAND & GARRETT. 1852. (*Lower right*) "Boy with a Rabbit", a best seller of the 1850s, by Copeland & Garrett.

22. *Comedy* in Worcester parian modelled by W. B. Kirk in 1853 to accompany the Shakespeare dessert service. 1853.

those made under the previous patent and those of still earlier origin.

The brown stoneware potters of Brampton in Derbyshire, long famous for their spirit flasks, now produced small image toy animals including horses, dogs of several breeds, cats, stags, cows and dubious-looking baby lions. These were never considered worth marking. A few may be noted with a two-colour finish, buff and ginger-brown—again characteristic of the spirit flask. They were sold at fairs and in the streets for a penny or two apiece. In view of their intense hardness and the hundreds of thousands produced by casting, it is remarkable that so few can now be traced.

From the 1860s Doulton made stoneware figures in brown, blue, green, claret red and white and from the 1870s was persuaded to co-operate with the Lambeth School of Art in applying the ware, still salt-glazed, still baked and glazed in a single kiln firing, to the new ideas of a younger generation of artist-craftsmen whose initials may be found and identified.

The Derbyshire interest in salt-glazed stoneware and especially in the creation of spirit flask figures dates from 1806 when a coaching road was being constructed from Derby to Alfreton. The navvies' picks and shovels revealed stoneware clay deposits of a quality eventually found to be the finest in Europe.

William Bourne, a potter at nearby Belper, immediately acquired the working rights of the land. Three years later his twenty-one-year-old son Joseph began working the new clay beds, founding what became the Denby pottery, the source of enormous quantities of salt-glazed stoneware including many of the spirit flasks that had a considerable vogue in the second quarter of the 19th century. Although designed for the rough wear of inns and taverns, these were of a quality which has earned them a place among collectors' pieces.

Makers' names often stamped on the more decorative pieces of this stoneware include BOURNE or BELPER & DENBY / BOURNE'S POTTERIES / DERBYSHIRE; BRIDDON (W.

Briddon of Brampton); BURTON (W. Burton, Codnor Park, until 1833); KNOWLES (Welshpool and Payne Potteries, Brampton); OLDFIELD (J. Oldfield & Co., Brampton, from 1838).

By 1815 Bourne's high quality stoneware had to face the competition of the Lambeth firm of Doulton and both establishments then included huge stoneware spirit jars among their products. These were used by the manufacturers of spirits, cordials and strong ales to convey their supplies to the inns and taverns, and the vessels' cheapness and durability led the same manufacturers to order flasks of similar material. With the decline in the popularity of punch and punch-houses in the reign of George IV they sought to extend their spirit trade in the taverns. With this in view they developed the shelf display of these attractively modelled flasks, carrying clearly incised descriptions of their contents such as "Spicer's Cordial" and "Old Tom".

While the capacious spirit jars possessed the natural grace of simple pottery form, these spirit flasks were fashioned by casting into more lively and popular imitative shapes. These ranged from barrels, pocket books and powder horns to pigs and grandfather clocks. Their colour still depended upon the chance quality of the unrefined clay mixed with sand and flint by each individual pottery, many vessels being partially covered with a wash of semi-liquid clay that burned to a different tone. Catering for a public long enamoured of the Toby jug, it was natural that such designs should lead to still more ambitious work, culminating in a wide range of figure subjects. In these the sturdy, flat-faced brown-and-buff bottles, varying in height between seven and eleven inches, were surmounted by busts and figures. And, just as the Toby design deteriorated from an individual portrait to a range of more generally agreeable stock characters, so the spirit flask figures began as highly individualistic portraits and it was only later that they were replaced by jolly sailors and the like.

Early in William IV's reign (1830–1837), there was intense political excitement associated with parliamentary reform, the inns and taverns witnessing many a stormy scene. Cordial and spirit merchants realised that the customers where such flasks were displayed would generally be on the side of reform and accordingly issued their liquors in stoneware flasks favouring Whig propaganda. Many of these early portrait busts were of political celebrities; others represented royalty.

The lower, plainly shaped body of such a flask might be impressed with the name of the individual represented, accompanied by an appropriate slogan such as "Reform Cordial", "The People's Rights", "Bread for the Millions" or "Irish Reform Cordial". In the Doulton flask representing Lord John Russell the sponsor of the first reform bill is represented holding a scroll impressed with the words "The True Spirit of Reform". Many thousands of Reform spirit flasks were issued in 1832 when the Great Charter became law.

Other portraits modelled on stoneware spirit flasks included William IV, Queen Adelaide, the Duke of York, the Duke of Wellington, Earl Grey, Lord Brougham and Vaux, Sir Francis Burdett, Sir Robert Peel and the Irish patriot Daniel O'Connell. Bourne's flask representing Sir Robert Peel shows a full length model of this statesman standing on a plinth.

In view of the popularity of such stoneware flasks for the sale of branded cordials and strong ales it was only natural that the work should be more widely developed, although the basic simplicity and cheapness of the material and its limited range of colours were maintained. Each manufacturer issued his own version of a jolly sailor seated on a barrel impressed with the name of the liquor concerned, such as the "Old Tom" found on the Oldfield flask. The Doulton firm kept twenty men working on these cordial bottles and issued representations of tipsy sailors dancing and of a man sitting on a barrel. Each was inscribed "All around my bar good customers I see". Figures representing "Smoking" and "Snuffing" came from the Vauxhall pottery; mermaid-shaped flasks were made by Stephen Green of Lambeth, whose marine subjects also included large fish about thirteen inches long. Such non-figure subjects continued to find favour in the less ambitious designs then proving acceptable. Another fish design emanated from Vauxhall, while the firm of Stephen Green produced a popular pistol design. These were all made during the 1830s.

Spirit flasks in the form of tipstaffs were made by Stephen Green during the early 1840s. The 15-inch examples have the letters V.R. in relief on one side, the insignia of the Order of the Garter on the other. Shorter tipstaffs bear the arms of the city of London in relief.

More ambitious models representing Queen Victoria were issued at the beginning of the new reign. The Denby version was a full length figure inscribed on the front "May Peace and Prosperity Prevail", and on the reverse "Queen Alexandrina Victoria". A more capacious model impressed "Queen Victoria 1st" was issued by Oldfield of Chesterfield. Prince Albert made his first appearance on a spirit flask in 1840, and later Jenny Lind and John Bull flasks had a considerable vogue.

Chapter Nine

BLACK BASALTES

WEALTHY Georgians delighted in the scholastic atmosphere given to their libraries by a display of bronze or marble busts on high shelves and bookcases, in niches and on elaborately carved and gilded wall brackets such as were illustrated in Thomas Johnson's design book of 1762. A few months after establishing his great pottery at Etruria in Staffordshire, Josiah Wedgwood suggested to his partner Thomas Bentley that their newly evolved black basaltes was an ideal material for portrait busts "for the Middling Class of People, which class we know are vastly superior in number to the Great. . . . Middling people will buy quantities at the much reduced price."

Black basaltes was composed of Staffordshire ball clay, calcined ochre and glassy slag from puddled ironstone, stained black with manganese dioxide. It was an intensely hard, fine-grain stoneware of uniformly dense texture. The black biscuit emerged flawless from the kiln, no bubbles, specks or undulations disfiguring its smooth surface. A permanent gloss was given by coating with potter's varnish and refiring to a red heat. When cool enough to handle the busts were polished by rubbing vigorously with a soft rag dipped in skim milk. The double firing caused the stoneware to become intensely hard so that it would polish to a brilliant reflecting surface at the lapidary's wheel. This finishing was a highly skilled process and for several years Wedgwood sent the plinths for his figures and busts to be polished by a Birmingham lapidary.

Plinths and busts, packed separately, were sent to the London warehouse for assembly by Palethorpe of Chelsea. At prices ranging from sixpence to one shilling and sixpence each he drilled holes in the basaltes and supplied and fitted wrought iron bolts and nuts. These are now scaly, rough and very black.

Many basaltes busts were made to closely resemble solid bronze by a process patented by Josiah Wedgwood on November 16, 1769. They were coated with gold bronze which was burnt in and afterwards polished. This gold bronze was unable to withstand intensive cleaning and in many instances traces of bronze are visible in the crevices of now otherwise black examples.

The Wedgwood-Bentley letters record that busts in black basaltes were marketed as early as 1771. On February 16 Wedgwood wrote: "The busts at the Academy are less hackney'd and better in General than the Plaisterers shop can furnish us with; besides, it will sound better to say— This is from the Academy than to say, we had it from Flaxman, Oliver as a plaister figure maker, in selling us the moulds, transfers his business to us and must therefore be p^d handsomely. I sho^d like to keep one hand constantly at Busts if you could dispose of them. The Marquis of R[ockingham] has some divine busts. Perhaps he wo^d lend you some either to mould in Town or send down here."

Busts and figures in black basaltes were taken from original marbles or bronzes, or from a model carved in wax, usually copied from a portrait in oils or a print. Plaster casts were taken, and from these moulds were made in Etruria. Hoskins & Grant, plaster figure makers, London, made the majority of Wedgwood's plaster casts.

Eliza Meteyard quoted several of Hoskins & Grant's bills for "Plaister Casts Prepared to Mould from". The usual cost for large casts was one guinea; ten inches and less, half a guinea. During March 1774 they delivered twenty-two plaster moulds to Wedgwood who exclaimed: "I had no idea of our having ordered so many Bustos from Hoskins and Grant . . . to make the moulds from these will be a great and long piece of work." However, in December thirty-four more models were delivered, thirty-two of them in matching pairs.

A further bill quoted by Miss Meteyard shows that

Hoskins & Grant had increased the price of their plaster casts by May 1779:

To a large Bust of Bacchus ..	..	..	£2	2	0
To a ditto of Ariadne	..	..	..	1 11	6
To a Large Antique Bust of Mercury	..	1 1	0
To a ditto of Alexandre	..	..	..	2 2	0
To 2 Busts of Shakespeare and Garrick	..	1 16	0
To a Bust of Julius Caesar ..	..	..	- 14	0

Existing Flaxman bills show that in 1781 he moulded busts of *Rousseau* and *Stern*, 16s.; *Dr. Fothergill*, £1 4s.; and *Mrs. Siddons*, £1 11s. 6d. Richard Parker modelled *Zingara*, and John Cheese, the celebrated sculptor in cement, made models of *Shakespeare*, *Plato* and *Aristotle*. These plaster moulds were vastly improved at Etruria by Wedgwood's chief modellers, Hackwood, Hollinshed and Keeling.

The Wedgwood-Bentley correspondence affords many glimpses into the intensive experimental work before production began on a grand scale. Because of shrinkage in the kiln vivid likenesses were difficult to obtain, although clothing and accessories remained excellently portrayed. Wedgwood complained because "seams rising in the fire plague me very much, but I am determined to conquer them . . . we proceed very slowly, it being a fortnight's work to prepare and mould one of these heads."

On the 16th August 1774 Wedgwood continued: "We are going on very fast with the Busts, four of our principal hands almost constantly employed upon them. You will find our Busts much finer and better finish'd than the Plaister ones we take them from—Hackwood bestows a week upon each head in converting it to what we suppose it was when it came from the hands of the Statuary." A month later he recorded that, "Busts will employ Hackwood for a year or two before our collection is tolerably complete . . . I hope in time to send you a collection of the *finest heads* in the World."

A few wholesale prices have been preserved in an invoice dated December 2, 1775: *Homer*, 25 inches, £3 3s.; *Cicero*, 20 inches, £2 2s.; *Venus de Medici*, 18 inches, £2 2s; *Vestal*,

Sappho, Horace, Cicero, Dryden and *Addison,* 15 inches, £1 11*s.* 6*d.* each.

Three successful busts and figures of *Voltaire* were made. He died on May 30, 1778 and three months later Wedgwood wrote to Bentley: "Voltaire was made in black before we received your last order. The Clergy will buy him in that color [an indication of the philosopher's presumed association with the devil] & we will make him in white [jasper] for the Laiety." On December 5 Wedgwood despatched to the London showrooms a jasper bust of Voltaire, a covering letter recording that "it is in white Jasper upon a Basalte Pedestal richly ornamented with the disconsolate Muse, her lyre unstrung at her feet & other suitable insignia." This shows that a full three months were necessary for a bust to develop from model to showroom, and that moulds intended for basaltes were unsuitable for white jasper.

Busts were often made in pairs. On September 2, 1779 Wedgwood wrote: "We are now modelling a head of Dr. Solander to match Mr. Banks, the second & large edition, which I think a very strong likeness, but the original does not seem to have sat in an over-pleasant mood. Can you think of a better match than Count de Caylus for our very good friend Sir Wm Hamilton. We have bosted him out the size of Mr. Banks, & I think a suit of eminent moderns and naturalists should be made in the same size and stile, & so form a constellation to attract the notice of the great and illuminate every palace in Europe." A few days later Wedgwood wrote complaining that the bust of Bacon, intended to pair with Robert Boyle, ". . . . will not be known without his *English ruff* & that will be incompatable with his companionship with Boyle."

The first busts to be made in black basaltes, according to Eliza Meteyard, were *George III, Horace* and *Cicero.* Later subjects were divines, philosophers, poets, physicians and naturalists. The female busts included *Cleopatra, Ariadne, Agrippina, Sappho* and *Julia.* The name of the subject might be incised on the back of the bust or cut into a decorative tablet placed immediately above the plinth. Some busts were made in several versions, not only in size, but in pose and characterisation.

23. Parian statuary busts. (*Top left*) *The Veiled Bride* after Raffaelle Monti. Made by W. T. Copeland for the Crystal Palace Art Union. Height 15 inches. 1861. (*Top right*) *Miranda* after W. Calder Marshall R.A., by W. T. Copeland. Height 10 inches. Mid-1850s. (*Bottom*) Portrait busts by Kerr & Binns of Mr. and Mrs. R. W. Binns, modelled by W. B. Kirk. Height 6 inches. 1853.

24. Parian statuary. (*Top left*) *Dorothea*, after John Bell, R.A. Marks show this figure to have been registered by Minton & Co. at the Patent Office, October 2 1847. It is also impressed with Minton date symbol for 1853. Height 14 inches. (*Top right*) *Go to sleep*, after J. Dunham. Made by W. T. Copeland for the Art Union of London in 1862. Height 19 inches. (*Lower left*) *The Vine Gatherer* impressed with the Minton date symbol for 1851. Height 15 inches. (*Lower right*) *Hermione*, cast in two parts from a translucent light-weight parian. Impressed W. C. MARSHALL R.A. Sculpt. PUB. June 1 1860.

Surprisingly there was an immense continental demand for basaltes busts, particularly in Holland, Russia and Germany. This followed the life-size production in 1779 of the *Prince of Orange, Grotius,* the *de Witts, de Ruyter* and *Baerhaave,* modelled from medals lent to Bentley by the Burgomaster of Amsterdam. The wholesale price for these 25-inch busts was four guineas each.

Josiah Wedgwood was the first potter to issue a catalogue, first published in 1773 with revised editions in 1774, 1777, 1779 and finally in 1787. Wedgwood recorded his own egotistic opinion of black basaltes in the 1779 edition. "The black Composition having the Appearance of *antique bronze,* and so nearly agreeing in Properties with the Basaltes of the Aegyptians, no Substance can be better than this for our Busts, Sphinxes, small Statues, &c., and it seems to us to be of great Consequence to preserve as many fine Works of Antiquity and of the present Age as we can, in this composition; when all Pictures are faded or rotten, when Bronzes are rusted away, and all the excellent Works in Marble dissolved, then these Copies will probably remain, and transmit the Works of Genius and the Portraits of illustrious Men to the most distant Times." The title page of the 1787 catalogue records that it was written by "Josiah Wedgwood, F.R.S. and A.S., Potter to Her Majesty, and to his Royal Highness the Duke of York and Albany".

The catalogued busts ranging from four inches to twenty-five inches in height, number more than ninety, but other subjects have been recorded. In the following list, compiled from the 1787 catalogue in the collection of Sir John Wedgwood, Bt., the date of the first catalogue entry is given, then a few wholesale prices and the names of modellers when known—H & G referring to Hoskins & Grant.

About 25 inches high:

M. Aurelius Antoninus, 1774; *Lord Chatham,* 1779; *Zeno,* 1774; *Plato,* 1774; *Epicurus,* 1774; *Junius Brutus and Marcus Brutus,* 1774, £8 8s. pair, H & G; *Pindar and Homer,* 1774, £8 8s. pair, Hackwood; *Cornelius de Witt* and *John de Witt,* 1787, £8 8s. pair.

About 22 inches high:

Antinous, 1744; *Antoninus Pius,* 1774, £3 13s. 6d.; *Augustus,*

1774, £3 13s. 6d.; *Palladio*, 1774, £3 13s. 6d.; *Minerva*, 1774; *Inigo Jones*, 1777, Hackwood; *Demosthenes*, 1777, H & G.

About 20 inches high:

Cato, 1774; *Seneca*, 1774; *Horace*, 1773; *Faustina*, 1774, H & G; *Socrates*, 1779; *Cicero*, 1773, H & G; *Rousseau*, 1777, *Josiah Wedgwood*; *Grotius*, 1779; *Mercury*, 1779, Hackwood; *Voltaire*, 1779; *Pindar* (from a marble in the possession of David Garrick), 1779, £3 13s. 6d.; *Zeno*, 1779; *Dean Swift*, 1779.

About 18 inches high:

Venus de Medici, 1777, H & G; *Lord Bacon*, 1777, £2 7s. 3d., H & G; *Raleigh*, 1777, H & G; *Boyle*, 1777, H & G; *Ben Jonson*, 1777, Keeling; *Newton*, 1777, £2 7s. 3d.

About 16½ inches high:

Young Germanicus, 1774, £2 2s., H & G; *Agrippina*, 1774, £2 2s., H & G; *Plato*, 1774, J. Cheese; *Young Marcus Aurelius*, 1774, H & G; *Fletcher*, 1775, H & G; *Dr. Fothergill*, 1787, by Flaxman in 1781.

About 15 inches high:

Homer, 1774, H & G; *Democritus*, 1779; *Vestal*, 1774, H & G; *Aristotle*, 1777, J. Cheese; *Zingara*, 1774, H & G; *Hippocrates*, 1777, H & G; *Galen*, 1777, H & G; *Chaucer*, 1777, H & G; *Beaumont*, 1777, H & G; *Cicero*, 1774; *Shakespeare*, 1774, J. Cheese; *Fletcher*, 1777; *Milton*, 1777, H & G; *Congreve*, 1777, H & G; *Newton*, 1777; *Prior*, 1777; *Swift*, 1779; *Plato*, 1774; *Pope*, 1777; *Sappho*, 1777; *Julia*, 1777; *Addison*, 1777; *Dryden*, 1777; *Horace*, 1777; *Jonson*, 1777; *Locke*, 1777; *Madonna*, 1777; *Spenser*, 1777; *Seneca*, 1777, J. Bacon; *Baershaave*, 1779; *Michael de Ruyter*, 1779; *Virgil*, 1777, from a gem. These all sold at £1 11s. 6d. each.

Between 10 and 11½ inches high:

Newton, 1777; *Locke*, 1777; *George II*, 1777; *Voltaire*, 1779, from Houdon's marble bust; *Cicero*, 1777, J. Bason.

Between 7 inches and 8 inches high:

Socrates, 1777; *Aristotle*, 1774; *Newton*, 1777; *Locke*, 1737; *Prior*, 1777; *M. Anthony*, 1777, H & G; *Congreve*, 1777; *Cleopatra*, 1777.

Between 4 inches and 4½ inches high:

Homer, 1779, H & G; *Bacchus*, 1779, H & G; *Ariadne*, 1779, H & G; *Rousseau*, 1787, by Flaxman in 1781; *Voltaire*, 1777; *Pindar*, 1779; *Aristophanes*, 1779; *Montesquieu*, 1777.

It will be seen from the above that large busts preceded

the smaller, which were made as the higher priced markets reached saturation point. Several versions, alike in size and subject, exist of a few busts such as Seneca, Homer and Shakespeare, but in others dimensions varied slightly because of unequal shrinkage in the kiln.

Wedgwood prepared fashionable suites of chimney ornaments in black basaltes, each including a pair of busts. Typical was the set composed of a statuette of *Venus de Medici,* busts of *Shakespeare* and *Garrick,* two boys from Fiamingo, and a pair of vase candlesticks. The wholesale price was £4 7*s.* for this set.

Basaltes busts continued to be made by the Wedgwood firm for a full century, new subjects being added from time to time such as the cleverly modelled bust of *Nelson* impressed WEDGWOOD and incised in flowing script "Pub^d July 22nd 1798. R. Shout, Sculp". Shout was head of a well-known plaster modelling family with showrooms in Holborn and workshops in nearby Red Lion Street.

Until the death of Bentley in 1780 busts were impressed WEDGWOOD & BENTLEY in a circular stamp. The pedestal of a large bust might be impressed WEDGWOOD & BENTLEY; ETRURIA between inner and outer circles. WEDGWOOD & BENTLEY in upper case letters and in upper and lower case letters were also used. From 1780 WEDGWOOD in upper case letters was also used. A pair of facing commas, horizontal or vertical and sometimes resembling a small semi-circle, were impressed beneath the name between 1800 and about 1830. From 1860 busts were additionally impressed with a date cypher composed of three letters.

At the end of this chapter is a list of priced statues, figures, busts and the like. This was quoted by Eliza Meteyard in *The Life of Josiah Wedgwood,* 1865, from Christie's sale catalogue, 1781.

Several other Staffordshire potters made busts in black basaltes, notably John Turner who operated at Lane End—now Longton—from 1762 to 1787. Few were marked, but they may be recognised by plinths resembling shining jet, encircled top and bottom with acanthus leaves.

Enoch Wood who potted at Burslem from 1783 to 1840, was an accomplished modeller. The quality of his basaltes was poor in comparison with Wedgwood's productions: they display a rather tawdry bluish-grey tint. This applies to an 8-inch bust of *George Washington* in the British Museum, impressed ENOCH WOOD and inscribed on the back, within a circle: WASHINGTON BORN 1732 DIED 1799 ENOCH WOOD SCULPST 1818. In the British Museum, too, is a 12-inch bust of the *Emperor Alexander of Russia* inscribed upon the back within a circle: ALEXANDER AET 35 MOSCOW BURNT EUROPE PRESERVED 1812 WOOD & CALDWELL BURSLEM STAFFORD-SHIRE. This is an inferior production by an unknown modeller. A popular pair were the 12-inch busts of *John Wesley* and *George Whitefield* on rectangular plinths with bowed fronts. Later he potted *William IV* and *Handel*.

John and Richard Riley who potted at Burslem from 1800 to 1827 made several portrait busts of unnamed subjects in a light-weight friable Egyptian black coated with a durable black lead glaze of dull gloss. These were impressed RILEY.

Reproductions of early models made by the Wedgwood firm during the early and mid-Victorian periods as a rule display more clearly cut modelling than 18th-century examples which, however, were made more finely finished and polished. Reproductions made by other Staffordshire potters during this period were poorly fired, lacked under-cutting, and were finished with a dull, bluish-black surface without the glow polishing.

STATUES, FIGURES, SMALL BUSTS, CANDELABRA, AND LAMPS DISPOSED IN SUITES FOR CHIMNEY ORNAMENTS, FROM CHRISTIE'S SALE CATALOGUE, 1781

		Ware-house	Reduced price after death of Bentley	Realised by auction
67	A suite of seven pieces: the centre a chased lamp, forming a tripod with Etruscan sphinxes, two Egyptian lions, two griffin candelabra.	£8 17 0	£5 5 0	£2 15 0
68	A suite of seven: one statue, Apollo; two busts Shakespeare and Garrick; two boys, from Fiamingo; two triton candelabra.	6 9 0		2 9 0

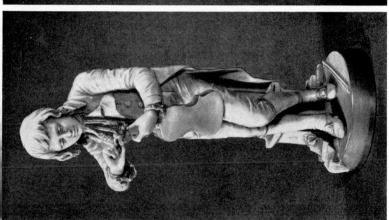
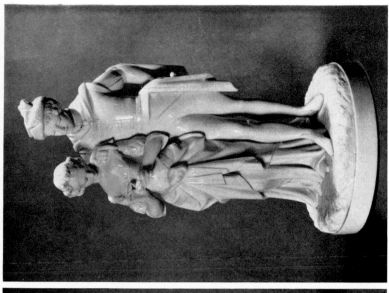

25. (*Left*). The *Volunteer in Khaki*, coloured in dry brown with gilding. Height 7⅞ inches. Made by Worcester Royal Porcelain Co. Ltd., 1900. (*Centre*) Violinist decorated in the old ivory porcelain style. Height 19¾ inches. Worcester Royal Porcelain Co. Ltd., 1895. (*Right*) *Faust and Marguerite* in undecorated ivory porcelain. Modelled by W. B. Kirk. Height 12 inches. W. H. Kerr & R. W. Binns, Worcester, 1858.

26. Ivory porcelain by the Worcester Royal Porcelain Co. Ltd. (*Top left*) *Venus Rising from the Sea*. Height 17 inches. About 1870. (*Top right*) Youth and girl in the style of Boucher rustics. Height 19½ inches. About 1870. (*Lower left*) Japanese man and woman decorated in matt colours and gold. Height 7¼ inches. 1873. (*Lower right*) Mermaid supporting an embossed nautilus shell, coloured in the Capodimonte style. Modelled by James Hadley. Height 15 inches. 1877.

		Ware-house	Reduced price after death of Bentley	Realised by auction
69	A suite of seven; statue of a boy on a pedestal; two busts, Montesquieu and Rousseau; two boys, from Fiamingo; two Egyptian sphinx candelabra.	3 15 0		2 2 0
70	Another: a statue, Venus de' Medici; two busts, Shakespeare and Garrick; two boys, from Fiamingo; two vase candelabra.	4 7 0		1 15 0
71	A pair of Grecian sphinxes, large	4 4 0	3 6 0	1 6 0
72	A fine figure of Ceres.	5 5 0	3 13 6	2 10 0
183	Two statues, Voltaire and Rousseau; two busts, Vestal and Zingara.	4 13 0		1 6 0
184	A suite of seven pieces for chimney ornaments; a bust, Venus; two boys from Fiamingo; two beakers with Etruscan borders; two Egyptian sphinx candelabra.	5 14 0		1 4 0
185	Two statues, Bacchus, faun; two griffin candelabra.	6 6 0		1 14 0
186	A suite of seven pieces, one chased tripod, with Egyptian sphinxes; two Grecian sphinxes; two triton candelabra.	7 16 0		3 8 0
275	A suite of seven for chimney ornaments; a statue of Mercury, two beakers with Etruscan borders; two boys, from Fiamingo; two Egyptian sphinxes, candelabra.			1 6 0
276	Two pairs of chimney ornaments: two pug dogs, from Hogarth; two candelabra.			2 0 0
277	A suite of five: one basalt vase, with figures in bas-relief: two sitting sphinxes; two candelabra.			– 18 –
278	A suite of seven: one bust, Voltaire; two boys, from Fiamingo; two busts, Garrick and Shakespeare; two small lamps.			– 18 –
374	A suite of seven pieces for chimney ornaments; a statue, Apollo; two busts, Zingara, Vestal; two boys, from Fiamingo; two sitting sphinxes.	6 9 0	2 6 0	2 6 0
375	A pair of small busts, Congreve Prior; another, Garrick and Shakepeare; two boys, from Fiamingo.	3 6 0	1 14 0	1 14 0
376	A pair of boys; a pair of sleeping boys, from Fiamingo; two sitting sphinxes.	2 17 0		– 16 6
377	A suite of five: a statue; faun; two sitting sphinxes; two vase candelabra.	3 9 0		1 3 0

		Ware-house	Reduced price after death of Bentley	Realised by auction
447	A fine figure of young Hercules choking the Serpent, the ground imperfect.	7 17 6		2 2 0
448	A suite of five chimney ornaments: a basalt vase, with bas-relief figures, Cupid and Psyche; two boys, from Fiamingo; two sitting sphinxes.	3 12 0		1 1 0
449	Three pairs of chimney ornaments: two griffin candelabra, two sitting sphinxes.	8 0 0	2 10 0	2 12 6
450	A suite of seven: a basalt vase, with bas-relief figures; two boys, from Fiamingo; two small busts, two candelabra.	4 4 0		1 10 6
530	A pair of elegant ewers with bas-relief figures; subject, birth of Bacchus, and Bacchanalian figures, very proper for a side-board.	1 16 0	– 18 –	1 12 0
531	A suite of five pieces for chimney ornaments: one vase with bas-relief figures; two statues; two griffin candelabra.	9 9 0	3 13 6	5 7 6
532	Another: one bust on a pedestal, George II; a pair of busts, Congreve, Prior; two vase candelabra.	4 4 0	1 14 0	2 2 0
533	A pair of Egyptian lions; a pair of triton candelabra.	5 0 0	2 6 0	2 6 0
534	A suite of five: one statue, Bacchus; two sphinxes; two vase candelabra.	3 12 0	1 8 0	2 5 0
535	A pair of large Grecian sphinxes; a pair of pug dogs, from a favourite dog of Hogarth's.	6 6 0	2 10 0	3 3 0
536	A suite of five: a chased tripod, a pair of pug dogs, and a pair of griffin candelabra.	11 11 0	4 9 0	8 12 6
676	A suite of five chimney ornaments: a basalt vase with bas-relief figures; a pair of busts, and a pair of tripod candelabra.	10 0 0	4 4 0	4 6 6
677	A suite of seven chimney ornaments: a bust, Venus; two boys, from Fiamingo; two beakers with Etruscan borders; a pair of Egyptian sphinx candelabra.	5 14 0	1 10 0	
678	Another, one bust, Voltaire; a pair of busts, Montesquieu, Rousseau; two boys, from Fiamingo; a pair of lamps.	2 15 0	1 10 0	1 10 0
679	A suite of five: a basalt vase with bas-relief figures; two boys, from Fiamingo; two sphinx candelabra; two handsome ewers, very proper for a side-board, the subjects in bas-relief, birth of Bacchus, and Bacchanalian figures.	5 0 0	2 2 0	2 6 0

		Ware-house			Reduced price after death of Bentley			Realised by auction		
767	A suite of five chimney ornaments: a basalt vase with bas-relief figures; a pair of busts; two sphinx candelabra.	3	18	0				1	16	0
768	Another: a bust of Cleopatra; two boys, from Fiamingo; two sitting sphinxes.	2	11	0				1	6	0
769	Another: a vase with ornaments in encaustic painting; two boys from Fiamingo; two vases.	2	11	0				1	2	0
872	A suite of five chimney ornaments: one boy on a pedestal; two boys, from Fiamingo; two sphinx candelabra.	2	15	0				1	5	0
873	Another: a bust of Cleopatra, two boys, from Fiamingo; two sitting sphinxes.	2	11	0				1	3	0
874	Another: a vase for a watch case; a pair of busts; two sphinx candelabra.	6	10	0				2	4	0
1068	A pair of griffin candelabra; a pair of Egyptian lions.				2	0	0	1	10	0
1069	Three pairs of small busts: Socrates and Aristotle; Locke and Newton; Congreve and Prior.				2	0	0	2	0	0
1070	A pair of capedunculae, a pair of griffin candelabra.				2	0	0	3	4	0
1072	Three small busts for chimney ornaments: Homer, Pindar and Aristophanes; two boys, from Fiamingo.							1	2	0
1073	A pair of patera, plain							–	17	–
1074	A suite of five small busts: Locke, Newton, Voltaire, Rousseau, Montesquieu.				1	10	0	1	11	6
1181	A suite of five chimney ornaments: a statue, Mercury; two boys, from Fiamingo; a pair of sphinx candelabra.				1	7	0	1	16	0
1182	Two pairs of chimney ornaments: two Egyptian lions, two Roman capedunculae.				1	10	0	1	10	0
1183	Three small busts: Voltaire, Montesquieu, Rousseau; a pair of candelabra.							1	4	0
1184	One vase with encaustic painting; Cupids wrestling; two boys, from Fiamingo; pair of sphinx candelabra.							2	18	0
1185	A pair of Egyptian sphinx candelabra; a pair of Grecian sphinxes.				2	2	0	3	12	0

Chapter Ten

A TEN-INCH FIGURE of a lady in the Fitzwilliam Museum, Cambridge, is initialled and dated *ISA 1679*. This striking figure is in the maiolica style of tin-enamelled earthenware usually known as delft ware and typified to the layman by pictorial platters with "blue dash" borders. The figure's painted colours include blue, orange, manganese purple and greenish turquoise; her hair hangs in curls tied with ribbons and rosettes and her full purple skirt is rolled up to show a flower-sprigged underskirt. Apart from the magnificent work of John Dwight, however, such early virtuosity appears to be exceptional. For the most part, even by the early-18th century, earthenware potters long skilled in making useful wares turned uneasily and clumsily to the fashioning of what they called "image toys". Continental figures in hard-paste porcelain were no more than a remote indication to them of what the public liked and their figures represent a distinct and lively craft, aimed at an uncritical, forthright market.

For convenience figures in salt-glazed stoneware and lead-glazed earthenware are treated separately here. But it must be realised that in all probability some potters made figures in both, treating the same body of clay and calcined flint with different degrees of heat. Only from the 1740s did greater specialisation develop. The stoneware eventually lost in competition with porcelain but the cheaper earthenwares continued less ambitiously and with the endurance of a fundamental craft-form.

For a long time in earthenware there was a tendency to restrict ornamental work to such toys as could serve some purpose: many cradles remain for offering christening gifts, their wide date range covering many changing processes and some with figures or busts modelled in relief, and there are money boxes topped with crudely-shaped hens and chicks. A splendid tawny slipware owl in the Fitzwilliam Museum—and another in the British Museum—with stylised feathers worked in lines and dots of differently coloured clays proves on inspection to be hollowed and handled as a jug with the head an inverted drinking cup. But for the most part remaining figures from this period testify to a considerable output of small image toys hastily created, probably often by nimble-fingered children.

No potter would have dreamed of marking such work and collectors today who label all their pieces with such familiar names as Whieldon or Astbury can usually claim no more than stylistic classification and the occasional brilliance of pose or delicacy of execution that suggests a master craftsman. The names that remain commemorate outstanding initiators of new ideas and processes, the men who made the 18th century fascinating and unique to the collector of these forthright figures, but it must always be remembered that such men worked in competition with many rivals in turning old skills to the requirements of new materials and techniques—and this applies also to the members of the Wood family who tend to dominate any present-day assessment of mid-Georgian earthenware figure work.

Collectors who divide 18th-century earthenware figures into the categories of salt-glazed and lead-glazed may further distinguish the lead-glazed group according to the composition of their body and of their glaze and the associated method of ornament. At the same time they trace the advance in construction through early finger manipulation to the use of moulds for shaping and for casting. As has been explained in a previous chapter, the earliest of these image toys were shaped by the potters' fingers so that each is unique. By the 1740s considerable use was made of moulds, the plastic clay being pressed into the hollow shapes, and from the mid-1750s this work followed the porcelain men's technique, parts of a figure being moulded separately and assembled with considerable individual modification, depending on the assembler's skill for final grace and liveliness.

The main technical advance of the 1740s in this work was the introduction of plaster of paris moulds, quickly shaped from figure models in oiled clay or wax and used for producing entirely uniform figures by casting. This technique was introduced from France by Ralph Daniel of Cobridge (see Chapter 8).

Early figures hand-modelled in local clays were always fragile and now are correspondingly rare. By methods described in Chapter 8 the clay was rolled and cut and pinched and tooled into head and limbs and clothing. The first conspicuous advance in their material was the introduction of calcined flints to strengthen and whiten the clay body to the yellowish tone known as cream-colour: this dates from 1728 but was a gradual change. Figures produced through the first half of the 18th century depended largely upon the range of colours acquired in the process of baking by various local clays. Only as the cream-coloured body was improved —conspicuously in Wedgwood's queen's ware of the 1760s—did potters develop methods of surface colouring comparable with figure work in porcelain. The ultimate triumph in an earthenware body was the pearl ware evolved by Wedgwood in 1779 and defined as "a whiter earthenware body containing a greater percentage of flint and white clay than cream-coloured earthenware with a small amount of cobalt added to the glaze to give a still further whitening effect."

The surface gloss was achieved by lead-glazing. In early work this consisted of sprinkling the unfired figure with finely powdered natural sulphide of lead, at the time known as smithum and to present-day collectors as galena. A single firing of moderate heat then baked the earthenware to the required tone of red or buff and fused the ore into a glossy yellowish glaze which left the figure-base bare. A less colour-tinged but more expensive glaze was produced with calcined lead ground flour-fine.

The most conspicuous advance in glazing came in about 1750 when Enoch Booth brought to the Potteries the glazing process patented by Frye of Bow for porcelain glazing in 1749 (see page 35). This was a more even, reliable glaze but required an entire change of process: the earthenware had first to be baked to an absorbent biscuit state then dipped into a liquid solution of lead oxide mixed with ground calcined flints and water and refired. Age has given this glaze a faint iridescence. A further advance in the quality of the glaze was made by John Greatbach in 1764.

It is well to accept such dates with reservation, however. Old methods died hard and figures in slipware made largely by hand, decorated by combining local clays of different colours and coated in rich yellow glaze were still being made in Sussex; Devonshire and elsewhere in the mid-19th century (see page 152). Those of the early-18th century show a wide range of simple ornament formed with the thinner, more fluid clay known as slip that gave this style its name. These slips, burning to various tones of light and darker red, white, buff, dark brown, were variously applied to the surface of the figure, laid on or pressed into the ground as required in trails and dots and all enriched and mellowed by the yellow smithum glaze. Not only did they serve to indicate facial features but a woman's skirt, for example, might be striped in red and brown, buff and white. Such figures, mainly shaped by hand and wholly or mainly dependent for their ornament upon the various coloured clays and slips, are usually named after Astbury of Shelton (1688–1743), who, as shown in the previous chapter, improved the quality of the earthenware mixture by incorporating ground flints and white Devon clay. But evidence is inconclusive as to whether he has greater claim to the engaging toys that remain than Joshua Twyford, say, or Thomas Wedgwood junior or Ralph Shaw.

As an alternative, a dark-burning common clay could be coated all over with a white slip. One form of decoration then consisted of incising patterns through this to the darker tone below. A cat of light red clay in the Glaisher Collection is coated with white slip incised to suggest a collar and flower ornament in the red tone.

The range of colours produced by firing natural clays prompted also the development of agate ware, in lead-glazed earthenware as well as in salt-glazed stoneware, probably introduced in about 1730 by Dr. Thomas Wedgwood junior (1695–1733) of Rowley's Pottery, Burslem, and developed conspicuously by Thomas Whieldon in the early 1740s. Whieldon used metallic oxides to stain his clays for more emphatic contrast—manganese for brown shades, copper for green, cobalt for blue. Flat slabs of different coloured clays were beaten upon each other until the solid, airless mass could be sliced, piled up and pounded together again, eventually showing a complexity of wavy striations suggesting marble or agate. It was difficult to turn the resultant unyielding mass but simple figures could be shaped by pressing into moulds then hand-polished and golden-glazed with smithum. Here, too, collectors note the change to liquid-dipped glaze in about 1750, and further improvement with a cobalt-tinged glaze in the 1760s, really suggesting the cold glint of agate. The marble effect is ill-suited to human figures but particularly appealing in models of tabby cats—crude, individualistic creatures of their period, with no pretty sentimentality about them.

Agate ware figures, however, may be regarded as a side issue. The main course in 18th-century lead-glazed earthenware figures consisted of the increasingly skilled use of metallic oxide colours on the surface of the ware. At its simplest the whole figure might be covered in a single colour. The green and green-and-yellow (cauliflower ware) brilliantly developed by Josiah Wedgwood was largely restricted to moulded and cast fruit and vegetable forms of useful wares but figures were made in the handsome black ware produced by staining a deep red body with manganese further darkened with cobalt. Some pieces resemble other models classed as Whieldon ware. Originally they must have been extremely attractive, splashed with patterns in gold leaf fixed with an adhesive containing linseed oil and mastic, but this has worn so badly that it is difficult to decide how much has been lost. Similar ware was made at Jackfield, Shropshire, in the second half of the 18th century: John Thursfield is reputed to have passed on the pottery to his son Maurice who worked it about 1750–70. It was bought by Rose of Coalport in 1780.

Wider possibilities were offered by earthenware coated with white pipeclay slip, sometimes known as engobe, to show the first attempts at surface colouring with metallic oxides. Under the powdered glaze of smithum or clearer calcined lead this amounted to no more than indiscriminate clouding used in combination with the more substantial coloured slips. As early as about 1710 at least six potters were applying clouded effects to their figures with manganese purple and manganese-iron brown, cobalt blue and grey, ochre yellow and copper green. Early figures now associated with Astbury, mainly modelled by hand and dating to the first half of the 18th century, show both the use of clays in different tones and some enrichment by clouding. A cobbler in the Glaisher Collection, for example, is in white clay, his shoes in red clay and his stump seat a lighter red, but the colouring is greatly enriched by the soft tones of green, blue, orange and purple dusted on to the ware under the powdered lead to create an effect of mottled glaze.

When Josiah Wedgwood first established himself, developing his green and cauliflower ware and the cream-coloured earthenware he eventually named queen's ware, his partner from 1754 to 1759 was Thomas Whieldon. This energetic figure was established as a master potter in 1740 and first known for small agate ware figures. He welcomed alike the improvements in cream-coloured earthenware and the technique of liquid glazing to improve his clouding effects, dabbing on the colour with small sponges. These distinctive dabs and streaks enriched by the clarity of the liquid glaze are now known as Whieldon work, although to his contemporaries the term was tortoiseshell ware. They well suited the familiar rustic models then expected of earthenware potters and wholly distinct from the sophistications of porcelain. Typical is a girl milking a blotched and mottled cow backed by a tree-stump holding watchful birds.

One notes delightful figures on horseback such as a lady and gentleman in Brighton Museum, the lady riding pillion, and formalised arbour groups of seated lady and gentleman backed by a solid plate of flowers and leaves in low relief. Frequent colour combinations are mottled green and brownish-grey; green, brown and slatey-blue; mottled grey, green, slatey-blue and yellow. The figure *Diana* dating to about 1755 in the Glaisher Collection is mottled in purple, greyish-blue and green but her eyes are dots of brown clay in the older slip tradition. There was a tendency in the more elaborate pieces of this tortoiseshell-ware to treat the plinth importantly, making it taller and hollow with slight relief work of flowers and leaves often tinted green. In the same group in the Glaisher Collection a Turk on a leafy base has a colour range of grey, green, yellow and purple but already one is aware of an attempt at greater sophistication: the design is taken from a Kändler Meissen figure and only the eyes indicate the still imperfect control of pigment.

The main advance consisted in the change from mottling or clouding to what potters term glaze enamelling. Whieldon, credited with the efficient methods that enhanced the quality of oxides and glaze, may also have introduced this technique. Colours were blended with the glaze and painted on as separate washes while only semi-fluid and unlikely to run. Many collectors regard this as the finest colouring achieved on earthenware figures and it may better be attributed to the older Ralph Wood. Certainly the main development of more sophisticated design associated with this treatment appears to have been led by the father and son Ralph Wood (1715–72 and 1748–95) who probably called on the services of the French modeller John Voyez when he worked as free-lance for the Staffordshire potters.

No figures are known bearing a Voyez mark such as that on his most famous "Fair Hebe" jug. But certain characteristics of face and pose, a certain sense of unspontaneous deliberation in the modelling are common to the figures in question. The majority, it appears, were adapted from the works of Paul-Louis Cyfflé, or direct from classical antiquity. The range of classical favourites includes *Apollo, Venus, Juno, Vulcan* and others. Such impressive figures as *Jupiter* with an immensely bold eagle well suited the Wood decoration in lustrous coloured glazes. *Apollo*, in the Stoke-on-Trent Museum, is typical in standing on a high, elaborately worked mound but in his case a small detail of the tooling has been interpreted as a group of trees suggesting a rebus on the name Wood. A group of shepherd and shepherdess in the same museum, also dating to about the third quarter of the 18th century, shows the mound taking the waisted form adapted by many 19th-century primitives, complete with a lamb lying in a sheltered niche.

By the second half of the century few earthenware figures were original, as compared with the numbers copied or adapted from English or Continental porcelain. Some early Wood figures from the 1750s continued the Whieldon technique or were associated with the simplest slipware, being coated with dark brown slip under the clear dipped glaze, but facial expression acquired a new charm and the pose a graceful ease. The soft greens, blues, greyish-olive and manganese purples may be noted displaying a wonderful clarity and harmony of tone. Careful inspection of a figure may show where colours have over-run each other but without mingling. By 1775 brown and orange had been added and an opaque green. Fine crazing is now frequent on this work.

The Woods worked for a middle-class market. Classical groups might be as ambitious as a mounted *St George* in armour poised over a prostrate dragon and many were large such as the familiar *Hudibras* from the Hogarth engraving. But the firm also met a demand for groups which the purchasers could associate with their own lives such as the girl waving goodbye to her sailor, typical of Napoleonic war pieces, and the various *Charity* groups showing a sweet-faced woman with either two or three children. This Charity group can be traced through many versions in 18th- and early 19th-century earthenware. The great religious revival was reflected by the introduction of such Old Testament favourites as *Elijah* with the raven and the *Widow of Zarephath* and New Testament parable figures such as the woman with a broom eagerly holding out the recovered piece of silver. Occasionally a mark is noted: R. WOOD is attributed to the older potter and R*a Wood* or R*a Wood Burslem* to his son.

Intense rivalry with the porcelain figure makers in the later-18th century prompted further developments, spurred on by the public's enthusiasm for the white daintiness of the translucent ware. The basic need was a white glaze and this was available from the early 1760s, made by grinding and mixing lead oxide with calcined flint and Cornish clay in water. This was off-white at first but removal of impurities in the ingredients and improvement in the technique for exploiting them came in 1764, introduced by John Greatbach, resulting in a whiter, smoother, harder and more brilliant surface. The biscuit effects of Derby were beyond the scope of the earthenware potters but the younger Ralph Wood issued a number of white-glazed earthenware figures as a cheaper substitute for the costly white statuary then in demand for interior decoration.

To the younger Ralph Wood, however, the main requirement of the time appeared to be for earthenware figures that could rival the clear bright colouring of porcelain. This challenge he met in two important ways. The Greatbach glaze was an excellent base for enamel colours applied over it in the porcelain decorator's style. Enamels had been applied to earthenware for a quarter of a century but it was Wood, apparently, who succeeded in preparing the metallic oxides so that on earthenware they matured to a lustre equalling the work of the porcelain decorators. Inevitably costs were increased since two firings were required to harden body and glaze and a third for the colours which themselves were of a higher, more expensive quality. Wood used his bright colours sparingly, therefore, except on occasional elaborate groups, but the method made him prosper and encouraged many rivals.

Typical of his ambitious work is a twelve-inch model of *Sir Isaac Newton* standing beside a globe and holding a telescope. Projecting from a book under the globe is a sheet of paper showing a comet and the date 1680. Newton wears an embroidered waistcoat and a long pink house robe, its white lining sprigged with flowers or marked to suggest fur, and there is a real attempt to give him the expression of a far-sighted thinker. A 12½-inch figure of *Chaucer* is equally attractive. Crazing now often blurs the exposed surfaces of such work but under a figure's base one may note the white glaze, slightly blued with the high quality cobalt known as smalt. Classical subjects were still popular but gained little from the sprigging of their somewhat shapeless draperies.

Andromache is here to be noted with her arms around the pedestal-mounted urn containing the ashes of Hector, a simpler design than the Derby porcelain model copied by Leeds and traced by Rackham to a Cyfflé design produced in Lunéville earthenware. The pair *Elijah and the Widow* are particularly attractive when given the dainty sprigged ornament of the late 18th century. It is interesting to note that each has a background of a formalised tree with a few branches and leaves in the manner developed considerably later by John Walton, who also produced this pair. A pair in the Nottingham Museum over 11 inches tall with the raven perched immediately above Elijah's head, and the widow accompanied by her son, are of particular interest for the impressed mark on Elijah of *Ra. Wood Burslem*.

For bright effects on a cheaper range of figures Wood sought colours that could be applied under the glaze and fired with it, in the two-firings manner used for the soft tones of earlier mottled and colour-washed figures. The heat of the glost or glazing oven had been found too great for most colours other than blue but in about 1790 Wood developed a palette of what are now known as high temperature colours including dull blue, pale yellow, thick ochre orange, olive green and purplish and greyish browns, often applied with a mottled or stippled effect and appearing noticeably opaque, due, Bernard Rackham suggests, to the blending of the oxides and perhaps an admixture of clay slip. Felix Pratt, third of the name working a family pottery at Fenton about 1802 to 1828, quickly seized upon Wood's technique and to modern collectors such figures are known as Pratt-ware, although Wood's method became common to other potters in Staffordshire and Sunderland and to the Herculaneum Pottery, Liverpool.

A large number of figures by Ralph Wood with impressed mould numbers were collated by Frank Falkner, including some impressed *Ra. WOOD BURSLEM*. The following list appeared in *The Connoisseur*, May 1910 and is reproduced by permission of the editor Mr. L. G. G. Ramsey, F.S.A. Those marked * were impressed with Wood's name.

Mould No.		*Height*	
1	Gardener, square base	6 in.	Coloured glazes
2	Lady gardener, square base	6 in.	Coloured glazes
3	Charlotte weeping for Werther	9¼ in	Coloured glazes; enamel colours
8	Gardener	—	Enamel colours
9	*Shepherd, "Lost Sheep"	9 in.	Coloured glazes; enamel colours; cream colour
10	*Woman, "Lost Piece"	8¼ in.	Coloured glazes; enamel colours; cream colour
19	Reclining hind	5¼ in.	Enamel colours
21	Venus and Cupid on pedestal	10¾ in.	Coloured glazes; enamel colours
22	Neptune on pedestal	10¼ in.	Coloured glazes; enamel colours
23	*St. George and the dragon	11 in.	Coloured glazes; enamel colours
25	David with harp?	12 in.	Coloured glazes
27	Sportsman with gun and dog (Companion to 97)	8 in.	Enamel colours
28	David with harp	12½ in.	Coloured glazes
29	*Jupiter with eagle	10½ in.	Coloured glazes
31	Youth leaning on a stick	6 in.	Coloured glazes
32	Lion, left paw resting on a ball	11 in.	Coloured glazes
33	Bull attacked by bull-dog	6 in.	Coloured glazes; enamel colours
36	Gamekeeper with gun, square pedestal	14¼ in.	Coloured glazes; cream colour
37	Van Tromp, square pedestal	10½ in.	Coloured glazes; enamel colours
42	Hudibras, equestrian group	11¾ in.	Coloured glazes; cream colour
43	Dr. Franklin	13½ in.	Coloured glazes; enamel colours
44	Apollo with lyre	8¾ in.	Coloured glazes
45	Cupid riding a lion	8¼ in.	Coloured glazes
46	Cupid riding a lioness	8¼ in.	Coloured glazes
47	Youth with gun, dog at base	7 in.	Coloured glazes; cream colour
48	Girl with bird	7 in.	Coloured glazes
49	Figure of a fruit boy, square	6½ in.	Coloured glazes; enamel colours
50	Figure of a girl with basket	6½ in.	Coloured glazes; enamel colours
51	*Toby, usual type, holding jug and cup to lips	10 in.	Coloured glazes
53	*Satyr-head jug, half figure on handle	8½ in.	Coloured glazes; enamel colours
54	Figure, "Old Age", man with crutches	8¾ in.	Coloured glazes; enamel colours. Mark: R. WOOD
55	Figure, "Old Age", woman with crutches	8⅝ in.	Coloured glazes; enamel colours
56	Figure, "Juno" with bird	8 in.	Coloured glazes
57	Figure, "Bacchus"	8 in.	Coloured glazes

Mould No.		*Height*	
59	Figure of a boy with basket of flowers (Companion to 66)	4½ in.	Coloured glazes
62	*"Vicar and Moses" in pulpit	9¼ in.	Coloured glazes; enamel colours
65	Toby, sailor seated on chest	11½ in.	Coloured glazes; enamel colours
66	A girl with basket of flowers (Companion to 59)	4½ in.	Coloured glazes
67	Figure of a girl with pitcher on head	8½ in.	Coloured glazes; enamel colours
68	Figure, "Peasant Worshipping"	6 in.	Coloured glazes; enamel colours
70	Probably companion to 71	—	—
71	Figure of a troubadour	8½ in.	Coloured glazes
72	Probably companion to 71	—	—
73	Figure of "Spanish Dancer"	8 in.	Coloured glazes; enamel colours
74	Figure of "Sweep Boy"	7 in.	Coloured glazes; enamel colours
79	Vulcan	10 in.	Enamel colours
80	*Bust of Handel	9 in.	Enamel colours; cream colour
81	*Bust of Milton	9 in.	Enamel colours; cream colour
83	An obelisk, granite coloured vase on top	14 in.	Enamel colours
84	*Another	19 in.	Enamel colours
88	*The Flute Player, shepherd and shepherdess	11 in.	Coloured glazes; enamel colours; cream colours
89	*The companion—Youth and bird-cage	11 in.	Coloured glazes; enamel colours; cream colour
90	Bust of Pope	—	Cream colour
91	Bust of Matthew Prior	—	Cream colour
93	Group of "Roman Charity"	7¾ in.	Coloured glazes
94	A stag standing	9½ in.	Coloured glazes
95	Companion—hind	9¼ in.	Coloured glazes
96	Figure of boy, arms folded	9½ in.	Coloured glazes; enamel colours
97	Archeress with bow, quiver and target (Companion to 27)	8 in.	Enamel colours
99	Figure of a Gasconian	—	Coloured glazes; enamel colours; cream colour
112	Bust of Shakespeare	9½ in.	Enamel colours
118	St. Peter, square pedestal	13 in.	Enamel colours
119	St. John, square pedestal	13 in.	Enamel colours
120	St. Paul, square pedestal	13 in.	Enamel colours
121	St. Philip, square pedestal	13 in.	Enamel colours
123	Bust of Voltaire	—	Enamel colours
127	Bust of Milton, small (Different model from No. 81)	7 in.	Enamel colours
132	Girl with musical instrument	—	Enamel colours; cream colour

Mould No.		Height	
133	Group, three children scuffling	—	Enamel colours; cream colour
134	Companion group	—	Enamel colours; cream colour
135	Figure of Cymon	—	Enamel colours
136	Figure of Iphigenia	—	Enamel colours
137	*Figure of Sir Isaac Newton	12¼ in.	Enamel colours
140	Mother and Child (child held in left arm)	9 in.	Cream colour
153	Group "Tenderness", boy and girl with lamb	6½ in.	
154	Group "Friendship", two boys with linked arms	6½ in.	
155	Figure of Chaucer	12¾ in.	
164	Flower holder formed as a tree, boy with dog and bird's nest	9 in.	
165	Companion, boy at foot of tree, squirrel in branches	9 in.	
169	Woman with cornucopia, inscribed in front, "Fortune"	10 in.	

Aaron Wood (1717–85), younger brother of the older Ralph Wood, was another important figure-maker, beginning as a carver of the early moulds painstakingly cut in alabaster and quick, therefore, to appreciate the advantage of plaster of paris moulds introduced in the 1740s. He was apprenticed to Dr. Thomas Wedgwood junior in 1731 but in 1746 joined Whieldon and by 1750 was established in a pottery of his own at Burslem. Here again was a potter who might be associated with salt-glazed stoneware, with the tortoiseshell effects now called Whieldon ware and the light underglaze high temperature work introduced by Ralph Wood (Pratt-ware). He is thought to have originated the full-length figure of Benjamin Franklin long copied and sometimes titled Washington or Wellington in gold upon the plinth.

Aaron's son Enoch Wood (1759–1840) made figures comparable with those of his cousin the younger Ralph, strongly coloured and frequently on bases painted to suggest marble. Many are large in size such as the striking 19-inch figure dating to the 1780s known as *Eloquence*, a stern-faced St. Paul leaning forward in a declamatory gesture. This may be impressed *E. WOOD*. It is thought to have been taken from a figure in Westminster Abbey by the sculptor Sir Henry Cheere. Typically, it has a square plinth painted

27. Birds in Bow porcelain. (*Top*) Parrots coloured in tones of green with flowery tree-stump supports. The central bird is an outstanding model. (*Bottom*) A pair of pheasants, colours ranging from the mauve-marked blue of their heads, through pink, red and yellow to the browns and yellow of wings and tails.

28. (*Top*) Lively cock and hen modelled at Bow in imitation of Chinese porcelain. (*Lower left*) Peacock perched on a tree-stump with flowers and leaves. Derby. (*Lower right*) Phoenix and flames, one of a pair, in Plymouth hard-paste porcelain.

to suggest marble. Another figure sometimes impressed *E. WOOD* is *Fortitude*, a somewhat formidable woman supporting a fluted column: the pair to this is a figure of *Prudence* holding a mirror and a snake. All these and similar early Enoch Wood figures are notably well finished, if occasionally academic rather than lively.

Henry Neale was another figure-maker of the late 18th century, acquiring Humphrey Palmer's business in Hanley in 1776 and being joined in 1786 by David Wilson whose mark of a C under a crown may be noted impressed. Their small figures mostly follow the classical style of their period, such as Apollo or Ceres. Their method was to shape the figures in two-piece moulds instead of casting, and to apply fine quality enamels with restrained delicacy, patterning their figures' gowns with dainty sprigs and spots. Finish was characteristically neat and careful, greatly enhanced by their use of square moulded plinth bases.

Typical are their *Seasons*. These are less than $5\frac{1}{2}$ inches tall overall, the figures themselves being little over 4 inches since each is seated upon a scrolled mound above the plinth, far more suggestive of porcelain than the usual incoherent tooling. Their hats and dress are coloured with great attention to detail as are the emblems of the seasons which they hold.

Two years after going into partnership Neale and Wilson changed from cream-coloured earthenware, not to a chalk formula as often stated but to the whiter pearl ware evolved by Wedgwood in 1779 which could be clear-glazed to suggest porcelain. Larger figures were in production by 1800 and some with lustre ornament. In 1801 the firm came under the control of David Wilson who so tinted the glaze to overcome any creamy hue that his figures appear bluish in tone. A *Tragedy* in the Glaisher Collection shows this blued glaze—a figure in classical robes, her face expressing horror, her hands clutching a dagger and a cup, while beside her is a tombstone carved with a skull. Marks, always impressed, include *NEALE* and *NEALE & WILSON*, and also *NEALE & CO* to indicate a piece from Neale's London warehouse. A delightful *Hussar* on a galloping horse in the British Museum has been attributed to Wilson. This is

10   145

particularly interesting as a rare example of a figure entirely coated with "silver" lustre over a fine pearl ware to suggest a statuette in solid metal.

Higher, plainly rectangular pedestals painted to suggest marble were characteristic not only of some Wood figures but of those by Thomas Lakin and Robert Poole of Burslem from 1791 to their bankruptcy in 1797. This firm may have made the difficult nude figure of Cupid grouped with Psyche after a classical model. The impressed mark LAKIN & POOLE has been noted on a number of classical groups including *Ganymede* with an eagle and *Cephălus* withdrawing an arrow from the wounded Procris. But a somewhat crudely composed *Assassination of Marat by Charlotte Cordé, 1793*, is a better expression of the firm's pleasure in the contemporary scene. They were among the many who issued the long-popular group *The Tithe Pig* adapted from the Derby version in porcelain. As with Neale and Wilson, the enamelling of Lakin and Poole is lively without being garish and their work shows a care and finish seldom noted among the gaudy unpretentious figures of 19th-century cottage and fairground.

Chapter Eleven

LEEDS

THE Leeds Pottery, Jack Lane, Hunslet, Leeds was especially celebrated for its cream-coloured earthenware or queen's ware and few collectors are aware of its considerable production of figures. It is commonly assumed that the pottery was established in 1758, but it was twelve years later that the *Leeds Mercury* of August 28, 1770, reported: "Last Tuesday a misfortune happened at the large Earthenware manufactury now erecting near this town, owing to one of the master bricklayers hurrying up one of the tall hovels too expeditiously, by which the top fell in when just finished, and drove two men and two boys before it. The boys were immediately carried to our Infirmary, and one of them, called Moses Hawkhead, soon expired. Richard Holmby, one of the men, it is thought cannot recover." It was further reported on December 11 that "Mr John Green, jr. of this town has subscribed two guineas a year to the General Infirmary," a gift prompted, no doubt, by the fatal accident.

The firm at that time traded as Humble, Green & Co. In 1775 they were joined by William Hartley who became the dominant force in management, eventually achieving fantastic success with cream-coloured earthenware. This was the ideal year for beginning manufacture of this ceramic for Cornish china clay and china stone had just been freed from the effects of a patent monopoly which had prevented their use in the manufacture of earthenware. The partners now traded as Humble, Hartley, Greens & Co., and from February 19 as Hartley, Greens & Co.

William Hartley and his six partners followed Josiah Wedgwood's lead in issuing pattern books to the china

147

sellers. The earliest was published in 1783, its title page reading: "Designs of Sundry Articles of Queen's or Cream-colour'd Earthen-Ware manufactured by Hartley, Greens & Co., Leeds Pottery: with a great Variety of other Articles. The same Enamel'd, Printed, or Ornamented with Gold to any Pattern; also with Coats of Arms, Cyphers, Landscapes, &c., &c., Leeds. 1783."

Cream ware, notably light in weight, was the staple product of the Leeds Pottery and was greatly in demand on the Continent. Several countries levied a customs duty on ceramics by weight: the lightness of Leeds cream ware gave it a tax advantage over its rivals and also reduced transport costs. The business became highly prosperous: Llewellyn Jewitt recorded that sales in 1791 exceeded £51,000. Apparently nine kilns were in operation. The frontispiece to *Leeds Pottery*, an illustrated booklet issued by the Leeds City Art Gallery in 1951, shows a Georgian portrait of "Mr. Green" against a background of a nine-kiln pottery: a plan of the premises drawn in 1847 also indicates nine kilns.

Figures are not referred to in the first or subsequent pattern books. The Victoria and Albert Museum, however, attributes the earliest figures to the mid-1770s. These were decorated in colours under the glaze in the manner associated with Thomas Whieldon. A group in the Museum represents a man and woman seated on a bench enlivened with green and brown under the glaze. The bench has a fan-shaped back ornamented with eleven identical flowers in relief similar to flowers illustrated in the Leeds pattern books as decoration on domestic ware.

Several examples of a pair of figures known as Hamlet and Ophelia are decorated with green and brown under the glaze and hat, shoes, stockings and tree trunk are decorated with applied flowers again similar to those illustrated in the pattern books. There are records, too, of crudely modelled birds and animals such as foxes and farmyard cocks and hens attributed to Leeds: these are enriched with green and sometimes also with yellow or grey.

Leeds figures in cream-coloured earthenware are lighter in weight and possess a thicker and harder glaze than is

29. (*Top*) One of a pair of Derby canaries, 5¼ inches; squirrel in natural colours; a Derby blue tit, similar to one in the Victoria and Albert Museum, about 1760. (*Centre*) A pair of White partridges and a parrot. Chelsea mid-1750s. (*Bottom*) A pair of sheep and a poodle in Rockingham bone china.

30. Staffordshire 19th-century earthenware figures. (*Top*) Rustic boy between a doe and a buck in the Walton manner. (*Bottom*) Flower vase inscribed "Success to the Hunt" and showing fox and hounds with a crude attempt at the hand-placed encrustations of contemporaneous bone china.

found on similar Staffordshire figures. The glaze is seldom crazed and at first was a golden yellow, pale straw or deep cream colour, some areas being more deeply hued than others on the same piece. By 1780 the tint was appreciably paler and a few years later acquired a faintly greenish tone, distinctly visible where drops have accumulated in crevices. This was the result of using lead oxide manufactured from lead mined in Derbyshire. This lead was exceptionally suitable for ceramic glazes, but marred by an impurity, well-known at the time but only cleared in about 1810 by a process invented by the firm of Blair, Stephenson, Tipton, Staffordshire.

Figures in undecorated cream ware date from about 1780. Those dating from 1790 may show enamel colours applied over the glaze in tones of yellow, green, red and blue, all capable of maturing with a single firing. They stand on square plinths and are hollow throughout. They are glazed inside as well as outside, a feature that distinguishes un-marked Leeds figures from those of Staffordshire. In such figures the plinth is open beneath and the four corners may be nicked, a manufacturing precaution to prevent the development of fire cracks. Draped figures were cleverly modelled as candlesticks with one or both hands steadying the sockets upon their heads. These figures stand on shallow inward-sloping fluted bases.

Most spectacular are the centrepieces, planned to give an air of grandeur to the dessert. The term used in the pattern books was *Grand Platt Menage*. Here the silversmith set the example with basket-hung epergnes, but could not offer the warm, light colour of the cream ware in which elaborate figures and cornucopias, dolphins and shells, presented their sweetmeats and suckets. A centrepiece might consist of four separate tiers topped with a carefully modelled figure such as a seated woman holding a cornucopia or a standing figure, partly draped, with putti at her feet. These centre-pieces were made in cream-coloured earthenware and might measure as much as four feet in height. Kidson illustrates an example containing four figures of seated musicians with four urn-shaped vases and a central vessel for dry sweet-meats.

Collectors should beware of the reproduction centrepieces made in the 1880s by a German potter: the glaze lacks the green tinge of Leeds and the body is much heavier. Kidson comments that "the glaze is more *glassy*, white and thickly coated. In some cases the piece is decorated with edging of a brassy-looking gilt" and this has proved permanent. Early gilding to about the mid-1790s was used sparingly and merely applied with gold size: little has survived the wear of more than a century and a half.

A proportion of cream ware figures was impressed LEEDS * POTTERY, but it is thought that the majority were not marked. The stamps for impressing the name were in hard stoneware, the face bearing the raised letters being arc-shaped.

Pearl ware, harder, more durable and whiter than cream ware, was invented in 1779 by Josiah Wedgwood and by about 1790 an improved pearl ware more suitable for figure work had been evolved at Leeds. This was more porcelaneous in appearance and of a consistency which enabled details to be modelled sharply and finely. The shallow square plinth, deeper than similar plinths from Staffordshire, was smooth on all surfaces and might be lined with gold. These figures display skilful craftsmanship closely resembling that of porcelain and were always decorated with fine enamels. The glaze, lustrous and thick, is tinged with blue, differing in texture and colour from that used on cream ware.

An exceptionally tall figure, more than a foot in height, is *Andromache Weeping over the Ashes of Hector,* formerly known as *Grief at an Urn,* which appears to have been adapted from a figure in Derby porcelain. Andromache leans against an urn wreathed with flowers and stands on a square, sparsely gilded base moulded with trophies in relief and mounted on paw feet. The whole is supported on a square plinth with fluted edges. This figure in various poses and sizes was also potted in Staffordshire. Geoffrey Bemrose has commented that "current Staffordshire best-sellers were cheerfully pirated by Leeds".

In a pair of *Musicians* measuring about eight inches in height and painted in various colours the man, in 18th-century dress with two large feathers in his hat, is playing a tambourine; the woman plays a hurdy-gurdy. These, too, were made in Staffordshire. *Mars* is shown as a helmeted warrior with banner and horn.

Leeds figures in pearl ware also include pairs of *falconers* in white and in coloured enamels, about $7\frac{1}{2}$ inches in height; *Venus* and *Neptune*, height $7\frac{3}{8}$ inches; *Minerva*, height $10\frac{1}{2}$ inches; *Sir Isaac Newton* in late 17th-century dress, with an apple at his feet, height 10 inches.

Several busts were made. Kidson illustrates an excellently potted bust of William Shakespeare, 18 inches in height, and a pair of "antique" bearded men. These are not marked. In the Victoria and Albert Museum are a pair of $6\frac{1}{2}$-inch busts painted in colours, a man emblematic of *Air*, with an eagle's skin about his shoulders, and a woman emblematic of *Water*, with a dolphin's head among her draperies. The cubical plinths have oil gilded garlands in relief. The man is twice impressed LEEDS POTTERY on the base. About twenty different subjects in pearl ware have been collated impressed LEEDS POTTERY: others are unmarked.

Large horses were made in pearl ware (see Chapter Sixteen). These were intended for display in druggists' windows, indicating that horse and cattle medicines were sold: in Victorian days plaster-of-paris horses were used. Kidson suggests that the Leeds Pottery moulds were eventually acquired by John Marsden, Bedford Row, Hunslet, who also made small chimney-piece figures of dogs, birds and sheep during the 1830s.

After the close of the Napoleonic wars in 1815 French faience potters began the manufacture of cream ware. A large proportion of the Leeds output had been exported and production drastically declined. After the death of William Hartley in 1820 the firm became bankrupt and was managed for the creditors by Thomas Lakin, formerly of Lakin & Poole, Burslem, who had also produced fine quality cream ware figures. After Lakin's death in 1824 the pottery was acquired by Samuel Wainwright who worked it until 1837.

Although at least thirty-five master potters worked at Leeds during the 19th century it is not known that any but Marsden made any figures.

Chapter Twelve

BEFORE continuing to trace the course of earthenware figures through the 19th century it is necessary to draw attention to a parallel development in slipware. Figures in this primitive ware were discussed in some detail in Chapter Ten. To the collector they have a special appeal because each is unique. But despite their rustic air many of these pieces date little earlier than the mid-19th century. The cradle continued popular, often as "gift wrapping" at a christening but also sometimes filled with the figure of a sleeping child as in the many more sophisticated specimens in painted earthenware. One obvious variant was the high-backed porter's chair, not unlike a cradle stood on end. Chests of drawers have been noted, too, sometimes with figures or half-figures on top, including some in the heavy clay associated with Halifax where several potteries were active such as that of the Halliday family, at work until 1889.

Rackham has noted the use of exceptionally heavy bright red clay with trails of white slip under a strong yellow glaze usually full of glistening particles. Chests of drawers from Burton-in-Lonsdale, Yorkshire, have been noted with similar lustrous yellow glaze: these are in a hard-fired dark red clay and white slip. Melling, Lancashire, five miles away, may have produced a figure in the Fitzwilliam Museum in dark red clay with outstretched arm and a dog at his feet and wearing the tall hat, long coat and trousers of about 1830. Many slipware animals and birds are to be noted (see Chapter 16) but also more ambitious chimney ornaments. Attractive figures probably dating to about 1820 include a *Samson and lion* group at the Victoria and Albert Museum which is thought to have come from the same potter as a seated woman in red clay holding a pudding in a dish on her lap and a companion figure of a beggar sitting on the ground with a dog beside him. Figures such as these in red earthenware with modelled, incised, or trailed ornament under a rich yellow glaze have been attributed to Sussex where potters were at work at the Dicker, near Hellingly; at Cadborough Pottery, Rye; at Brede, near Hastings, and at Chailey.

Watchstands in slipware remain, 8 inches tall, impressed G. FISHLEY, FREMINGTOWN (Fremington, North Devon): the family worked as potters from the end of the 18th century until 1912. In these the detail consists of a screen with a socket for a watch and in front a figure of Napoleon among animals. One in the Fitzwilliam Museum also has a figure of a negro holding a bird. Other slipware figures of *Napoleon* show him with a dog at his feet and in half-length, seated with other figures at a fruit banquet, the detail modelled in red, white and brown. Busts of *Wesley* dating to the mid-19th century include a small slipware example with red and white details and a greenish-yellow glaze. Wesley wears a gown and strips of white clay to suggest a stole.

Wesley was one of many popular preachers to appear again and again in enamel-painted earthenware. Staffordshire figures in this medium at the end of the 18th century tended to be mainly imitations of porcelain, usually lacking the grace and delicacy of the more expensive work but lacking also the forthright simplicity and jollity of the old potter's toy. It was some time before this particular branch of the craft found itself again, the porcelain man's neoclassical elegancies forgotten in an abundance of gaudy little souvenirs—of royalty, politicians, soldiers, sportsmen, criminals. These sold cheaply among people new to town life and to contact with the world around them: they were appreciated at the time both as glossy, light-catching ornament and as evidence of a newly awakened personal interest in the happenings of the day. Yet today they are avidly collected for their engaging ugliness and their remote unreality.

As explained in previous chapters, the usual method was to shape the figures in plaster of paris moulds. An elaborate figure might require many moulds but as the 19th century progressed, design was modified to simple outlines so that a figure and its plinth could be shaped quickly and with a minimum of material by pressing the soft earthenware into a single two-part or three-part mould, using a press-mould design invented by an American in about 1830. Firing in the oven then transformed the "greenware" into brittle, absorbent biscuit, ready for underglaze painting, glazing, over-glaze enamelling, gilding. The associated process of casting was also continued to some extent, using earthenware in the wet condition known as slip. But this wet clay slip quickly spoilt the sharp edges of the plaster moulds, necessitating frequent renewal from the master mould. A figure may sometimes be found with an open base, as distinct from a base containing a small hole for escaping hot air: this has been cast in a single mould.

The fine white earthenware known as pearl ware was available and was used for some 19th century figure work of considerable quality. This was particularly effective when contributing to the brilliance of gold or ruby lustre. But the use of cheap brittle earthenwares for most 19th-century figures must be blamed for the fact that so comparatively few remain of the hundreds of thousands made.

Regarding the colours of 19th-century figures, a characteristic for many years was a splendid underglaze blue, so typical that it became known as Staffordshire blue. Cobalt oxide, in the form of zaffre or more costly smalt, was for long the favourite colour among decorators of all kinds of ceramics since it could be protected from flaking and wear by being applied under the glaze, remaining unaffected by the great heat involved in the glazing process and it appears in innumerable coats, gowns, uniforms of late Georgian and early-Victorian ceramic grandeur.

Because few 19th-century figures were marked the named potters have assumed more importance than may be their due. Collectors will usually be able to date their pieces more easily by subject matter than by any individual characteristics of design or workmanship. It cannot be stressed too often that these figures were turned out by the tens of thousands, many by children with piece-work haste: I have referred before to the *Report on the Employment of Children in Factories*, 1842, which quotes the evidence of a nine-year-old, William Cotton of Longton, who made forty dozen small figures a day at a piece-work rate of one penny for ten dozen. Some small potteries concentrated largely on these ornaments, relying on their small size and light weight for wide distribution by country packmen.

Of the potters mentioned individually in the previous chapter, Enoch Wood continued until 1840. His partnership with James Caldwell lasted from 1790 to 1818 when Wood continued as Enoch Wood & Sons. He largely adapted and copied from statuary and porcelain. His later pieces never reached the standard of the famous *John Wesley* modelled from life in 1781, and are generally dismissed as mediocre and often clumsily massive—as much as 21 inches tall. But they tended to be more carefully detailed than those of his contemporaries. For example, he issued a bust of *Napoleon* in 1802 and one of the Russian *Czar* in 1812 and commemorated the end of the Napoleonic wars with an ambitious figure of *Peace*, over 17 inches tall, enriched with gold and rose lustre.

Some figures marked WOOD & CALDWELL remain from the partnership, such as a vigorously modelled *Falstaff* in plumed hat and with sword and buckler: this was copied from porcelain models by Bow and Derby inspired by McArdell's engraving of James Quin. A figure of *Flora* on a square plinth impressed *W* is also attributed to this period. This is nearly 13 inches tall, in classical dress sprigged with flowers, with a wreath in her hair and flowers in her arms. A somewhat similar figure is known, painted in high temperature colours underglaze. Some Wood & Caldwell figures are enriched with lustre such as *Mark Antony* in Roman armour touched with the silver lustre produced from about 1805 with platinum. A pair of *Tritons* in copper lustre and a 17-inch *Cupid* in purple lustre have been attributed to the same firm.

Less well finished figures, in cruder colours, are associated with Enoch Wood after he bought out Caldwell in 1818. Here again the figures include such popular subjects as *Elijah and the Widow of Zarephath* on marble-coloured square plinths, but the widow lacks her son, the tree stump supports are less shapely and the colouring more crude. One notes sentimental groups such as the *Widow and Orphans*: the widow, carrying a baby, has a coin in her outstretched hand, a boy carrying wood at her side and a girl preparing a fire.

Enoch Wood is credited with the extremely popular *Vicar and Moses* figure group showing a cleric slumbering in his pulpit while his clerk below him reads the lesson—or perhaps the vicar's lengthy sermon. It is thought that both Ralph and Enoch Wood supplied figures to the Wedgwood firm such as the *Faith, Hope and Charity* groups modelled by Mrs. Landre for Wedgwood and copied by others such as Hartley of Leeds.

It is interesting to note the Wood & Caldwell use of lustre. At this time lustre was an important decorative medium to the potter of useful wares, its metallic glitter having an immediate appeal and showing up well in the ill-lit cottage. Particularly effective use was made of the silver (platinum) lustre. White or red earthenware figures covered entirely in the metallic glaze suggested statuettes of silver. Ephraim Wood, cousin of Enoch, was making pottery figures from about 1805 to 1830 at Burslem and was noted also as a lustrer. A silver lustre version of the armoured equestrian *St. George* with the slain dragon and a figure of *Napoleon* have been noted by Haggar and tentatively ascribed to him—extremely effective so long as no chipping spoiled the illusion of solid metal. Other lustre-brightened figures were produced by Elijah Mayer of Hanley, at work until 1830, and by the firm of Bailey & Batkin, Longton, at work in the 1820s. Solid effects in copper-brown lustre and the various pink-to-purple shades were also produced in Staffordshire but are now generally classed as Sunderland work (see page 161).

Another type of ornament too narrowly attributed is the so-called Pratt ware used by Felix Pratt III from about 1802 to 1828 but probably introduced about 1790 by Ralph Wood (see page 141) and adopted by many potters. Such figures are richly dabbed and mottled with a range of colours that could be applied under the glaze, being able to endure the

31. Salt-glazed stoneware busts by John Dwight of Fulham. (*Top left*) Life-size bust of Prince Rupert wearing the collar of the Order of the Garter, gilded. (*Top right*) Charles II in grey stoneware. Height 7 inches. About 1680. (*Lower left*) Believed to be a portrait of Mrs. Pepys. Height 7 inches. (*Lower right*) Recumbent effigy of John Dwight's daughter Lydia, inscribed "Lydia Dwight. Dyed March 3rd 1673." Length 10 inches.

32. Neptune by John Dwight of Fulham. In salt-glazed stoneware coated with a bronze-tinted slip and salt-glazed. Height 12¼ inches.

high-temperature firing—dull blue, olive green, thick orange yellow, pale yellow and greyish and purplish browns. The style dates from the 1790s well into the 19th century.

Little is known of the Felix Pratts, working at Fenton until the 1860s, and early 19th-century figures in this treatment cover a wide range of subjects and style from figures of *Ceres* in spotted dresses to the comedy Irishman riding his saddled and bridled pig among shreds of earthenware representing straw, in the Willett Collection at Brighton Museum. In this style, too, one meets the cavalry officer on a rearing horse, *Charity, Flora,* the *Seasons,* farm groups and shepherdesses. A group at Brighton of a strange, ungainly rearing horse which has thrown its rider, is marked *T* in relief and has been ascribed tentatively by Haggar to the Tittensor family, perhaps Jacob or William: he notes that Charles Tittensor, working as a potter through the first quarter of the 19th century, has been associated with some rustic figures impressed *TITTENSOR.*

Much of this early 19th-century work tended to be dominated still by the traditions of figure modelling in porcelain. Only from the 1830s or 1840s did earthenware figures acquire the distinctive characteristics of the Victorian chimney ornament. A potter associated with a transitional phase was John Walton, of special interest because he frequently marked his figures and groups and in any case possessed a talent that enabled him to find a market at a period of widespread depression in the trade, meeting it with designs and prices that ensured success.

Walton worked at Hadderage, Burslem, from the 1800s until his death in 1839 when his widow Eliza continued his craft. He gradually developed a style of standardised design and heavy colouring with a "dry" texture that was coarse and crude enough for cut-price production and for the same reason he used a cheap, brittle earthenware that could be shaped at high speed for his aim to sell cheaply and in quantity at fairs and markets and through hawkers in the streets. There is little here to suggest the grace of porcelain and his style is sufficiently individualistic to be recognised today and to have been shared or imitated by his contemporaries.

Walton continued the country subjects that recognised the uprooted factory workers' longing for imagined good old days of rustic simplicity, as well as for domestic peace and religious reassurance. He made a model of the Royal Arms with lion and unicorn supporters to mark the coronation of George IV—not very accurately—but in general his figures lack the topical interest that became usual among his successors, ranging instead among such themes as sentimental lovers and children bird-nesting, farm pieces such as a farmer feeding his cow, or animal groups. In subject much of his most attractive work still copied or adapted porcelain originals and he often showed a fondness, too, for their bright rich colours with occasional rough attempts at sprigged patterns and early examples suggest an obvious link between the careful potting of Enoch Wood and the cruder, more stereotyped, mass-production style which he appears to have developed, presumably as an economic necessity.

A notable detail was his adaptation of the porcelain *bocage* as a decorative support for figures that went back to the idyllic rustic mood of the mid-Georgian's arbour groups. Some have suggested he was by no means the originator of this earthenware simplification of porcelain delicacy. It is noted on Staffordshire salt-glaze conversation pieces of the mid-18th century and on such popular Wood figures as Elijah as described above. Walton's *bocage* was no more than a formal representation of a tree stump rising behind the figures or group and supporting a few stunted branches thickly covered with large conventional leaves stamped from the clay, not always cleanly, and placed by hand, each group of leaves centred by a coloured conventional flower. Sometimes the outlines suggest oak leaves and acorn cups but this was contradicted by his colourists. This notion was common to other early 19th-century potters, continuing until the end of the Georgian era.

The bases of Walton's figures, too, suggest association with porcelain work. At first he used the marble-painted plinths of his contemporaries but more typical are his tall, imposing mounds, often roughly rocky. Thus a figure of a sheep may include a lamb sheltering in a rocky recess of the green base. Characteristically a Walton base includes rounded scrolls picked out in blue and often incorporating a title on the front—frequently an entirely obvious title such as *Tenderness* or *Lovers* or *Lion*—and on the back an impressed mark *WALTON*.

Another name sometimes noted is *SALT* impressed above or upon a raised scroll, usually marking a figure in the Walton style with a tree stump setting and a substantial, slightly waisted rocky base. Ralph Salt (1782–1846) began making domestic pottery in 1812 at Hanley. By 1820 he was issuing small painted figures such as *bocage* pieces and sporting dogs and in 1834 built a larger pottery in Shelton. His modelling was clear-cut, his colours including metallic lustres and his subjects covering *Dr Syntax* figures as well as the usual domestic range. A figure of a tailor riding a goat in Hanley Museum has been ascribed to him. His son Charles (d. 1869) also impressed his name on the back of his figure plinths but it appears that even when he used his father's moulds his work was less well finished.

John and Ralph Hall of Swan Bank, Tunstall and the Sytch Pottery, Burslem, occasionally impressed a figure with the mark HALL but less is known of their figures than of their blue-printed wares for the American market. Their partnership dated from about 1800 to 1822. Ralph Hall continued at Tunstall into thé 1840s; John and his sons at the Sytch Pottery became bankrupt in 1832, being followed by the firm of Barker, Sutton & Till. The names of Edge & Grocott are associated with a few early 19th-century *bocage* groups but it appears that after about 1820 they continued figure-making independently. John Dale impressed J. DALE BURSLEM on figures such as a bust of *John Wesley* and a set of four *Elements* at the Victoria and Albert Museum and in the same group of potters may be mentioned the very small figures impressed with the name of Turner & Abbott, Lane End, potters to the Prince of Wales in the late 18th-century and Bott & Co., known for their bust of *Shakespeare*.

Further yet from the porcelain style was the work associated with Obadiah Sherratt of Burslem, at work by 1810. Characteristics of presentation and a sense of showmanship link a number of pieces now ascribed to this potter and suggest that he was quick to sense the moods of his day and present them with a laugh or a guffaw. These include the familiar ugly bull-baiting scenes recording a barbarity which was legal until as late as 1835, and the straightforward scriptural and classical groups of much early 19th-century pottery but also more lively, down-to-earth humour typified by the husband and wife deciding "Who shall ware the Breeches". The pair *Teetotal* and *alebench* show a finely dressed family taking tea in elaborate elegance and in contrast a husband belaboured by his wife among broken ale bottles. The term tee-total dates the pieces as no earlier than 1834. *Polito's Menagerie* was a notably elaborate piece, considered a triumph of shaping and firing in the flat. The scene is the menagerie entrance with seven figures grouped below the elaborate façade announcing "Polito's menagerie of the wonderful burds and beasts from most parts of the world". Some time after Polito's death the same façade was named for Wombwell's circus.

A feature common to these pieces is the unusual base, square or rectangular and raised on corner feet in the bracket-shape of contemporaneous chest furniture. Other pieces sometimes ascribed to Sherratt include *The Death of Monrow* on a flat plinth showing Lt. Munroe being seized by a huge tiger.

Sometimes, too, he is credited with a particularly popular crime piece of 1828, now rare, which shows the figures of *William Corder and Maria Marten*—murderer and victim—standing outside the notorious red barn at Polstead, near Bury St. Edmunds. He was succeeded by his son Hamlet in about 1846 and from about 1850 until the late 1850s by his widow Martha. For very many other late-Georgian figures, however, it is impossible to ascribe an origin—religious groups such as the Virgin and Child, conversation pieces, classical figures such as Venus and many different Cupids, shepherds, gardeners. Occasionally a portrait of a living personality was produced, not only Nelson and Napoleon but briefer celebrities such as *John Liston* the actor dressed as a Dutchman or carrying a hat box as Paul Pry in a play first staged in 1826. Some figures that remain are in plain white earthenware but in general the tendency of this period was

33. Staffordshire white salt-glazed stoneware. (*Top*) Figures of sitting cats, marbled with dark brown clays, touched with blue inside the ears and on the body. Heights 5 inches and 5½ inches. About 1745. (*Bottom*) Pew group showing a man in a curly wig playing bagpipes, seated beside a woman with a pug dog on her lap, on a bench. The high back of the bench is decorated with incisions inlaid with dark brown slip and there are twisted threads of brown and white clay along the arms. Height 6¼ inches. About 1745.

34. Staffordshire white salt-glazed stoneware. (*Top*) Pair of busts, the Empress Maria Theresa and her husband Francis I who wears the Order of the Golden Fleece over armour. Eyes represented by beads of dark brown slip. Height 7½ inches. About 1745. (*Bottom, left to right*) Woman with wide-hooped skirt impressed with pattern and flouncing, eyes touched with brown slip. Height 3¾ inches. About 1745. Chung-li Ch'uan, one of the Taoist Eight immortals, with a fan in one hand and a peach in the other. Height 7¼ inches. About 1750. Youth with dog on high moulded square pedestal. Based on an English 17th-century bronze. Height 6 inches. About 1745.

to cover the many flaws in cheap wares by an abundance of rich colouring: the earthenware figure left mainly white with touches of black and gold was largely a Victorian development.

Although Staffordshire was the main source of 19th-century figures there are records of considerable production elsewhere. The Herculaneum Pottery, Liverpool, made figures decorated with high-temperature underglaze colours: as might be expected, their portrait busts included famous Americans and Navy heroes. The impressed mark *HER-CULANEUM 2* has been noted on a white earthenware pedestalled bust of *Lord Duncan of Camperdown*, painted in enamel colours. This has been dated to about 1800 and a bust from the same mould has been noted in brown stoneware. Figures attributed to Leeds were considered in Chapter Eleven. Leeds figures in cream-coloured earthenware and the whiter pearl ware are difficult to distinguish from Wood's work unless marked. Emblematic figures of *Hope* with an anchor, *Peace* with an olive branch and *Charity* with two small children are typical of known Leeds work.

It is thought that other Yorkshire figures may have come from Swinton, near Rotherham, but this is uncertain for no marks have been found on the lions and other conventional favourites in the rich purplish-brown manganese glaze known as Rockingham glaze but used widely elsewhere. The name HAWLEY on an occasional figure such as a simple version of Wood's *Good Shepherd* parable figure, noted in the Yorkshire Museum, is associated with William Hawley who was at work from 1790 to 1810 at Rawmarsh, also near Rotherham, and was followed by his widow who continued until 1844.

Sunderland has become the generic term for certain styles of lustre ware made also in Staffordshire, Liverpool and Bristol and this has tended to obscure any local individuality of design. This lustre ranged in colour from pale pink to purple, produced with gold chloride and tin chloride in varying proportions over a white body or glaze. Characteristically it was speckled, mottled or sponged, an effect achieved by spattering the ware with small droplets of oil. At its best the lustre was applied over a body of fine pearl ware but more figures were produced in coarse earthen-wares, with the lustre usually restricted to small touches on dress or plinth.

The endless coming and going of seamen, both local and foreign, ensured in Sunderland an exceptional demand both for souvenir figures of local interest and for sentimental gifts that would convey affection and fidelity. For example, Sunderland claimed—and modelled—*Jack Crawford*, hero in the 1797 Camperdown incident of nailing the colours to the mast. Such an outward-looking region also offered a sure market for topical celebrities, from *Garibaldi* to *Napoleon*. A large bust of Napoleon, now a rarity, was made from a 35-piece or 40-piece mould at Low Ford, South Hylton, owned by John Dawson (1769–1848) and his sons and grandsons until 1864. A splendid bull, entirely in glossy copper-brown lustre, in the Sunderland Museum, is attributed to this pottery.

The Sunderland or Garrison Pottery, under John Phillips, Robert Dixon, William Austin and members of their families, produced and marked many inexpensive figures from 1800 ranging from *Queen Victoria* and *Wellington* to *Joan of Arc* and *Napoleon* and the *Child Samuel* and busts of such celebrities as *Wesley* and *Nelson*. They followed convention by producing also more generalised subjects such as the *Seasons* in simple shapes and quickly coloured detail: a set in Sunderland Museum are impressed Dixon, Austin & Co., dating them to 1820–6. A pink lustre watch-stand in this collection, similarly marked, is in the shape of a grand-father clock flanked by two child figures. In the Fitzwilliam Museum is a figure in a flowered, blue-trimmed robe entitled *Aesculapius*, leaning on a club and holding up a scroll. This is taken from a Derby porcelain model. Dixon, Austin & Co. made some of the many figures of *Elijah and the Widow of Zarephath*, about 10 inches tall and mounted on square plinths. Here the raven is offering food to Elijah who wears a blue cloak and flowered robe; the widow wears a blue hood and spotted gown and holds a cake. Highlanders were made here as well as in Scotland and shepherds and shep-herdesses.

In Wales the Cambrian Pottery, Swansea, issued figures

under the management of Llewellyn W. Dillwyn, 1802–50. A *Florow* in the National Museum of Wales, Cardiff, is ascribed to this pottery: this Flora is in the usual robes with flowers in her hair and in her hands and in this model has a lamb at her side on the high base.

In Scotland the Portobello factory, Midlothian, was responsible for some brightly coloured "dabbities" as they called them, spotted and stippled with the underglaze blue, green, orange, yellow and browns. The factory was acquired by Thomas Rathbone in about 1808. His small figures, crude but engaging, included the fishwives and shepherds that would have the local familiarity to ensure wide sale and more romantic soldiers and sailors including, it is thought, some in simplified *bocage* settings. It must be accepted, however, that it is virtually impossible to distinguish between English and Scottish work, only the fishwives from Portobello or neighbouring Prestonpans showing a distinctive local character. A shepherd in tartan in the Willett Collection is marked *Portobello*. Watch-stand groups attributed to Rathbone followed the style of other earthenware potters of the 1820s: a group of figures on a substantial base flanked a niche designed to receive a pocket watch, transforming it temporarily into a table clock. The early Victorian detestation of blank spaces prompted the inclusion of painted watch faces on some of these groups, robbing them of their original purpose: Victorian pulpit models of famous preachers by Sampson Smith and others sometimes incorporate these useless clock faces. Rathbone was followed by his son Samuel until a trade depression temporarily closed the factory in 1837. Bo'ness (contraction of Borrowstoun-ness) potteries were noted, too, for their chimney toys in bright underglaze colours including animals (see Chapter Sixteen).

English majolica was devised as a novel ceramic experiment for the Great Exhibition, 1851, by Leon Arnoux, chemist and art director to Minton & Co. Catalogued as "imitation majolica ware" it bears little resemblance to the original Italian maiolica, a soft reddish or greyish earthenware of poor quality clay, tin-glazed in lustrous opaque white and painted in colours. Minton used the Anglicised form of the Italian name, calling his ceramic majolica. This was a hard earthenware painted with thick coloured glazes. Under gas illumination majolica displayed a richly lustrous glow.

The foundation of Minton's majolica was a fine cane-coloured stoneware that could be modelled into high relief with clear sharp detail. The shaped figure was dried and fired to a biscuit and later dipped into a bath of white enamel glaze composed of pure silica, oxide of lead, oxide of tin and water. The cane colour of the biscuit so tinctured the film of white glaze that it enriched the colour glazes painted upon it. These glazes were technical improvements on those used on late 18th century figures, being of greater brilliance and purity. The colours included red, pink, blue, green, purple, orange, yellow and brown in various tints, obtained by adding colouring oxides to clear glaze possessing a thermal expansion similar to that of the basic ceramic. If their thermal expansion differed the glaze eventually became disfigured with numerous fissures known as crazing.

At this time Mintons were commissioning work from celebrated sculptors for reproduction in parian statuary. Among these was Baron Marachetti, who also modelled several large figures for reproduction in imitation majolica. The firm continued the trade names "imitation majolica ware" and "majolica style" until about 1861 when competitors entered this profitable branch of the pottery industry. The name majolica then became general and remained fashionable for more than thirty years. Majolica, like other Minton figures was impressed with the firm's trade mark and date symbols.

In 1860 Mintons introduced parian statuary porcelain as the basic ceramic for majolica figures. The creamy richness of this hard porcelain increased the brilliance and clarity of the glaze and gave a delightful softness to flesh tints: crazing was avoided. Typical of the centrepieces that immediately became fashionable were the delicate openwork dishes supported by graceful nude figures mounted on pedestals.

George Jones established himself as a manufacturer of parian statuary in 1861 at Trent Pottery, Stoke upon Trent,

35. Figures of Doulton & Company, Lambeth. (*Top*) *Going to the Derby*, a group in salt-glazed stoneware modelled by George Tinworth in about 1880. (*Lower left*) Bust of William Pitt modelled for the centenary of his birth in 1906 by John Broad. In dark grey terracotta. (*Lower right*) Figure of Napoleon in salt-glazed stoneware. Early 19th century.

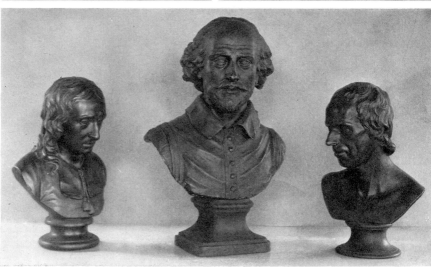

36. Portrait busts in black basaltes by Josiah Wedgwood, Etruria, Staffordshire. Impressed Wedgwood & Bentley. (*Top left*) Ben Jonson with his name mis-spelled on tablet and (*right*) an unknown sitter. Height 18 inches. 1787. (*Bottom*) Three English poets. (*Left and right*) John Milton and Alexander Pope modelled by Hoskins & Grant in 1777: (*centre*) William Shakespeare from the Chandos portrait modelled by John Cheese in 1774.

also using this as a basis for majolica figures notable for their careful modelling and the lustre of their glazes. Jones was awarded gold medals for his majolica at the exhibitions of Paris, 1867, London, 1871 and Vienna, 1873. Until about 1880 he impressed his majolica with the monogram GJ, sometimes within a circle: after taking his sons into partnership " & SONS" was added in a crescent beneath the monogram. Among other potters who combined parian statuary with coloured glazes was Thomas Bevington, Hanley, from 1862 to 1877 when production ceased. Bevington's mark was a six-pointed star containing a crown and flanked by the initials TB.

John Adams & Co., Hanley, made majolica figures from 1860. From 1871 Adams made flower vases measuring four feet in height, their huge bowls supported by substantial cupids. The firm traded as Adams & Bromley from 1875 to 1894. Early majolica was impressed ADAMS & Co and, from 1873, ADAMS & BROMLEY or A & B. Daniel Sutherland & Sons, Longton, established in 1863 a pottery specialising in parian statuary and majolica figures. The mark S & S was impressed on early productions.

Edward Steele, Hanley, established as an earthenware potter in about 1850, became also a specialist in parian and majolica during the early 1860s. The body of his majolica was sharply modelled and finished with colours of outstanding hue and lustre. His main productions in majolica were dessert services with elaborate figure centrepieces, figures and much purely ornamental work. The mark was ETRUSCAN MAJOLICA in a circle enclosing the monogram ESH.

Chapter Thirteen

EARTHENWARE: VICTORIAN PORTRAITS

THE watch-stands referred to in the previous chapter are of more than passing interest since they tended to follow a style of ornament particularly associated with the Victorian era. Because such a piece was designed solely for presenting one face to the world the back was not elaborated. Also, its purpose required a stability best met by a wide-based design tapering more flatly above with a minimum of out-jutting ornament. Vases for spills or matches with figure supports followed the same outline and soon more and more figures and groups were evolved with detail of moulding and colour concentrated to the front: these are now known as flatbacks. Uncomplicated flat-back figures could be shaped extremely quickly and economically in press moulds as already described. Characteristics are the white body and brilliant glaze with the lovely Staffordshire blue still dominating the early colour schemes.

Collectors soon discover varying qualities of moulding and ornament in figures basically identical. A sharply moulded piece was given most careful decoration; specimens from a worn mould would be finished hastily for a cheaper market. Many a popular model, too, was issued in several sizes ranging from perhaps five to nineteen inches. A small figure of the *Duke of Wellington*, for instance, sold for as little as fourpence and a complicated equestrian figure of *Garibaldi* for about eight shillings.

The colours used overglaze to augment the blue on early-Victorian figures are nearly as stereotyped as the subsidiary details that offer clues to the identity of the figures—the anchors supporting sailors, the guns and shot behind the soldiers, the books held by literary figures, the long frock

166

coats of the politicians, the pulpits for preachers—but no lamp for "Miss Nightingale". One notes the characteristic use of light red and orange for cloaks—and for Garibaldi's shirt—green for trimmings unless ermine is used to signify royalty, black for shoes etc., chestnut or white for a horse.

Reference has been made already to some portraits among early 19th-century figures. More than a dozen different models of *John Wesley* were issued and there were figures of the nonconformist *W. Thorn* (dated 1826) and *George Whitefield*. An enduring favourite was *John Wilkes* seated on a rock holding a scroll that declared "The rights of the people". War figures and busts included many of *Nelson*, a bare-headed *General Sir John Moore* (d. 1809), *Admiral Duncan, Admiral Sir William Sidney Smith* and others. *Napoleon* is found in many poses and even *Francis II* of Austria and *Alexander I* of Russia. A topical variant of the popular ornamental china cottage was a cottage and lighthouse with a small boat in the foreground containing tiny figures of *Grace Darling* and her father, commemorating her valour of 1838.

On the other hand, chimney ornaments throughout the Victorian era continued many standard popular figures. These included religious groups such as the flight into Egypt and the return, the sacrifice of Isaac, St. Peter healing the lame man and figures of Old Testament prophets, the Evangelists with their symbols, and the like. There were many rustic figures still—shepherds, lovers, music-makers and innumerable children, simpering, scuffling or grouped with their pets. These may be dated by comparison with the treatment of figures more briefly popular.

Such figures as may be found belonging to earlier centuries are usually easy to recognise as romantic Victorian conceptions. There are, for example, several equestrian figures of *William III* (1650–1702) who is also found engraved on early 19th-century wine glasses in connection with lodges of the Orange Society.

Figures and busts of royalty had appeared early in the 19th century when public emotion warranted, such as those of the ill-fated *Princess Charlotte* (d. 1816) and the figures and busts of *Queen Caroline* that expressed public sympathy during her trial in 1820, issued in stoneware (see Chapter Eight) and white earthenware. *William IV* is to be found in white, with and without *Queen Adelaide*. But among flat-back portraits the earliest examples that can be dated exactly are a pair of *Queen Victoria and Prince Albert*, issued to commemorate their marriage, February 1840. Among the last of note was the figure marking Victoria's diamond jubilee and even this was taken from a model of 1870.

With these flat-backs it is usually impossible to attribute individual makers and even a model's identity is sometimes in doubt unless it is titled for often there is little enough attempt at a portrait likeness. Such titles may be included in the mouldings so that they appear as raised letters, or impressed into the soft clay before firing, but many more were added overglaze in hand-painting or transfer-printing and with occasional inaccuracy, such as the confusion of Washington with Benjamin Franklin.

Collectors trace an increase in average size among these figures through Victoria's reign as they gradually lost their rich colours and lively, complicated poses. By the 1870s they were fast losing, too, the characteristic air of individuality that came of an inborn skill in model designing and considered, if rapid, brushwork. Overglaze colours, which consisted mainly of red, yellow, green and black, tended to flake off when applied thickly and they appeared less and less on later figures, which depended for effect on their clear white gloss relieved only by flesh tints and quick dabs and lines of black for hair and details of dress, set off by gilding. This gilding became important when potters found they could use the liquid gold process invented by William Cornelius in 1853 to replace the costly and unhealthy mercury gilding. No reason has been suggested for the omission of Staffordshire blue from later figures, but the glitter of gold and white well suited the candle-lit cottage.

One potter known to have been associated with these figures was Sampson Smith (1813–78), Sutherland Works, Longton, reputed to have started potting in Longton in 1846: subsequent potters continued to trade under his name. A marked group of a gardener and his wife, press-shaped in a two-piece mould, may be noted at the Victoria and Albert Museum. This is interesting for few of his figures were marked. Occasionally a mark by this firm includes the date 1851 but as on other ceramics this indicates a date important in the firm's history and not that of the figure's manufacture. Regarding this firm, some confusion has been caused through the rediscovery of some of the old moulds in 1948 and the re-issue of some sporting figures, animals and cottages. The cautious collector must note, too, that the firm of William Kent (Porcelains) Ltd. has been producing figures almost without a break from 1878, still using the old models and methods.

John Lloyd was another figure maker who marked some flat-backs LLOYD SHELTON impressed in two lines at the back or underneath. Lloyd was at work from 1834 to 1850 and was followed by his widow Rebecca using the same mark. His workshops were at Market Street, Hanley, and subsequently at Marsh Street. His shepherds and shepherdesses were popular and there are marked specimens in Hanley Museum and the Fitzwilliam, Cambridge.

Following the success of the 1840 Victoria and Albert figures came the group of the queen and consort with the baby *Princess Royal,* born in November of that year. A charming figure of *Victoria* in the Willett Collection nursing her baby is touched only with pink, black and gold, obviously the popular rendering of a contemporaneous figure in white biscuit porcelain. Thereafter many further glimpses were offered of the royal pair and even of *Balmoral* and *Windsor Castle*. Their children, and especially the *Princess Royal* and the *Prince of Wales*, appeared again and again, typical being the group showing them asleep, watched by a guardian angel. Another favourite was the Prince of Wales in a sailor suit from Winterhalter's painting of 1847.

During this first decade of wide popularity a wonderful range of finely designed and coloured portrait figures was put upon the popular market. These included such statesmen as *Wellington*, in frock coat now, less striking than the familiar figure on horse-back titled *Up Guards and at Them*, though another figure in military uniform marked his death; *Richard Cobden* seated beside a wheatsheaf or a cornucopia; the *Earl of Shaftesbury* with a small boy to signify his work for ragged schools; *Sir Robert Peel*; the Chartist *T. S. Duncombe*; *Daniel O'Connell*; the Irish nationalist *William Smith O'Brien* wearing the manacles that signified his transportation to Australia and paired by his loyal wife. One meets the Quaker philanthropist *J. J. Gurney* in a fur waistcoat and the eccentric *Jemmy Wood* (d. 1836) who left fruitless legal wrangling instead of an intended £200,000 to the city of Gloucester.

For the romantic there was *Sir John Franklin* who discovered the North West Passage but perished in the Arctic in 1847: his wife, paired with him, financed several of the many expeditions that searched for him. These earthenware figures may have been first issued as late as 1850, but the 1840s can claim the introduction of such romantic authors as *Robert Burns* who appeared again and again, bare-headed and usually wearing a plaid. His *Highland Mary* is paired with him in later issues. *Sir Walter Scott* was modelled from the Edinburgh statue: a heavy tartan plaid across one shoulder looks somewhat out of place with his tidy blue coat, heavy necktie and close-fitting pink trousers. *Lord Byron* is a more laboriously glamorous figure of this period. *Eliza Cook* holds a book to declare her passing fame as a poetess in a ringleted figure of around 1850 but is completely overshadowed by all the figures of the Swedish singer *Jenny Lind* who was wildly popular in the late 1840s. Among the most appealing, it seems, was her characterisation of Maria in *The Daughter of the Regiment*: this figure shows her with hand raised to her stiff little hat in a somewhat casual salute and her feet neatly coloured in red boots. In another version she is found as Alice in Meyerbeer's opera *Robert le Diable*, a part she first took in 1847. She may be paired with her impressario *Louis Antoine Jullien*, the French conductor who produced operas at Drury Lane in 1847 and long continued popular in England.

Other stage figures include *Edmund Kean* in the Richard III nightmare scene and *William Macready* and the figure of *Will Watch* that sometimes puzzles a collector but which commemorates not so much the smuggler himself as the rip-roaring play *Will Watch and his Black-eyed Sue*. The highwaymen *Dick Turpin* and *Tom King* make an attractive equestrian pair in contrasting colours.

The most popular drama of the decade, however, would seem to have been a murder that prompted the various crime pieces centring around *James Rush* who was hanged in April 1849. Here some attempt has been made to contrast his chubby countenance with the lean austerity of *Emily Sandford* his chief witness in the murder of Isaac Jermy and his son: enthusiasts collect also the model of *Stanfield Hall*, scene of murders, and *Potash Farm* near Wymondham where Rush lived and which was mortgaged to Jermy who was threatening foreclosure. The naming of these buildings is somewhat casual. Comparable in popularity were the figures of *Frederick George Manning* and his wife *Maria* who in 1849 murdered her lover Patrick O'Connor and was hanged in November of the same year. Seven years later the poisoner *William Palmer* of Rugeley prompted the issue of two further crime pieces, of the criminal and of a trim villa *Palmer's House*.

Sportsmen of this decade include two top-hatted cricketers, wicket-keeper *Thomas Box* and batsman *Fuller Pilch* and the pugilist *Benjamin Caunt* who appears in a huge bust dated 1844, to be found, for instance, in Brighton Museum.

The 1850s began with an outburst against Popery which produced a number of figures, some with transfer-printed wordage and others showing more imaginative propaganda such as the burning of *Cranmer* and of *Latimer and Ridley*. Groups of children were modelled to mark the formation of the *Band of Hope Union* in 1851, to be followed later by other popular efforts to encourage total abstinence such as the *Independent Order of Good Templars* represented by at least two figure groups. Popular visitors to England in 1851 included the Hungarian patriot *Louis Kossuth,* and dress-reformer *Mrs. Amelia Bloomer* who caused much merriment, duly remembered in quaint little caricature figures titled merely *Bloomers*.

In the following year there was Wellington's death to commemorate, but the decade is dominated by the outbreak of the Crimean War in 1854. Here was abundant opportunity for the patriotic figures, the gay uniforms, the emotional outbursts that best suited this peasant art. Loyalty to the crown was declared by such groups as *TURKEY ENG-LAND FRANCE* showing a crowned Queen Victoria clasping the hands of Abdul Medjid, Sultan of Turkey, in red cap and frock coat, and Emperor Napoleon III, in blue tunic and high boots. Another group *THE ALLIED POWERS* shows Victoria between Napoleon and the King of Sardinia. Similar gestures may be noted among the troops, such as a French soldier fraternising with an English blue-jacket, a pile of shot between them. One finds various leaders of the fighting services—*Field-Marshal Lord Raglan, General Sir James Simpson, Marshal Saint-Arnaud, General Canrobert, General Pelissier, Omar Pasha* and many others with their flags, guns and similar accepted ornament. Some of them are also to be found on horseback. Even the fortress of *Sebastopol* is recorded.

Admirals Napier and Dundas were issued as a pair during 1854 and are unusual in being decorated with underglaze jet black, rarely used because of the difficulty in obtaining black from metallic oxides. The admirals stand bareheaded in naval uniforms flanked by guns and shells. Their names *C. NAPIER* and *DUNDAS* are in raised capitals on the plinths. Dundas (1785–1862) commanded the Mediterranean fleet in 1853–54 and Sir Charles Napier (1786–1860) the Baltic fleet 1854–55. Another version shows Napier with telescope in his right hand and his left foot on a gun.

On a less exalted level, wonderfully colourful soldiers and sailors were turned out in great numbers under such titles as *BRITAIN'S GLORY* and *SCOTLAND'S PRIDE* with bright details of uniforms from kilts to fezzes. Even the most familiar figure of *Florence Nightingale* shows her accompanied by a dashing wounded soldier, but several other portraits and busts of her may be found.

The Indian Mutiny in 1857–59 contributed a few more military leaders to the array of earthenware flat-backs and at least two different versions of the dramatic incident when *Highland Jessie* heard the bagpipes and exclaimed "The Campbells are coming" as the soldiers under Sir Colin

37. *Mercury on the Rock*. A figure in black basaltes impressed WEDGWOOD.
Height 18 inches. Made at Etruria in 1787.

38. Stoneware and terracotta figures by Doulton & Co., Lambeth. (*Top left*) *Atalanta* in white
stoneware modelled by John Broad. Late 19th century. (*Top right*) *The Potter* throwing a vase.
In terracotta, modelled by John Broad. Height 27 inches. Dated 1883. (*Lower left*) Queen
Victoria in state dress at the time of her jubilee. Modelled in terracotta by John Broad. 1887.
(*Lower right*) Winter, in dark green stoneware modelled by A. Beere. Height 7 inches. Late
19th century.

Campbell (another figure) marched in to relieve besieged Lucknow.

Brief respite from the theme of war came with the marriage of the *Princess Royal* to *Prince Frederick William of Prussia* in 1857. A later figure notes the Prince's new status of Crown Prince, acquired in 1861. For one marriage group the Prince is bareheaded, in uniform, and the Princess is a most gracious little figure at his side, her status declared by bands of ermine around her flower-sprigged dress. There are splendid equestrian figures of them too. These were soon followed by figures of the *Prince of Wales* celebrating his engagement to *Princess Alexandra of Denmark* in 1862, a somewhat less attractive pair here, perhaps, than his sister and her husband although there is no difficulty in observing a fine array of figures of the Prince throughout boyhood and youth as he graduated from kilt and Shetland pony to the fashionable dress of a man about town on a lively horse. The potters obviously enjoyed his gay taste in flowered waistcoats. His sailor brother *Alfred* may be noted as the pair for some of these figures.

This was the decade of the American Civil War (1861–65) and a few potters seized the opportunity to produce contrasting figures, white and negro. One finds *John Brown* with a couple of small negro children and several versions of *Uncle Tom with Little Eva* from *Uncle Tom's Cabin*.

By the 1860s, however, it appears that the greatest demand for new figures was over, or perhaps these later figures never commanded the affection that ensured preservation. The visit of *Garibaldi* to England in 1864, however, produced a rush of figures including a particularly lively model in which he stands beside his horse. In one model his companion is *Colonel Peard* and in another the two are paired. In 1870 pro-German feeling was roused briefly over the Franco-German war and figures were issued of *King William of Prussia, Queen Augusta* and the *Chancellor Bismarck*. The same decade produced figures as varied as the American revivalist preachers *Moody* and *Sankey, Pope Pius IX, Cardinal Manning* and a caricature of the Channel swimmer *Captain Webb*.

Impressive figures marked the marriage of *Prince Alfred,*

Duke of Edinburgh, to the daughter of the Czar of Russia in 1874 and yet another royal betrothal was recorded in 1891 with a delightful figure of *Princess May*—Princess Mary of Teck—whose fiancé, the Duke of Clarence, died before their wedding. *Gladstone* was modelled in the 1870s and as late as the 1890s. The 1880s included figures of *General Gordon*, one mounted on a massive camel, and as late as 1900 figures were still being issued of military heroes such as *Kitchener* and *Baden-Powell* but these generally lack the quality to arouse much enthusiasm today.

Such a list indicates no more than the general scope of these Victorian chimney ornaments. In his book *Staffordshire Portrait Figures of the Victorian Age* (1958) Thomas Balston lists a collection of nearly two hundred different characters in something like five hundred variations and always there is the hope that more will come to light as collectors look anew at their long-despised Victoriana.

Chapter Fourteen

PSEUDO-CLASSICAL figures and groups and portrait busts in porcelain suggesting the tones and texture of marble statuary ornamented innumerable early- and mid-Victorian middle-class drawing rooms, studies and vestibules. This graceful statuary was reminiscent of the ivory-tinted marbles quarried on the Island of Paros or the white carrara marbles of Tuscany and was known under the generic name of parian statuary. Two qualities were made: a soft-paste or frit parian and a hard-paste non-frit variety.

The earliest of these highly vitrified porcelains to be developed was the soft-paste parian, the culmination of long and arduous experiments by several Staffordshire potters. Success was first achieved by Copeland & Garrett, Stoke-upon-Trent, under the direction of Thomas Battam, art director of the firm from 1835 to 1864. The earliest figure in this ware to reach the china-sellers was *Apollo as the Shepherd Boy of Admetus* after the full-size marble statue by R. J. Wyatt, R.A., in the collection of the Duke of Sutherland at near-by Trentham Park. The duke was enthusiastic over his presentation copy and became Copeland's patron of this ware, which the firm referred to as porcelain statuary. Copeland released the *Shepherd Boy* to the London china-sellers on August 3, 1842, a date important in the annals of the Potteries as establishing a branch of ceramics which continued in its finest expression until the mid-1860s. The demand for lesser quality parian continued until early in the present century.

Simultaneously Herbert Minton & Co. were experimenting towards a similar objective, success being realised in 1844. They named their productions parian statuary. Later,

Josiah Wedgwood & Sons evolved a whiter but less translucent variant which they named carrara porcelain.

The Jury of the Great Exhibition, 1851, studied statements from Alderman W. T. Copeland and Herbert Minton and concluded that "whichever party may have actually been first in producing articles in this material, both were contemporaneously working with success towards the same result". The Jury also placed on record that Copeland's statuary porcelain, Minton's parian statuary and Wedgwood's carrara were merely less costly modifications of the white biscuit statuary made in the second half of the 18th century at Sèvres, Derby, Meissen and Berlin.

The *Art-Journal*, November 1859, declared that fifteen years earlier the magazine had been responsible for introducing porcelain statuary to the Art-Union of London at a time when it seemed possible that manufacture would be abandoned. "When we visited the works of Mr. Alderman Copeland—then Copeland & Garrett—at Stoke-upon-Trent, we witnessed the first efforts to secure popularity for the new art of Porcelain sculpture. Two statuettes had been produced in it, one a graceful female bust, and the other 'the Shepherd Boy', after Wyatt; but they had not 'sold'. The public showed no sign of being prepared to acknowledge the real worthiness of the novelty; and it is improbable that the process would have proceeded further, had it not been our good fortune to urge upon Mr. Garrett the wisdom of perseverance. A meeting was, in consequence, arranged by us between several sculptors, of whom Mr. Gibson was one, and Mr. T. Battam, the artist of the works. The two honorary secretaries of the Art-Union of London were also present. After a careful examination of the new material opinion was decidedly in its favour, Mr. Gibson declaring it to be 'the material next best to marble that he had ever seen', his brothers in Art agreeing. Mr. Gibson, at the same time, expressing a hope that some work of his might be suitable from Mr. Battam to produce in the Statuary-Porcelain. A commission from the Art-Union of London followed; and thus the new art of Parian sculpture was rescued from a peril, that might have proved fatal in the first infancy of its career."

39. An exceptionally finely modelled figure in Staffordshire earthenware.
Height 21 inches. About 1790.

40. Staffordshire earthenware figure of Ellen Bright, niece of George Wombwell, who became "The Lion Queen" in his menagerie at the age of 16. A year later whilst performing at Chatham in a cage with a lion and a tiger she was mauled to death by the tiger. Height 15 inches. 1850.

Thereafter lively competition existed between the Copeland and Minton firms as to which produced the finer parian until Worcester entered this field in 1853. Figures, groups and portrait busts were commissioned from celebrated sculptors, thus inaugurating a period of artistic animation unknown to the Potteries since the days of Josiah Wedgwood (d. 1795). Sculptors who responded to the demand included J. H. Foley, R.A., John Gibson, R.A., W. Calder Marshall, R.A., R. J. Wyatt, R.A., John Bell, R.A., Count D'Orsay and Baron Marochetti. More than three thousand models are known to have been made, measuring from two inches to nearly three feet in height.

The Staffordshire potters also supported several independent modellers to the trade such as Albert Carrier-Belleuse who supplied models to Copeland, Minton, Wedgwood, Brownfield, Mayer and others. Among the most skilful was William Beattie, Boothen, Stoke-upon-Trent, who modelled for Josiah Wedgwood & Sons from about 1850 to 1864; for Bates, Westhead & Co., Burslem, 1858 to 1862; for Sir James Duke & Nephews, Burslem, and for William Adams & Sons, Tunstall. Giovanni Meli, Rome Street, Stoke-upon-Trent, worked as an independent modeller at Little Fenton from the early-1840s before establishing his own parian factory in 1852. The name G. MELI has been noted impressed on several figure groups. He exhibited at the London International Exhibition, 1862. Two years later he sold his goodwill, plant and moulds to Robinson & Leadbeater and then returned to Italy. A year or two later he emigrated to Chicago where he established a successful terracotta factory. Joseph Brookes, David Chetwin, William Haslehurst, Noah Nash and George Reade were well-known figure modellers of the 1850s.

Reduced copies of original statuary were made from 1850 by the Benjamin Cheverton mechanical process. This patented machine was seen in operation at the Great Exhibition and is now in the Science Museum. The Jury awarded Cheverton a gold medal for his alabaster reduction of the equestrian figure of Theseus from the Elgin collection of marbles in the British Museum. It was later reproduced in parian statuary by Minton. This accounts for the inscription *Cheverton Sc* sometimes impressed with the original sculptor's name beneath the plinth of a piece of parian statuary.

Two qualities of parian ware were made: a soft-paste or frit parian and a non-frit hard-paste variety. These were fired by different methods: for frit porcelain air was introduced plentifully into the kiln and excluded for hard parian except for the minimum essential for combustion. Only highly skilled potters could handle the detailed work required by the costly frit formula. John Mountford, a Derby figure-maker employed by Copeland at the time that frit parian was invented, claimed to have evolved the hard-paste parian. The resulting statuary was distinctly inferior to that from the original formula but also much less costly.

It has been wrongly assumed by some authorities that the method of making parian statuary has been lost. Yet the entire process was detailed in *The Catalogue of the Great Exhibition*, 1851, by Thomas Battam and the accuracy of this has been confirmed to me by Mr. Gresham Copeland.

The body of frit parian statuary differed from biscuit in that it contained a larger proportion of felspar. The formula called for 40 parts felspar, 36 parts china clay and 24 parts frit: the frit contained 57 parts white sand, 11 parts Cornish stone and 8 parts potash. Each master potter tended to deviate from the standard formula however, with the result that makers of unmarked parian statuary may be identified occasionally by comparison with marked examples.

Air was introduced abundantly into parian kilns; thus the ware was fired in contact with an excess of carbonic acid. Small quantities of oxide of iron contained in the felspar oxidised when heated in this gas, the result being the formation of silicate of peroxide of iron, reddish brown in colour. This spread in small quantities through the mass and produced the pleasing tint that contributed so highly to the beauty of early parian statuary.

The original model was copied in wax or alabaster and this was cut into sections from which moulds were made. The mould-maker arranged that the castings should come from their moulds marked as little as possible with the "seams" that indicated where the parts of a mould were joined. A single figure might be represented by twenty or thirty moulds each containing a separate unit such as head, arm, leg, body, part of the drapery or other detail. Water was added to the finely powdered ingredients until the mass was of the consistency of thick cream ready to be poured into the hollow moulds. As explained in Chapter Eight the mould was made from plaster of paris and this quickly absorbed moisture from the creamy slip so that a solid coating formed upon its interior surface. When a suitable thickness had been deposited the surplus was returned to the casting jug. Evaporation converted the slip into a clay cast strong enough to bear its own weight when taken from the mould and sufficiently solid to be handled by the figure-maker or "repairer" who arranged all the pieces on a slab of plaster before him.

The casts were trimmed and assembled into a reproduction of the original model. The parts were attached by slip similar to that used for the casting, which softened the clay surface just enough to secure adhesion so that a perfect joint could be made, superfluous slip being removed with a camel's hair brush. Every part of the figure liable to warp or move during firing was supported by a network of props made from strips of clay of exactly the same composition and therefore subject to similar shrinkage in the kiln. The ends of the props were coated with powdered calcined flint to prevent adhesion.

Contraction during firing was one of the great difficulties encountered in the craft of porcelain manufacture, and castings contracted more than pressed work. Contraction ratios are known to the potters and a modeller made appropriate allowances in preparing the model which was proportionately larger than the finished figure. Shrinkage between the original model and the final figure approximated one-quarter, caused by loss of water and fusion of the particles. A figure originally 24 inches high emerged about 18 inches high having lost 1½ inches by contraction of the slip in the mould; 1½ inches through evaporation in the drying oven, and a further 3 inches during vitrification in the kiln. Sharpness of detail was accentuated by this shrinkage.

After standing in a warm room for two or three days the figure or group was ready for the biscuit kiln or drying oven, being by then sufficiently dry not to crack under heat. This firing continued for sixty to seventy hours: the fires were then drawn and the oven allowed to cool gradually. After removal the figure was released from its network of props and rubbed clean of scars.

It was then embedded in a sand-filled saggar and refired at a still greater heat. Although further contraction took place, the bedding of sand proved adequate support during vitrification, a process which gave statuary porcelain its distinctive surface texture. Parian has no visible glaze, yet to the touch there is a suggestion of dull polish.

The deep cream tint was lightened in much porcelain statuary from about 1853 by the introduction of near-pure felspar imported first from Ireland and later from Norway. W. H. Kerr & Co. of Worcester bought a considerable consignment of Irish felspar and in the spring of 1853 were advertising "Irish Statuary Porcelain Figures" (see Chapter Fifteen).

By then there was a tendency for the frit process to be replaced by a non-frit formula composed of 33 parts Cornish china stone and 67 parts felspar. Great heat was necessary to fuse these materials and air was excluded from the kiln. A single firing produced a hard-paste porcelain and the distortion hazard was greatly reduced. This statuary lacked the silky surface texture but smear-glazing produced a smooth dull surface closely resembling that of parian statuary. The glaze was introduced into the saggar either in a small cup or thickly painted over the walls of the saggar which was then tightly sealed. As the temperature increased, the glaze volatised and settled as fine mist on the surface of the ware. This parian could be fired repeatedly in a manner impracticable with the softer frit parian, thus permitting decoration in colours and gold.

Since the ware was developed to supply less costly imitations of marble statuary the subjects naturally tended to follow the lead of classical and neo-classical sculpture. Nude figures were immensely fashionable among middle-class Victorians: more than a hundred models have been

41. Staffordshire portrait figures: Crimean War 1854–56. (*Left and right*) Admirals Napier and Dundas were first issued during 1854 in 15-inch and 16-inch pairs. Admiral Sir Charles Napier (1786–1860) commanded the Baltic Fleet 1854–55. The figure bears the name C NAPIER in raised capitals. This figure has been wrongly attributed and named General Napier. Admiral Sir James Dundas (1785–1862) commanded the Mediterranean Fleet 1853–54. The figure is named DUNDAS in raised capitals. These figures are unusual as they are decorated with underglaze black, rarely used because of the difficulty in obtaining jet black from cobalt, manganese and iron oxides. (*Centre*) Queen Victoria with Victor Emmanuel II, King of Sardinia, at the time of his state visit to England in 1855.

42. (*Top left*) Spill-holder in the form of a hen in English majolica by Minton & Co., modelled by John Henk. (*Top right*) Spode comfit holder enamelled in indian red, yellow, green and blue. Marked Spode in red script. Height 6 inches. (*Bottom*) Derby figures in bone china, enamelled in colours. Modelled by Edward Keys in about 1830. Their wholesale price was seven shillings and sixpence each. (*Left*) Dr. Syntax landing at Calais. Marked N11, incised. Height 4⅝ inches. (*Right*) One of a pair of Canton girls. Height 5 inches.

noted, many from the Copeland firm. A celebrated Copeland nude was *The Greek Slave*. The original marble statue by the American Hiram Powers was a sensation at the Great Exhibition and was bought by the Duke of Cleveland for 1,800 guineas. A full-size model was made from this by Bruccini and casts were sold. One of these was exhibited in Copeland's Bond Street show rooms from April 1852. But by then this had already been reduced by the Cheverton process and reproduced in parian statuary: many thousands were sold during the next twenty years. Statuettes of *Venus* were in constant demand until the early 1860s. The Copeland firm issued at least seven: *Venus de Milo*, *Venus de Medici*, *Venus of the Capitol*, *Venus at the Bath*, and others after Canova, Thorwaldson and John Gibson. The Copeland figure *Narcissus* after John Gibson, R.A., is interesting as the first piece of parian statuary to be commissioned—in 1846—by the Art-Union of London, an organisation established in 1836 and legalised by incorporation ten years later to comply with the lottery laws. Subscribing members participated in an annual draw for prizes ranging from oil paintings priced at several hundred pounds to inexpensive steel engravings in limited editions. Parian statuary was included among the lesser prizes. Those commissioned were issued in editions of fifty with plinths impressed ART-UNION OF LONDON. The Art-Union awarded one hundred guineas to J. R. Foley, R.A. for the excellence of his reduced model *Innocence* which was reproduced in parian statuary by Copeland and sold at four guineas. In 1859 the Art-Union commissioned from Copeland thirty groups of *Venus and Cupid* and sixty statuettes of *The Dancing Girl Reposing*, both by Gibson.

Equestrian figures are now rare: although many were made few have escaped accidental destruction. Copeland's *Emanuel Philibert, Duke of Savoy*, after the Baron Marochetti, continued in demand for many years. This was first issued in 1844 and exhibited in 1851.

Lady Godiva, after J. P. McBride, was commissioned in parian statuary in 1850 by the Art-Union of Liverpool. Minton's equestrian figures included *Amazon* after Fauchere and *Theseus*, both issued in 1851.

The Veiled Vestal, after the marble by Raffaelle Monti, exhibited at the Great Exhibition and acquired by the Duke of Devonshire, represents a kneeling girl with a thin veil thrown over her face. The Jury remarked that "extraordinary skill is shown in the execution of this veiled figure, true judges of art must, however, always esteem it a mere specimen of dexterous workmanship". The bust from this figure, known as the *Veiled Bride*, was reproduced in parian by Copeland in 1861, fifty copies being impressed CRYSTAL PALACE ART UNION. This very popular bust was described by the Art-Journal as "a work of great beauty, wondrously executed".

Parian statuary was a considerable feature at the Great Exhibition, 1851. The list of "works in porcelain statuary" displayed by William Taylor Copeland, Stoke-upon-Trent and 160 New Bond Street, was catalogued as follows, the dates in brackets being the years of original production:

Group of Ino and the Infant Bacchus after J. H. Foley, R.A. from the original model in the possession of the Earl of Ellesmere (1849).
Group of the Prodigal's Return after William Theed (1850).
Sabrina and *The Last Drop* both after W. Calder Marshall (1849). The original marbles were exhibited at the Royal Academy in the previous year.
The Goatherd after the late R. J. Wyatt, R.A., from the original marble in the possession of the Duke of Sutherland.
Sappho after W. Theed, from the original marble.
Rebecca after W. Theed.
The Indian Girl and the Nubian Girl after Cumberworth (1849).
Head of Juno, life size, from the antique (1850). *The Astragali Players, The Girl with Scorpion.*
The Dancing Girl Reposing by W. Calder Marshall, R.A., executed for the Art-Union of London, 1859. This was advertised as in production 1860 and sold at four guineas.
Sir Walter Scott, reduced copy after John Steel, R.S.A., from the original colossal statue on the Calton Hill, executed for the Edinburgh Association for the Promotion of Fine Arts.
Group of *Graces* and group of *Cupids* as Kanephoroi.
H.R.H. the Princess Alice, as Spring; *H.R.H. the Princess Royal,* as Summer; *H.R.H. the Prince Alfred* as Autumn; *H.R.H.*

the Prince of Wales, as Winter all after originals commissioned by Queen Victoria from Mrs. Mary Thorneycroft (1848).
The Sea Nymph.
Group of *Paul and Virginia* after Cumberworth (1845).
Sir Robert Peel after Westmacott (1850).
Lord George Bentinck after Count D'Orsay.
Jenny Lind after Durham (1847).
Shakespeare (1846).
The Lady Clementina Villiers after M'Donald. An example has been noted impressed with the registration mark for December 4th, 1845.
H.R.H. the Princess Helena after Mrs. Thorneycroft.
Duke of Wellington after Count D'Orsay (1849).
Duke of Sutherland after Francis (1850).
Sir Henry Havelock after Morrison (1856).
The Return from the Vintage, an ambitious group consisting of seven youths bearing on their shoulders a vine-decked basket in which sits a laughing girl with a tambourine.

Popular parian statuary continued in production for many years. For instance, the Copeland figure of H.R.H. the Princess Alice, modelled by Mary Thorneycroft and issued in parian from 1848, appeared again thirty years later with the inscription "Mary Thorneycroft Sc Art Union of London 1879 Copeland".

The Copeland show rooms in New Bond Street during December 1859 devoted a corridor to the display of parian statuary. The *Art-Journal* of that month reported:

The groups, statuettes, busts and other compositions are arranged in two long lines on either side of the corridor, some of the more important specimens being brought together to form groups. In the adjoining saloons other specimens may be seen. Of the busts several are of the full life-size of the original marbles. The Queen and the Prince Consort are among the most successful. [The originals were carved at Osborne by Joseph Durham in the summer of 1855.] But the work that is the more admirable is the parian reproduction of the well-known Greco-Roman bust in the British Museum, known as *Clytie,* with the hair brought down so low on the forehead and the figure represented as if rising from a bud of the lotus. [This sold at three guineas.] The busts of *Juno* and *Ariadne,* of full size, are of great excellence; and those of *Ophelia* and *Miranda* by Calder Marshall are also very beautiful; and the reduced models of

183

them are more beautiful still. Among the busts of this smaller size is a charming one of *Jenny Lind*. A group of busts of Indian heroes, with Havelock at their head, require no special notice. Other busts of *Nelson* and *Wellington* range consistently with them: they include an admirable figure of the great Duke.

The exhibits may be divided into three classes: of these the second group consists of facsimile reproductions of well-known statues and groups on a greatly reduced scale; the second comprises a variety of original figure subjects modelled expressly for the statuary porcelain; and in the third group may be included miscellaneous subjects such as groups or figures of animals, vases, jugs and other similar objects.

Many are the familiar forms that we have known before of larger proportions, as *Sabrina*, *Sunshine* and the *Greek Slave* . . . our readers will find every subject here, from *Venus at the Bath* to *Paul and Virginia* and from the *Wounded Soldier* to the *Boy with a Shell*. There are some spirited dogs and noble horses.

Copeland issued several outstanding pieces of parian statuary in 1861. *The Toilet* (height 16 inches), a group after W. Calder Marshall, R.A. sold for five guineas. Copeland also made four busts for the Crystal Palace Art-Union, for sale at one guinea each: *Oenone* after W. Calder Marshall, *Enid, the Fair and Good* (of the Idylls of the King) after Felix Miller and *Peace and War* after Durham. These were also available on marble pedestals and enriched with gilding and partial tinting at two guineas each. Regarding the tinting the *Art-Journal* commented that it was "executed with a cautious delicacy that commands admiration even if it fails to establish a recognition of the legitimacy of colour in sculpture". At this time Copeland made wall brackets for supporting busts from a design by David Roberts, R.A. These sold at one guinea. *Caractacus*, an unusual statue by J. H. Foley, R.A., carved in marble for the Egyptian Hall, Mansion House, was reproduced by Copeland in 1861. *Night* and *Morning* by Monti were illustrated as the Copeland entry in the catalogue of the Exhibition of 1862. These ostentatious figures are on tall plinths with rectangular classical figure panels, front, sides and back.

Copeland issued a bust of H.R.H. Princess Alexandra modelled by F. M. Millar and commissioned by the Crystal Palace Art-Union and registered at the Patent Office on

February 23, 1863. The Princess was married to the Prince of Wales on March 10 of that year.

Alderman W. T. Copeland, M.P. in 1859 presented to the Museum of Lichfield a selection of statuary porcelain then in production at his works. These included eleven portrait busts: *Queen Victoria*; *Emperor Nicholas of Russia*; *Duke of Wellington*; *Lord Nelson*; *Lord John Russell*; *Lord Charles Bentinck*; *Sir Robert Peel*; *General Havelock*; *Samuel Donald O'Connell*; *Jenny Lind*. There were also eight decorative pieces of statuary: *Mother and Child*; *Fox and Terrier*; *The Bather Virginia*; *Boy and Shell*; *Boy and Rabbit*; *Modesty*; *Little Nell*.

At the Great Exhibition Minton displayed forty-six groups and figures: the dates in brackets are the years of first issue:

Two groups of *Children with Goat* after Carrier (1850).

Statuettes after John Bell: *Dorothea* (1847); *Miranda* (1850); *Una and the Lion* (registered October 4, 1847); *Triton and Nautilus*; the *Babes in the Wood* (1849); *the Infant Neptune* after H. J. Townsend; *the Distressed Mother* from the statue by Sir R. Westmacott; *Cupid Indignant* with pedestal festoons of raised flowers; *Temperance* (1849); *Flora*.

Groups: *Love Restraining Wrath* after William Beattie (1850); *Naomi and her Daughters-in-Law* (1848); *the Flight into Egypt* (1849).

Statuettes: *Mercury* after Thorwaldson; *Shakespeare* after John Bell (1848). The original marble was on view in the sculpture court. The likeness of the face had been taken from the bust over the poet's tomb at Stratford-upon-Avon. *Sir Robert Peel* (1850); *the Prince of Wales*.

Busts of *Michael Angelo* and *Raphael* after John Bell (1850). Statuettes: *Ariadne on a Panther* after Daneker (1847); *Atala and Chactas* (1850).

Candlesticks with figures in the costume of Louis XV.

Minton parian figures from 1862 included: *Bacchus* incised 355; busts of *Queen Victoria* and the *Prince Consort* incised 355 and 356; *Prince Alfred with his Shetland Pony* by Marochetti, incised 357; bust of *Clodian* incised 359; *Lady Godiva* incised 383; *Autumn* and *Summer*, a pair by Carrier-Belleuse, incised 384 and 385; *Perseus* and *Adromeda*, incised 425; *Dr. Livingstone*, incised 445; *Elaine*, incised 429;

Canadian Trapper, incised 465 ; *Pandora Opening the Fatal Box*; *Mercury Preparing to Stay Argus* after Thorwaldson; a pair of figures in the dress of Louis XV touched with gilt, mounted on pedestals touched with imitation gems.

The Jury of the Paris Universal Exhibition, 1855, recorded in their report several now rare parian figures by Minton. "The finest specimen in the Palais de l'Industrie seems to have been the bust of the Empress, modelled by the Count de Nieuwerkerke and executed by Mintons; and the superiority of the material which we use over that employed in France was clearly shown by the comparison of the large busts of the Emperor, one of which was produced by Mintons and the other by M. Gilles. . . . From among the vast number of works we would select for special mention Mr. Copeland's group of *Ino and Bacchus,* after Foley, Mr. Minton's *Highlanders,* his group *Cain and Abel* and above all his charming statue of *Lady Constance Grosvenor.* As far as regards beauty of form and admirable execution, it seems difficult to make any further progress."

Summerly's Art Manufactures, founded in 1847, commissioned in that year two parian figures from Minton, *Una and the Lion* and *Dorothea,* both after John Bell. The plinth of Dorothea is marked with a relief pad stamped JOHN BELL with Felix Summerly's cypher above and the Minton ermine mark below. A second pad is stamped with a diamond-shaped mark showing the design to have been registered at the Patent Office October 2, 1847. In the hollow of the base is the hand-incised Minton ermine mark; an arrow head with three dots at the point used on parian statuary until 1855; and No. 189. Impressed marks included the horseshoe-shaped year mark for 1855 and the letter N. The example illustrated has several firecracks.

The amazing success of Copeland and Minton in this branch of ceramics prompted many other Staffordshire potters to make parian figures but few used the frit formula which gave sharpness of detail and fine surface texture.

Josiah Wedgwood & Sons, Etruria, gave the name carrara to their statuary. The catalogue of the Great Exhibition records the following:

Figures from the antique: *Venus and Cupid,* 27 inches;

Cupid, 24 inches; Infant *Hercules*, 20 inches by 17; *Morpheus*, 24 inches long; *Venus*, 19 inches high; *Mercury*, 17 inches high; *Faun with Flute*, 17 inches high.

Figures: *The Preacher on the Mount*; *Crouching Venus*; *Nymph at the Fountain*; *Cupid and Psyche* group; *Cupid with Bow*.

Busts of *Washington*; *Shakespeare* on pedestal; and *Venus*. *Sleeping Boys*.

In addition the *Art-Journal* 1849 referred to *Triton*, *Diana* and an *Infant Bacchus*, and later there were figures of Venus, nymphs and copies of antique statues and *Charity* by Carrier-Belleuse. The *Art-Journal* of 1859 reported that Wedgwood's "bust of Stephenson, reduced from the bust by E. W. Wyon is certainly the best likeness of the great engineer." This was marked WEDGWOOD & SONS.

Many companion pairs of parian figures were made by Charles Meigh & Sons, Hanley. Their Great Exhibition display included: "Statuettes (Parian) of various kinds: *Templar and Companion*; *Falconer and Companion*; *Bather and Companion*; *Cupid and Venus*; *Dancer and Companion*; *Flora*; *Prometheus*.

"Ornamental clock, subject *Night and Morning*, with a figure of Silence on the top."

"Heads of *Dr Adam Clarke*, *Sir Robert Peel*, *Shakespeare* and *Napoleon*."

The impressed mark C M & S has been noted on *The Templar*.

The catalogue of the Great Exhibition lists the parian statuary displayed by several other potters.

T. & R. Boote, Burslem, showed: "Parian allegorical group and figures. *Rustic* group. Statuettes in parian, about 20 inches high, *Shakspeare*, *Milton*, *Venus*, &c. Parian bust of *Sir Robert Peel*, from the painting by Sir Thomas Lawrence. This has been noted with the impressed mark T & R B. Allegorical group, *Repentance, Faith and Resignation*," 1850–60.

Keys & Mountford, Newcastle-under-Lyme, announced as designers, inventors and manufacturers of porcelain statuary, exhibited: "Statuettes of *Flora*, *Prometheus Tormented by the Vulture*, *Venus Unrobing at the Bath*, *Venus Ex-*

tracting a Thorn, and two Circassian slaves. Group of *Two Dogs, Setter and Pointer with Game.* Group of *Three Greyhound Dogs.*"

Thomas, John & Joseph Mayer, Dale Hall, Burslem, showed: "Bust of Wesley, from the original mould belonging to the late Enoch Wood, Esq., the sculptor" (see page 155). This bust should not be confused with the parian bust of Wesley by T. Hughes, modeller and designer, Cobridge. Albert Carrier-Belleuse who modelled many statuary groups and figures for Minton, also modelled for the Mayer firm. Following the lead of Copeland, this firm might add touches of colour, blue, pink and green, to their parian statuary.

John Rose & Co., Coalbrook Dale, Ironbridge, Shropshire (Coalport) listed: "Parian—pair of wrestling figures; *The Pleides adorning Night;* large group, *Puck and Companions* from 'A Midsummer Night's Dream'." Already in 1849 Rose had issued *The Cornish Wife at the Well of St. Keyne* and *Bacchus and Ariadne.* After the death of the Duke of Wellington in 1852, Coalport reproduced his bust after Weigall and a statuette after Abbot showing the duke seated and wearing a plain frock coat. These bear the name of Daniell, New Bond Street, by whom they were commissioned. At the Dublin Exhibition 1855 Coalport displayed a group from *The Faerie Queene.* A bust has been noted inscribed on the front of the plinth *H.R.H. P of Wales* and on the back *John Rose Coalport February 18th 1863.*

Robinson & Leadbeater, Stoke-upon-Trent, originally professional modellers, specialised in parian ware and for many years made nothing else. In 1864 they bought the moulds, plant and machinery of Giovanni Meli of Rome Street (see page 177). Robinson & Leadbeater used a frit body and their productions were usually in the original cream tint. L. Jewitt in 1878 listed some of their groups, figures and busts: *Innocence Protected, Penelope, The Power of Love, Cupid Betrayed, Cupid Captive, Golden Age, Rock of Ages, Edwardian Angel, The Immaculate Conception, Christ and St. John, Virgin and Child.* Their busts included *Clytie,* 22 inches in height; *Gladstone; Disraeli; Cobden; Dickens; Tennyson* and other celebrities. *Abraham Lincoln, Charles Sumner* and *Governor Andrew* had extensive sales in the United States.

43. (*Top*) Pair of Staffordshire earthenware figures of the prize-fighters. Tom Crib, world champion 1811–1821, and the negro Tom Molineaux. Early 19th century. (*Bottom*) Horse in pearl-ware, standing on oblong plinth. Eyes, nose, ears, mane, tail and hooves painted black; harness painted yellow with blue medallions; plinth green, blue and purple. Height 16 inches. Leeds Pottery, about 1800.

44. Early English figure pottery. (*Top, left and right*) Lion and lioness in olive coloured glaze mounted by Cupids, height 8 inches; large model of a lion in natural colours on green and brown plinth, height 9¾ inches, length 12 inches. (*Second shelf, centre*) Whieldon owl on rocky base, in deep rich brown glaze. Height 9 inches. (*Third shelf*) Ralph Wood camel in rich brown glaze, on rectangular plinth in white and brown. Height 7½ inches. Whieldon water buffalo in cream ware mottled in brown and white glazes, copied from a Chinese model. Height 6 inches. About 1755. Elephant in natural colours. Height 7½ inches. (*Bottom shelf, centre*) Large figure of a stag by Ralph Wood in white glaze splashed chocolate brown, on shaped plinth with acanthus leaves in green and slight traces of blue. Height 13 inches.

Robinson & Leadbeater, like Copeland and Minton, made portrait busts for private sale. Their mark was R & L impressed.

Bates, Westhead & Co., successors of John Ridgway, Shelton, in 1859 produced a parian bust of George Frederick Handel. This was modelled by William Theed from Roubilliac's famous statue to mark the centenary of the composer's death. The *Art-Journal* reported that the bust was produced in three sizes and impressed B W & Co.

J. Bell & Co., Glasgow, 1842–80, was perhaps the only Scottish pottery to manufacture parian statuary. Although ornamental domestic ware was shown at the Great Exhibition, no figures were included. But at the Dublin Exhibition, 1853, they showed statuettes of *Dante, Petrarch, Kilmeny* (from the Queen's Wake and modelled by Mossman), and a bust of Jenny Lind. These were impressed with a bell bearing the initials J.B.

Among the hundred or more potters of parian statuary the following have been selected as typical:

Adams, William & Sons, Stoke-upon-Trent. Made statuary after models by William Beattie and Giovanni Meli until 1864. Mark: ADAMS impressed.

Alcock, Samuel, Hill Pottery, Burslem. Made biscuit and parian statuary, late 1840s to 1859. Impressed S A in monogram, S A & Co. or SAMUEL ALCOCK.

Bailey, John, Hanley. Made at least three figures of Venus. Early 1860s. Impressed J.B.

Beech & Podmore, Burslem. Parian chimney ornaments and toys for the home market and for export to America, the East Indies and Australia. 1864 to late 1870s. Impressed mark B & P.

Dudson, James, Hope Street, Hanley, 1850s to 1882. Japanese figures impressed J.D.

Duke, Sir James & Nephews, Hill Pottery, Burslem. This pottery was taken over from Samuel Alcock in 1859. In 1861 they potted a full-length portrait statuette (height 17½ inches) of *Lord Elcho* in the uniform of the London Scottish. Copied from a marble by Beattie, this figure was

Facsimiles of the key to the registration marks used at the Patent Office Registry of Designs 1842–83 (see page 192)

Registry of Designs

Index to the letters for each month & year from
1868 to 1883

Year		Month	
1868	X	January	C
1869	H	February	G
1870	C	March	W
1871	A	April	H
1872	I	May	E
1873	F	June	M
1874	U	July	I
1875	S	August	R
1876	V	September	D
1877	P	October	B
1878	D	November	K
1879	Y	December	A
1880	J		
1881	E		
1882	L		
1883	K		

(Registration Marks brought in with W for the Year on them see 1st to 6th of March 1878)

Class

date

Parcel

year

month

1878

From 1st to 6th March the following Registration Mark was issued

Rᴰ W instead of Rᴰ D 1878

G   W March

H.S.C. Kingsford
16 October 1884

described in the *Art-Journal* as "an excellent example of miniature portrait sculpture and a characteristic likeness". At the London International Exhibition, 1862, this firm exhibited *Innocence Protected* also after Beattie.

Grainger, George, St. Martins, Worcester, whose figure *Medusa* is impressed with her name and GEORGE GRAINGER 1845 was probably the first model made outside Staffordshire. Parian statuary continued in production until the firm was absorbed by .the Royal Worcester Porcelain Company in 1889.

Sale, William, Bryan Street, Hanley. Made coloured and white parian statuary during the 1860s. Impressed w SALE.

Stanway, Horne & Adams, Joiner Square, Hanley. Specialised in cheap parian figures, groups and portrait busts. Jewitt recorded that at least 400,000 pieces were sold in a year, the quality and the body being good and modelling clever. *Commerce* seated was one of their most effective figures. 1859 to 1880s. No mark.

Steele, Edward, Hanley. Jewitt recorded that this firm made "some hundreds of different single figures, groups, busts and animals, many of large size". Mid-1870s to 1889. No mark.

Sutherland, Daniel, Longton. Established 1865. Early productions marked S & S.

Turner, Bromley & Hassall, Stoke-upon-Trent. Exhibited groups and statuettes at the London International Exhibition, 1862. No marks.

Wardle, James, Hanley. Specialised in portrait busts. Mid-1860s to 1879. Impressed marks J W and WARDLE & CO.

Wayte & Ridge, Longton. Mid-1860s. Impressed mark W R above L noted by Haggar on the figure of a beggar wearing the Victoria Cross.

The diamond-shaped registration mark found impressed upon some parian statuary and usually accompanied by the potter's name shows that the design was registered at the Patent Office and so obtained three years of protection against copying by competitors. Although this mark does

45. Sporting figures: (*left to right*) Sportsman with dog on a rocky base and square plinth. A hare hangs at his right side. Black hat and boots, mauve coat, olive green breeches. Height 9 inches. Third quarter of 18th century. Rare Ralph Wood bull baiting group. Height 8½ inches. Cockerel on shaped green base, with red comb and white ground splashed with green, yellow, brown and blue. Height 8 inches. Pair of boxers, both representing Gentleman Humphreys the prize-fighter. The left hand figure is in white except for yellow-splashed tunic and brown shoes; in the other, the tunic is splashed blue, brown and yellow, breeches blue, hair and tree-stump brown, base green. Height 8 inches. (*Front*) Whieldon fox reclining on a rocky base, right forepaw resting on a fowl. The fox is brown, the base splashed green, blue and brown. Height 2½ inches. About 1760.

46. Whieldon and early Ralph Wood figures. (*Left to right*) Unique pair of Whieldon figures of a shepherd and shepherdess on tall plinths, tortoiseshell glazed. Height 6½ inches. Seated figure of a Chinaman in plain manganese and blue-grey glazes. Height 3 inches. By Whieldon, about 1750. Agate ware cat decorated with yellow, orange and brown marbled clays in plain lead glaze, the base unglazed. Height 6¼ inches. About 1730. Pieman, one of the earliest Ralph Wood figures, probably modelled by Aaron Wood, with clear glaze, the pies in brown clay. The typical early Ralph Wood impressed markings round the base. Height 6½ inches. About 1745.

not display a date, its symbols may be interpreted to give the exact day of registration. The earliest of these marks so far noted in connection with parian statuary appears on Copeland's *Philibert, Duke of Savoy,* registered November 4, 1844 (see pages 190 and 191).

Chapter Fifteen

WORCESTER PARIAN AND IVORY PORCELAIN

THE Royal Worcester Porcelain Works under the direction of the Chamberlain family during the 1840s passed through a period of intense depression. In 1851, however, just a century after its foundation by Dr. John Wall and his fourteen partners (see page 80) the decaying business came under the sole control of W. H. Kerr of Dublin who invited Richard W. Binns to join him as artistic director. Binns had been practising as a designer of ceramics at No. 58 Baker Street, London. At the Great Exhibition he displayed a "miniature fountain for conservatory, with group of parian statuary in the centre throwing water. The vase and pedestal of Japanned slate." Use of the term "parian statuary" suggests that the group was made by Minton.

Considering it unwise to continue old styles and traditions, Kerr and Binns introduced a prestige-building programme. Binns later recorded that they "attempted to revive in Worcester the pure lines of Grecian vases and another departure was the modelling of statuettes". New techniques were introduced into mills, kilns and workshops and buildings were modernised.

A department was established for the modelling of figures in the form of parian known at the time as statuary porcelain (see previous chapter). Kerr's attention was drawn to the fact that large deposits of felspar were available on the Castle Caldwell estate near Fermanagh in Northern Ireland, and were claimed to be virtually pure. Early in 1852 experiments on test consignments confirmed that the Irish felspar was indeed of greater purity than any known English deposits. This discovery had far-reaching effects upon Worcester porcelain throughout the Victorian period.

Kerr immediately began the manufacture of statuary porcelain and by the spring of 1853 skilfully modelled figures were in production. In the catalogue of the Dublin International Exhibition of that year the firm was entered as W. H. Kerr & Co., Royal Porcelain Works, Worcester, although later advertisements perpetuated the name of the former proprietors in the works title "Chamberlains Royal Porcelain Works". Their chief exhibit was a magnificent dessert service for twenty-four persons in a combination of statuary porcelain and lead-glazed bone china, enriched with relief ornament and gilded with Irish gold. This was known as the Shakespeare service, the free-standing statuary constituting the supports of epergnes and tazze representing characters from *A Midsummer Night's Dream*. Designed by R. W. Binns and modelled by W. B. Kirk, son of a well-known Irish sculptor, the service was catalogued as "manufactured from materials principally the produce of Ireland". Other statuary porcelain exhibits were busts of the *Duke of Leinster, W. Dargan* and *Sir Robert Kane* by J. E. Jones, and *Uncle Tom and Eva* by W. B. Kirk who later in the year modelled portrait busts of Mr. and Mrs. R. W. Binns for private circulation. The demand for statuary porcelain created by the Irish Exhibition prompted Kerr & Binns to establish three depots or sales branches in Ireland and the United, States of America: James Kerr & Son, Dublin; W. J. Kerr, China Hall, New York, and W. J. Kerr, Philadelphia.

Groups and figures made at Worcester during the Kerr-Binns period ending in 1862 were: *Lady Macbeth*, 15 inches, and *Hafid and the Fireworshippers* from Moore's "Lalla Rookh", 14 inches, both by Kirk in 1855; *Faust and Marguerite* by Kirk, sometimes slightly gilded, 12 inches, 1858; *Paolina Bonaparte as Venus*, after Canova, 23 inches long, 1860; *Venus Rising from the Sea*, 15 inches, 1860; *Plenty* (group), 10½ inches, 1860; *Peace*, 12½ inches, 1860; statuette of *Robert Stephenson* by Durham; bust of *James Watt*, 1862, described by George Wallis as "the best portrait statuette ever produced in parian".

These figures usually bear the firm's standard trade mark, a circle containing four script Ws with a Worcester crescent and the figure 51 in the centre. This might be impressed or transfer-printed over the glaze. A mark occasionally used during the mid-1850s was a transfer-printed crown within two concentric circles enclosing the name w. h. kerr & co, worcester.

Figures made when the firm had been converted into a joint stock company, after Kerr's retirement in 1862, under the name of the Royal Worcester Porcelain Company include: *Autumn* and *Winter*, a pair, 20 inches, 1870; *Boy* and *Girl*, figures of Boucher rustics, a pair, 20 inches, 1870; *Seated Boy and Girl*, dressed in the Kate Greenaway style, modelled by J. Hadley and decorated in dry colours and gold, 4 inches, 1884. The mark then included a crown.

The standard mark was retained as above. Until 1867 the crown was open-cage topped; from 1868 to 1890 the crown possessed a velvet cap with the top bars enriched with laurel leaves. Beneath this was a date letter: a Gothic A for 1867 changing each year to Z in 1888, O in 1889 and a lower-case a in 1890. Thereafter the top bars were enriched with pearls.

The production of hard statuary parian at Worcester prompted the development of a variant, achieved in 1856 and named ivory porcelain. This was ideal for figures, groups and ornamental ware. The first specimens were decorated in the style of Italian Capodimonte porcelain of the 18th century and promoted by Worcester as Raphaelesque porcelain. Original Capodimonte figures were in a cold white soft-paste porcelain, sparsely decorated, the slight colouring accentuating the beauty of both form and glaze. The soft ivory tone used in the Worcester version tended to enrich colour effects.

Experiments were carried out over a long period in an effort to find a glaze that would give the surface of this porcelain the texture of ivory as well as the tone. By 1872 this had been achieved. Professor Archer in the *Art-Journal*, July 1873, described it as "a variety having instead of the creamy yellow of ordinary English parian [frit-parian] an equally soft pearly grey like freshly cut ivory".

This invention was made early in the quarter-century when industrial art was dominated by the vogue for the style then termed Japanesque. The ivory porcelain, resembling the tint of Japanese Satsuma porcelain, was ideal for such work. *The Times*, June 4, 1873, reported of Worcester's Japanesque figures in ivory porcelain that "the draperies, enamelled in colours, have a flow and freedom not to be found in native models". The *Art-Journal* in 1873 commented on the difficulty of making figures in ivory porcelain, "half a dozen failures occurring before a faultless work is produced. This once overcome, the peculiar ivory appearance is given by a warm, almost cream-tinted enamel, the process of firing being stopped at an intermediate state between biscuit and glaze. . . . We must note two exquisite figures by Hadley, of a Japanese lady and gentleman, remarkable alike for modelling and decoration."

The ivory porcelain formed a delicate ground for gold alloyed to various tints such as yellow, green and bronze in imitation of the Japanese style. Several unusual varieties of decoration requiring outstanding technical skill were introduced with ivory porcelain. Handsome figures were made by combining this porcelain with oxidised metal, particularly silver, also in association with the pale willow-green glaze known as celadon.

Ivory porcelain figures include: *Faust and Marguerite* by Kirk, 12 inches, 1858; *Infant Bacchus and Companion* in colours and gold, 2¾ inches, 1860; the *Boy Jesus and the Boy St. John the Baptist,* decorated in oxidised metal, 4½ inches, 1865; *Youth and Girl* in the style of Boucher rustics, 19½ inches, 1870; *Mermaid and Merman* holding shells modelled by J. Hadley, 15 inches, 1877; pair of *Boys on Dolphins* decorated in the Capodimonte style, 5 inches, 1875; four *Putti* in the Capodimonte style, 7 inches, 1878; pair of *Putti with Trumpet and Cymbals,* undecorated, 6 inches, 1877; *Violinist,* 19¾ inches, 1899. A collection of Worcester ivory porcelain figures shown at the Chicago Exhibition, 1893, which received widespread praise included the rare bust of *Queen Victoria* mounted on a tall pedestal decorated in relief.

During the early 1870s figures and portrait busts were potted in a coloured porcelain imitating terracotta. The statuettes, draped in an exceptionally smooth turquoise blue enamel glaze, were modelled by James Hadley, chief modeller until 1875. Hadley resigned to become an independent modeller but for twenty years he worked almost exclusively for the Royal Worcester Porcelain Company.

Worcester's spectacular success with statuary porcelain and ivory porcelain figures incorporating Irish felspar in the formulas was directly responsible for the establishment in Ireland of a parian pottery. This was built at Belleek, Co. Fermanagh, on a small island in the River Erne, about six miles from the sea and accessible to small coastal craft. This adjoined the Castle Caldwell estate from which Worcester drew its supplies of felspar. Here about 90 per cent of raw materials and also ample fuel were immediately available without costly transport problems. A 100-horse-power water-wheel made by Fairbairn of Manchester provided power for operating machines for grinding, mixing and the like.

By the autumn of 1857—the date printed on the firm's notepaper heading—the pottery was in production, trading as M'Birney & Armstrong. David M'Birney, a wealthy Dublin tradesman, proprietor of a store then advertised as "the Largest and Most Complete in the Three Kingdoms", was the financing partner and the first retailer of Belleek porcelain.

At first they manufactured "ordinary useful goods in parian" but soon they began to make statuary parian, some of it incredibly large and complicated, such as *The Prisoner of Love*, height 25½ inches, the magnificent equestrian group *Richard Cœur de Lion* from Marochetti's statue facing the House of Lords, and *Erin Awakening from her Slumbers,* height 18 inches. A Belleek modeller of outstanding skill was William Gallimore. Unfortunately by the bursting of a gun he lost his right arm. Moving to Staffordshire he set up as an independent modeller at Hanley and excelled in portrait busts. Jewitt, whose portrait bust he modelled for William Henry Goss, records that modelling carried out entirely with his left hand was far better than his earlier work.

The Belleek firm found that they could give their parian an entirely smooth surface by glazing it with a pearly white lustre, then newly patented by a Frenchman, Jules Brianchon. This resinous lustre gave Belleek parian an iridescence suggesting pearl shell. Slight decoration in enamels and gold might be added, commonly green and pastel pink which could be fired together in a muffle kiln at a temperature too low to melt the lustrous glaze.

M'Birney and Armstrong ploughed back the profits and more into their statuary parian work, employing outstanding modellers and highly skilled operatives to a number exceeding two hundred. Both partners died in 1884 and the pottery was sold as a running concern to a group of business men seeking profit rather than artistic kudos.

Belleek parian statuary was invariably marked. Early pieces were impressed BELLEEK POTTERY beneath the base. From about 1865 a transfer-printed trade-mark was usual, composed of an Irish wolf hound, harp and round tower with the name BELLEEK below in a ribbon flanked by shamrock leaves. BELLEEK, CO. FERMANAGH might be impressed on the rim of the plinth.

Chapter Sixteen

ANIMALS AND BIRDS

FIGURES of animals and birds have always appealed to the potter, results ranging from superb little primitives to attempts at individual portraiture, expressed in every kind of ceramic ware. Subjects have included lions, usually royal or heraldic rather than ferocious and more rarely other exotics such as elephants and buffaloes taken from Chinese porcelain, monkeys from Meissen and a few, such as giraffes in the 1820s, modelled to mark the arrival of such curiosities in this country. Farm animals abound such as cows and goats and astonishingly numerous sheep. Chelsea, for example, made delightful sheep to set among their idyllic pastoral figures and earthenware potters copied the sheep more successfully than the shepherdesses. Horses belong mainly to figure groups but other domestic animals are plentiful, ranging from occasional rabbits and guinea pigs to cats and far more numerous dogs.

Birds are a specialist study on their own, covering alike the whole range of the gentleman's aviary and game preserves and the cottagers' canaries and barnyard fowl. Owls, like captive bears, have always suggested vessel forms, found in early Lambeth wine pots, for instance, and in the golden brown stoneware jugs of Nottingham, "rough cast" with shreds of clay in the manner associated, for instance, with the Morley firm through much of the 18th century.

For a chronological survey the student can begin with primitive slip ware of as early as the 17th century. A vigorous 17th-century hen on a posset pot lid in the Fitzwilliam Museum has been attributed to Donyatt, Somerset. This piece is interesting for an unusual method of representing

200

the plumage—crucial consideration in bird figures. Here the red clay body has been covered in white slip and this has been scored with a sharp tool to show feather patterning in underlying red. A 17th-century cream pot in the same museum in light red clay is treated in a more usual manner, the surface striped and spotted with applied slip in white and red: this takes the form of a plump cat, sitting on its haunches, remarkable for its air of complacency. In the main however existing slipware animals date to the 19th century (see page 152).

A rarity of the early 18th century in the Fitzwilliam Glaisher Collection is a hound in Lambeth delft ware, a medium seldom applied to figure work. This is spotted in blue and yellow and red, its collar inscribed *ANN WITTIN 1717*. Appropriately, this watch dog is a money box: animals made solely as ornaments only gradually came into fashion when English porcelain men took up the Meissen notion of making ornaments to garnish the tables for fruit banquets and desserts in place of perishable figures in wax and sugar and marzipan.

Chelsea of the early raised anchor and red anchor periods (1747–56) issued some splendidly modelled soft porcelain birds and such animals as mountain sheep with long silky-looking wool and dogs, especially pugs in the Meissen manner. These are now museum rarities that may sell for many hundreds of pounds (see Chapter One). Bow, Derby and Longton Hall, too, issued birds, lions, pug dogs in the 1750s: these may be found in the white or splendidly coloured in enamels. William Duesbury's account book, 1751–53, lists many pheasants, parrots, goldfinches, owls and the like which passed through his hands when he was still a porcelain decorator in London.

Even in the mid-18th century there was still a tendency for the potter to find some purpose for a bird or animal figure and Chelsea and Bow introduced such models as impressive covered tureens: the Chelsea list of designs includes various game birds, swan, hen with chicks, fish, rabbit, boar's head. The sitting hen in particular continued popular far into Victorian days as an egg holder and can be collected in a range of ceramics and qualities. Chelsea also made small scent bottles shaped as squirrels, pug dogs and birds. But the most delightful of these early soft porcelain creatures are the bird figures intended merely for table and cabinet ornament—hawks, partridges, parrots and the like which possess a lively vigour of pose and colour that were never equalled by the more laborious and charming Derby peacocks on flower-encrusted stands and finches among flowering branches. Longton Hall is credited with a few birds and some powerful models of a phoenix, coloured and in the white, are found in the hard porcelain of Plymouth.

The fashion for birds in porcelain was all too brief but the theme was taken up by the earthenware potter catering for cottage folk wanting representatives of familiar hens and roosters, and for their successors in the factory towns with nostalgic memories of the wicker cage by the cottage door. The mannered style of porcelain was revived to some extent in early 19th-century bone china, however, when Derby, for instance, issued meticulously painted birds among delicate flower encrustations. Spode made some small bone china birds such as thrushes and occasionally a Chamberlain Worcester parrot comes to light, brilliant in plumage of red and green and yellow. Rockingham made miniature parrots some two and a half inches high in the 1820s but is more famous for its poodle dogs. Both Derby and Rockingham issued sheep in the Chelsea manner with notably woolly fleeces, these animals being colourless except for their bright green bases. Derby made bone china squirrels, too, now nearly as rare as their well modelled animals in white biscuit porcelain.

Most obvious imitation of porcelain in the mid-18th century was white salt-glazed stoneware and some splendid bird figures with alert heads and considerable surface detail were made in this ware by the methods described in Chapter Eight. Animals are to be noted, too, in obvious imitation of porcelain models, such as pugs and poodles.

The earliest creatures in the white stoneware menagerie may be all white except for eyes of brown slip. Successive styles produced white birds with eyes, beaks and a few details of legs and plumage touched in blue and the most brilliant specimens painted in enamel colours. A pair of swans in the Victoria and Albert Museum have necks and bodies painted purple and turquoise blue and wings in blue, green, red, orange and yellow. William Duesbury's account book makes reference to such "swiming swans donn all over".

Contemporaneous with these and in striking contrast were the birds and animals in lead-glazed earthenware issued by Whieldon and his rivals in the mingled colour glazes known as tortoiseshell ware. Simplicity of outline and formal incised detail well suited the soft mottled greens and greys and browns of these owls, hawks, pigeons, game birds and animals now attributed to Whieldon. Animals of the 1750s–60s included lions, monkeys, deer, such dogs as greyhound and spaniel and cats that were peculiarly well suited by the soft marking in manganese purple and brown. The horses in tortoiseshell ware equestrian figures are worth noting for their lively, representational treatment, such as the delightful model dated to about 1745 in the Victoria and Albert Museum carrying a lady riding side-saddle.

The alternative for animal figures at this period was agate ware (see pages 135 and 136). This resulted in some re-markably effective dogs, deer and again most especially cats for which the blended clays produced suitably haphazard markings, frequently supplemented by touches of blue. Sometimes an agate cat holds a grey or brown mouse: this was an endlessly popular theme, now too often assumed to be early work but found, for example, as late as the mid-19th century in a red and white slipware specimen made by Fishley of Fremington, North Devon, now in the Fitz-william Museum.

When Ralph Wood and his contemporaries in the 1770s–80s brush-applied these limpid colour-glazes the emphasis was still on decorative effect rather than naturalistic exacti-tude. A lion, say, or a fox carrying a rabbit, might be slate blue, green and purple as well as tones of brown and yellow.

The introduction of high-temperature underglaze colours in the 1790s (see page 141) resulted in many more prosaic bird and animal figures such as the crudely shaped cock and hen in the Victoria and Albert Museum whose colour scheme is dominated by the thick orange tones applied to combs, beaks, legs and tails in contrast to bodies streaked with blue, and blue and brown feathers in wings and tails. The Glaisher Collection of animals in these high-temperature colours includes a tiger, leopard and cat mainly in tones of brown and another cat more interestingly dabbed in blue and orange and olive green.

Cow milk jugs were popular for nearly a century and many are to be noted in this style of ornament. The design was introduced by the silversmith John Schüppe in the 1760s. The animal's tail serves as a handle and its mouth for pouring and there is a lidded opening on the back for filling. The vessel was difficult to clean thoroughly and went out of favour when the 19th century became hygiene-conscious with the cholera epidemic of the 1850s. Probably it was used mainly as an ornament for other cow models in Staffordshire earthenware are legion and, like the jugs, include many reproductions. The collector looks for the more imaginative models such as one with head turned to a raised back leg where sometimes a snake is attacking. A familiar design with a pair of cows propping up small subsidiary human figures is attributed to the Pratt firm of Fenton.

When potters devised economical ways of colouring their birds and animals overglaze their bright colours and gilding were rivalled only by the peculiarly effective metallic lustres associated with the years around the Regency. Among subjects, lions continued popular, especially the model with one forepaw on a globe. Leeds made many of these in several sizes up to twelve inches long and sometimes coloured. But their origin has been ascribed to many potters and possibly they may have been inspired by the marble lions at the Loggia de' Lanzi, Florence. Many farm animals were made and again especially sheep and lambs. But dogs were already becoming more popular and tend to dominate the animal figures in the white glazed earthenware of the Victorian chimney ornament.

Marks are rare among pottery animals and birds and similar models were popular throughout the industry. A collector's choice must depend upon his appreciation of good design, clean potting and imaginative colour work. Some large horses in pearl ware about eighteen inches tall and fifteen inches long may be ascribed to Leeds, however. These fine animals were intended for shop display by those dealing in horse equipment, foodstuffs and medicaments and date mainly 1800–20. They all appear to have been made from the same mould with head turned to the right and stand on oblong plinths. Colours vary between white and buff tones, and they are usually piebald. One in Leeds City Art Gallery has eyes, ears, nose, mane, tail and hooves painted black, yellow harness decorated with blue medallions and a plinth in green, blue and purple. Those potted after 1820 were coarser and heavier than earlier examples. A named model of a horse in earthenware is a rarity, such as the eighteen-inch *Eclipse* in the Willett Collection.

Lions are among the animals especially associated with Thomas Rathbone of Portobello (see page 163) and have been noted measuring as much as ten and a half inches long. But it is evident that he made a range of domestic animals and birds. Lions were also issued by the Scottish Bo'ness Potteries: in 1836 Jameson & Co. introduced Staffordshire workers and methods and the firm specialised in chimney ornaments until its closure in 1889, including also cats and rabbits, cockatoos, ducks, hens and other birds, comforter dogs and various other breeds including specimens which stood on four feet without pedestals.

Lions in the posture described above but in a rich brown manganese glaze are too narrowly attributed to Rockingham who made no monopoly of the so-called "Rockingham glaze". Similarly, in copper-brown lustre these lions were made in many potteries besides those of Sunderland associated with such metallic glazes. Obviously demand was stimulated by the souvenir figures associated with the coronations of George IV and William IV. A lion and unicorn in heraldic posture by John Walton have been noted, with the inevitable Walton leafy tree stump to support the lion's tail. Even in early 19th-century slipware conventional lions are to be found. A pair in the Fitzwilliam Museum are marked H. DAVIES and one also PILL POTTERY, assumed to be the pottery at Pill, near Bristol. A flat-backed lion eleven and a half inches long in nut-brown stoneware with white eyes and teeth in this Museum is attributed by

Rackham to Nottingham. Sunderland animals now in the Sunderland Museum include a cat and some cow cream jugs ornamented in colours and pink lustre from the Garrison Pottery and a magnificent copper lustre bull probably by Dawson & Co.

More marked animals of the early 19th century were made by John Walton, such as a cow with a calf and a sheep with a lamb in many variations. Rams with decorative horns were enormously popular at this period and can be found in wide variety. Walton's sheep on high mounds may be more effectively woolly-looking than those of his rivals when he used chippings from the turner's lathe instead of the surface tooling noted, for example, on marked specimens by Ralph Salt and his son Charles (1820s–64).

Both Walton and the Salts issued models showing a tiny lamb in a niche below the sheep or ram and both used supporting backgrounds of tree stumps bearing stamped leaves and flowers applied separately by hand. The name HALL was impressed on some animals made by John and Ralph Hall, of Swan Bank, Tunstall, between about 1800 and 1849 and yet another name occasionally noted is J WALLEYS WARE, on animals including sporting dogs, but little is known of this early 19th-century Burslem potter. Among Victorian potters, Sampson Smith is thought to have produced many dogs from about the mid-19th century and a later maker was William Machin of Percy Street, Hanley, from 1875 to 1912. The name I RIDGWAY transfer-printed over a pottery kiln is a rare mark noted on a delightful group of a spaniel sitting on its haunches entirely unresponsive to a cat's attempts to make it play: the firm, John Ridgway, was noted by the Great Exhibition Jury to be one of the most important in Staffordshire.

Some mid-19th-century slipware figures of both birds and animals have been attributed by Bernard Rackham to Fishley of Fremington, N. Devon, but even unmarked and wholly anonymous birds are comparatively rare among 19th-century earthenwares. Those in slipware were sometimes hollowed as whistles such as a specimen in the Fitzwilliam Museum in light red earthenware marbled with white under the typical deep yellow glaze and possibly made in Sussex. A more elaborate group from Yorkshire in this collection consists of a tree full of whistle birds with a nest among leaves suggested by shreds of slip; this has two small children below. Simplest of all, however, are the animals in brown salt-glazed stoneware. Many cats, dogs, cows, deer and the like were made by the Derbyshire stoneware potters, a few in two-colour brown and buff effects, and there was a considerable output by the Portobello firm of Milne, Cornwall & Co., established 1830–40.

A few birds are to be found in the Victorian white earthenware with brilliant glaze and dabs and streaks of bright gold among sparsely applied colour. An eagle is often noted, large and on a high rocky base. But the collector soon realises that dogs were by far the most important animal figures at this period. Bone china potters set the fashion with spaniels and the pugs and bull terriers of Derby and Chamberlain's Worcester and, in the 1820s, the cushion-pampered poodles of Rockingham. Rockingham succeeded in conveying the poodle's curly coat with extremely fine china threads in a manner that defeated the earthenware potters who applied small granules of earthenware glazed to the surface like sandpaper.

Rockingham dogs are generally small, such as spaniels and lap dogs on tasselled cushions, white or richly coloured. These and some white woolly dogs that may be unclipped poodles often show their tricks by carrying baskets of flowers in their mouths. This factory was one of the few to break away from the conventional dog models—standing, sitting, lying and fawning, with little variation save for the occasional introduction of a second dog on a longer base, centred with a spill holder or inkwell. Rockingham, it may be mentioned here, also made dogs in earthenware, including the greyhounds and spaniels then expected of every animal figure maker.

In bone china the dogs often appear to be mongrel types but the miniature mastiff is a recognisable breed taken from Meissen, modelled with head turned to the right and tongue hanging out and known to the early 19th century as the mops. These bone china models may be outstandingly lifelike and given considerable elaboration of setting such as pedestals encrusted with flowers. The Copeland firm made some even more lifelike, sitting on their haunches, without any form of support, such as pugs in the Meissen-Chelsea manner and also St. Bernards: these were impressed COPELAND & GARRETT between 1833 and 1846 and COPELAND LATE SPODE between 1847 and 1867. But these are only a few among the countless thousands produced unmarked in earthenware between 1810 and 1870, largely made and sold in pairs for symmetrical display on Victorian mantelpieces.

These earthenware dogs were coloured individually by hand and such details as eyes may decide the quality of a specimen but there is comparatively little variation from the white, fawn, tan and grey tones of more or less naturalistic colouring. The top of the oval base is usually green and there may be a gold line around the edge. Of the dogs modelled, the majority were the sportsman's choice. The favourite, it seems, was a rather poor-looking spaniel, lacking the quality of today's breed, but close rivals were the far more elegant greyhounds and whippets. These delicately limbed hounds were often modelled sitting on their haunches or lying down with crossed paws, often holding or guarding the hare just killed. Fawning greyhounds are sometimes found, their graceful motion excellently modelled. A standing figure required considerable support under its chest and behind the legs and slender tail. The most usual colouring was a reddish tan or salmon-orange with features picked out in black but those classed under the generic term of Jackfield are of red earthenware covered with a lustrous black glaze usually enriched with markings in gold that has proved all too fleeting. In callous Victorian days coursing was a national pastime, and a familiar pair of these dog models are *McGrath* and *Pretender,* winner and runner up in the Waterloo Cup of 1871. The model *Dog Tray* was prompted by the poem *The Harper* published in 1809 by Thomas Campbell (1777–1844).

Game dogs include the pointer standing over its game; the heavier Spanish pointer may be noted too, usually all white or all black. There are setters with thickly curled hair, foxhounds, harriers, staghounds and springers. The spotted dalmatian carriage dog was a conspicuous favourite,

47. (*Top*) Ralph Wood peasant models including, right and left, a pair of a sailor and his lass. Height 7¾ inches. (*Centre*) Ralph Wood models. (*Left and right*) Admiral von Tromp and gamekeeper on square pedestals with medallion ends, height about 10½ inches; (*centre*) Charity—group. About 1780. Height 9¾ inches. (*Bottom*) Astbury figures. (*Left to right*) Unique slipware woman: face in cream slip, remainder in slip marbling reaching almost to bottom of skirt. Height 6½ inches. About 1700. Fiddler entirely in brown and white clay, with lead glaze. Height 5½ inches. About 1730 Rare mounted soldier. Height 8 inches. About 1740. Standing piper with cream-splashed jacket, cream kilt splashed green and brown, plaid leggings and brown shoes. Height 6½ inches. About 1740. Unique figure of a man seated in a pew, reading a book. Pew in brown clay, the figure in cream clay with traces of green glaze, book in brown and white clay. Height 5½ inches. About 1735.

48. *The Parson and the Clerk*, an Enoch Wood model in enamel surface colours, black, pink and blue. Height 9 inches. About 1790.

but the greatest contrast to the outdoor sporting dog was the cross between a Maltese dog and a King Charles' spaniel, the "spaniel's gentle or comforter" made in vast numbers, especially between 1850 and 1870 when it tended to become outmoded by the renewed enthusiasm for pugs.

This was the lady's lap dog, always shown sitting up with turned head, and made in opposing male and female pairs, the dog showing the longer whiskers but both with insipid wide-open eyes, drooping ears and long silky coats usually heavily spotted with red or occasionally with gold, copper lustre or rarer black, brown, grey, even green. These animals were intended for symmetrical display either on the mantelshelf or, in summer, filling the front of the covered hearth and were made as tall as eighteen inches, the largest of five sizes down to about six inches. The most popular was nine inches tall. A feature of the comforter was the small gold padlock hanging from its collar on a thin gold chain.

Such popularity has inevitably resulted in many reproductions, usually just missing the colours of the originals. Even by mid-Victorian days the frequent insipidity of the animal chimney ornament was prompting individual potters to experiment, however. Resultant birds and animals ranged from the handsome brown stoneware of the Doulton firm's young artist-craftsmen to the individualistic contortions of the Martin brothers, not yet antiques but already eagerly collected. And a late 19th-century piece in the Fitzwilliam Museum, made at Castle Hedingham, Essex, is a crocodile which harks back to the most primitive style of yellow-glazed red earthenware in which men first sought to associate themselves with the creatures that shared their working lives.

SHORT BIBLIOGRAPHY

BRYANT, G. E., *Chelsea Porcelain Toys*, 1925

HURLBUTT, FRANK, *Chelsea Porcelain*, 1922

KING, WILLIAM, *Chelsea Porcelain*, 1922

MACKENNA, F. SEVERNE, *Chelsea Porcelain*: The Triangle and Raised Anchor Wares, 1948

MACKENNA, F. SEVERNE, *Chelsea Porcelain*: The Red Anchor Wares, 1951

MACKENNA, F. SEVERNE, *Chelsea Porcelain*: The Gold Anchor Wares, 1952

BEMROSE, WILLIAM, *Bow, Chelsea and Derby Porcelain*, 1898

HURLBUTT, FRANK, *Bow Porcelain*, 1927

LEWER, H. W., *Bow Porcelain Early Figures*, 1919

TAIT, HUGH, *Bow Porcelain 1744–1776*, 1959

GILHESPY, F. B., *Crown Derby Porcelain*, 1950

GILHESPY, F. B., *Derby Porcelain*, 1961

HASLEM, JOHN, *The Old Derby China Manufactory*, 1876

HURLBUTT, FRANK, *Old Derby Porcelain and its Artist-Workmen*, 1925

HYAM, E. E., *Early Period of Derby Porcelain*, 1926

WILLIAM DUESBURY's London Account Book 1751–53. MS in the British Museum. (Published as an English Porcelain Circle Monograph, 1931)

BEMROSE, WILLIAM, *Longton Hall Porcelain*, 1906

WATNEY, BERNARD, *Longton Hall Porcelain*, 1957

BARRETT, F. A., *Worcester Porcelain*, 1955

MARSHALL, H. R., *Coloured Worcester Porcelain of the First Period*, 1954

HURLBUTT, FRANK, *Bristol Porcelain*, 1928

MACKENNA, F. SEVERNE, *Champion's Bristol Porcelain*, 1947

MACKENNA, F. SEVERNE, *Cookworthy's Plymouth and Bristol Porcelain*, 1946

OWEN, HUGH, *Two Centuries of Ceramic Art in Bristol*, 1873

POUNTNEY, W. J., *Old Bristol Potteries*, 1920

BALSTON, THOMAS, *Staffordshire Portrait Figures*, 1958

BEMROSE, GEOFFREY, *19th Century English Pottery and Porcelain*, 1952

BLACKER, J. F., *The A.B.C. of English Saltglaze Stoneware*, 1922
BURTON, WILLIAM, *English Earthenware and Stoneware*, 1904
CUSHION, J. P. and HONEY, W. B., *Handbook of English Ceramic Marks*, 1959
GRANT, M. H., *The Makers of Black Basaltes*, 1910
HAGGAR, REGINALD G., *English Pottery Figures 1660–1860*, 1947
HAGGAR, REGINALD G., *Staffordshire Chimney Ornaments*, 1955
HONEY, W. B., *English Pottery and Porcelain*, 1947
HUGHES, BERNARD and THERLE, *English Porcelain and Bone China, 1743–1850*, 1955
HUGHES, BERNARD and THERLE, *The Collector's Encyclopaedia of English Ceramics*, 1956
HUGHES, G. BERNARD, *Victorian Pottery and Porcelain*, 1959
HUGHES, G. BERNARD, *English and Scottish Earthenware*, 1961
HUGHES, G. BERNARD, Numerous articles in *Country Life*, 1942–64
JEWITT, LLEWELLYN, *The Ceramic Art of Great Britain*, 1876
KING, WILLIAM, *Porcelain Figures of the 18th Century*, 1925
LUXMOORE, C. F. C., *Saltglaze*, 1924
MACKINTOSH, SIR HAROLD (Viscount Mackintosh of Halifax), *Early English Figure Pottery*, 1938
NIGHTINGALE, J. E., *Contributions towards the History of Early English Porcelain from Contemporary Sources*, 1881
PRICE, R. K., *Astbury, Whieldon and Ralph Wood Figures and Toby Jugs*, 1922
RACKHAM, BERNARD, *Animals in Staffordshire Pottery*, 1953
RACKHAM, BERNARD, *Early Staffordshire Pottery*, 1951
READ, HERBERT, *Staffordshire Pottery Figures*, 1929
RHEAD, G. WOOLLISCROFT, *The Earthenware Collector*, 1920
ROSCOE, W., *English Porcelain Figures 1744–1848*, 1947
STONER, FRANK, *Chelsea, Bow and Derby Figures*, 1955
TOWNER, DONALD, *English Cream-coloured Earthenware*, 1957

Index